The
Family Handbook
of Adolescence

The Family Handbook of Adolescence

by
JOHN E. SCHOWALTER, M.D.
and
WALTER R. ANYAN, JR., M.D.

ALFRED A. KNOPF   NEW YORK   1981

3738

THIS IS A BORZOI BOOK
PUBLISHED BY ALFRED A. KNOPF, INC.

Copyright © 1979 by John E. Schowalter, M.D., and Walter R. Anyan, Jr., M.D.

Library of Congress Cataloging in Publication Data
Schowalter, John E., [date]
The family handbook of adolescence.
Includes index.
1. Adolescence.   2. Youth—Diseases.   3. Youth—Health and hygiene.   I. Anyan, Walter R., [date] joint author.   II. Title.
RJ140.S34   1979   613'.04'243   79-2136
ISBN 0-394-41774-7 (hardcover)
0-394-73724-5 (paperback)

Manufactured in the United States of America
Published October 23, 1979
First paperback edition August, 1981

To

Carol Ann and Ellen,

and to our children,

Bethany, Blair, Jay, and Walter

Contents

Contents

The relationship between physical growth
  and sexual maturation   18
Menarche   19
Masturbation   21

General Factors in Adolescent Health   23

Nutrition   23
Exercise   30
Sleep   31
Dental health   35

Social Issues   39

Friends   39
Sexuality   46
Siblings   60
School   64
Clothing   73
Driving   79
Sports   84
Hobbies   88
Religion   93
Employment   99

Parental Issues   105

Rebellion   105
The impact of other important adults   112
One-parent families   114
The impact of "losing" one's child to adulthood   116

Medical Care   119

At the doctor's office   119
The physical examination   121
Planning additional studies and treatment   126
Genetic screening   130
Immunizations   131

Contents

Acknowledgments

We would like to thank Shirley Morgan, Betty Murray, and Ellen Schowalter for their help in preparing the manuscript for this book. In addition, Alice Atkinson, Shirley Morgan, Betty Murray, Ellen Schowalter, and Dr. Albert Solnit read various drafts and offered many helpful suggestions and criticisms. We also appreciate the encouragement, support, and help of Charles Elliott, our editor.

Preface

There are two eras in their children's lives that parents usually find most difficult. One is infancy; the other, adolescence. These are the two stages of life when growth both in body size and in body development is greatest. Health is generally good during both eras. But with so many physical changes going on, parents are often baffled as to what is happening, whether or not what is happening is normal, what is and should be their role in it, and what meaning these changes bode for the future.

The infant, of course, does not think about the consequences of undergoing so many physical and mental alterations. Other people will do the worrying about them. The adolescent, on the other hand, is constantly aware of being an adolescent. Not only changes in body size and configuration, but also changes in style of thought, changes in desires, and changes in social relationships are constantly redefining his or her existence. Parents care, but the adolescent cares strongly, too.

There are many books available about adolescence and about adolescents. Most common are books that focus only on the behavioral problems encountered in adolescence. Also popular are self-help books that present a particular perspective on and advocate a particular approach to being an adolescent or an adolescent's parent. This book aims at being broader in scope and is written from a medical perspective, with an emphasis on the evolving developmental periods within adolescence. Because it is intended to be used for reference, it includes all the more common health, psychological, and social issues faced during the decade between ages 10 and 20. No rigid routes are laid out, no orders given. The aim of the book is to inform, not to direct. Although written primarily for parents, this book will undoubtedly be read by adolescents as well. This is fine, since we believe that people of all ages make personal decisions best when they are most knowledgeable.

The
Family Handbook
of Adolescence

Arriving:
Childhood to Adolescence

What is meant by the term *child* is often a matter of opinion. So is what is meant by the term *adolescent.* To our parents we remain children forever. On the other hand, most junior high (middle) school students don't appreciate being referred to as children.

Nature and society are unfortunately of little help in clarifying these issues. Puberty refers to the body changes that take place when an individual becomes a mature person physically and sexually. The timetable for this accomplishment, however, is highly variable. For example, during the past century pubertal development, at least as measured by the average age of the onset of menstruation (**menarche**, pronounced men-arr'-ky, is the technical term), has been occurring increasingly early. There is variation between the sexes, with girls reaching puberty on the average of two years before boys, and also wide variation within the same sex. Some boys will have completed puberty before others have even started.

The onset of adolescence in terms of social and psychological maturity is at least as hard to pin down as the physical onset of puberty. In some cultures there is a ceremony that makes the transition clear. Before the ceremony the person is considered a child; immediately after the ceremony he or she is considered an adult. In our society there are many definitions for adulthood. Depending on the law in a particular state, at the same time as a person may be considered an adult and be able legally to buy beer, obtain an abortion, or act in a pornographic movie, he or she is also considered a minor who is legally unable to buy vodka, get married, or buy a ticket for a pornographic movie.

In short, adolescence is a process rather than an event. It begins, progresses, and ends uniquely for each individual. Although we may expect all persons of the same age to be roughly equal in maturation, in fact there is no other developmental period in our lives when this assumption is so likely to be wrong as in adolescence.

Preadolescence

Some psychologists find it useful to think of the year or so before the actual change in the sexual organs as preadolescence. During this time children become more aware of sexuality, but are at the same time quite embarrassed about it. Reading erotic magazines, sex talk with peers, and scavenging medical books for sex information are common, but all are done secretly. There is mimicry of teenage elders' dress and style, but the mimicry is expressed mainly in a bravado that rings false.

Personalities often change before bodies do. Just when parents believe they have finally trained their child to be neat, polite, and thoughtful, the clock seems to begin running backwards. Dirtiness in tongue and temperament is a common result of this tendency of the preadolescent to act younger but in an older way. Preadolescent children often decide that their clothing, body, and room should be cleaned as infrequently as possible. A distraught mother once told me that she feared her 11-year-old son was growing up to be a 2-year-old.

Dirty words are also common, and cussing seems to offer more pure pleasure than it ever will again. Bathroom words are savored first, with sexual words arriving somewhat later.

The variation in the time of onset of adolescence causes preadolescence to be an especially confusing time. Even if you are aware that it is not a sign of disorder that your 10-year-old daughter has begun to menstruate (see p. 19), you will probably have some feelings of being robbed of your child prematurely. Likewise if your 15-year-old son looks more like an 11-year-old, it is hard not to worry even after your doctor has confirmed the fact of your son's good health and normal development.

For the child, puberty has to be faced firsthand, and doubts and uncertainties about it are frequent. Almost all young people fear because of the timing or the intensity of their adolescent changes that they are abnormal in body, mind, or both. Because of these fears they often become very secretive, especially about their body and with their parents.

Relationship with the doctor

As your child grows older, you may notice that the doctor wishes to see and talk with you less. You may feel deserted just when you desire the doctor's closeness and counsel most. After all, you originally picked the doctor and are still paying for the visits.

One reason for this attitude on the doctor's part is that the older child can now provide sufficient and reliable information that a parent previously had to provide. Another is that the older child is more familiar with the doctor and with various aspects of medical care and no longer requires the presence of a parent for support. The most important reason is that the adolescent requires a more personal relationship with a doctor than a younger child does.

Many physical changes occur at the time of puberty, and the greatest changes are in those body parts having to do with sex. Adolescents find these changes and their meanings stimulating as well as mysterious. Just as adolescents want increased privacy at home, many also want it in the doctor's office. This is not only true for the physical examination but for the discussion part of the consultation as well. Experience has shown that a physician who is trusted by parents but not in close communication with them is more likely to obtain an adolescent patient's confidence and therefore be able to remain helpful during a time when most adults may be shunned. Even those physicians who wish to have an increasingly exclusive relationship with their adolescent patients, however, still usually appreciate a parent's comments when the parent believes the doctor will be aided by knowing certain information.

It is natural that many parents find it difficult to allow their offspring increasing independence in the area of medical care. The parent not only still retains responsibility but must often encourage the reluctant adolescent to consult the doctor appropriately. In the long run, however, increasing independence usually allows the adolescent to use the health care most effectively and supports a model of doctor-patient closeness that will prove important throughout his or her life.

What kind of doctor?

In general, family doctors see patients of all ages, while pediatricians restrict their care to children and adolescents, and internists, or specialists in internal medicine, restrict their care to adults. When does an adolescent no longer use a pediatrician?

There was an old-time pediatrician, and this is a true story, who was made nervous by adolescents. To protect himself he sawed off the foot of his examining table. By age 13 or 14, most of his patients began to dangle off the end when they lay down. When this happened, the old gentleman would comment that they were obviously too big to see a pediatrician and he would refer them to an internist.

Efficient as this method was, there is a better way. The

patient's opinion is very important in making the change from pediatrician to internist or family doctor. Most adolescents switch at the time of leaving high school, but many do before and some do later. Again, one faces the fact that there is no one time for reaching adulthood.

It is helpful around age 10 or 11 for the patient and pediatrician to spend some time together talking about the various changes that are occurring and will occur during puberty. If this talk does not occur, a parent should suggest it to one or both parties. As part of this discussion, the pediatrician often raises the issue of the adolescent's switching to an internist or family doctor. Pediatrician and adolescent may decide ahead of time that when the patient reaches a certain age the change will take place, or they may as the patient nears the end of high school assess the pros and cons anew each time the adolescent comes for a regular checkup.

Whom the patient will want to switch to should be discussed by parents and adolescent. Parents may assume that their child will see the parents' doctor, and this may certainly be suggested along with the reasons, but the adolescent may wish to go to someone else. The pediatrician may be asked to mention the names and give to the adolescent a description of a few doctors in whom he or she has confidence. At times, as with adults, the adolescent's choice will be based on word-of-mouth recommendations from friends. The selection, with the parents' endorsement, of an adolescent's new doctor is an important step toward independence.

The importance of privacy

One of the first personality changes usually seen in adolescence is a move toward greater secrecy. So many changes take place in body and thought that adolescents fear their strength, question their normality, and want to sort out their meanings before showing these changes to others, especially to adults and, most especially, to parents.

This increased sense of privacy is also reflected in the adoles-

7

cent's attitude toward medical care. While questions and concerns about the body increase, so does the reluctance to admit them. We humans seem to have a strong tendency, if we fear something is wrong with our body, to avoid confirming that fear. For this reason many adolescents begin to avoid physical checkups. When they do see a doctor, privacy is very important. Girls are usually self-conscious when a male doctor first notices evidence of sexual maturation. Boys often have similar embarrassment when the doctor is a woman or when a female nurse is present during the examination.

Changes in the doctor-patient relationship

As already mentioned, adolescents have difficulty talking to adults—*any* adults. Since the major developmental task of adolescence is to become an adult apart from parents, parents must be kept at a distance. Teachers and club leaders can become confidants, but they have not known the adolescent over a long period of time. Besides neighbors and relatives, the family doctor or pediatrician is one of the few adults who has a knowledge of the adolescent over the whole course of his or her life. In addition, there is usually a long-standing feeling of trust. Although the physician has been picked and approved by the parents, the child also has a separate relationship with the doctor that has been strengthened by having been through times of stress together. It is this longitudinal knowledge by the doctor of the patient and of the family circumstances that makes him or her such a valuable resource. It is also why most early adolescents prefer to remain with their pediatrician rather than switching to an internist or a specialist in adolescent medicine.

Is adolescence always a problem?

Since most people are not inclined to spend money for this type of book when family relationships are only a pure delight, it is assumed that readers are searching for help and understanding. Because of this there is an emphasis in the book on the meaning of problems and possible approaches to them. However, the fact is that for most of the time for most adolescents, the teen years are positive and without major difficulty. Although this point will perhaps not be repeated as often as it might, it is a comfort that should be kept in mind.

The Growing Body

One song from the popular show, *Fiddler on the Roof,* contains, in six terse lines, several nicely posed questions about physical growth and sexual maturation during adolescence:

> *Is this the little girl I carried?*
> *Is this the little boy at play?*
> *I don't remember growing older, when did they?*
> *When did she get to be a beauty?*
> *When did he grow to be so tall?*
> *Wasn't it yesterday when they were small?*

To provide answers for these provocative questions, the discussion that follows is separated into three parts. First there is a brief review of the growth process experienced by a child between birth and adolescence. Then there is a discussion of growth during adolescence. And finally there is a review of one of the most important achievements of the adolescent era, sexual maturation.

From birth to adolescence

During infancy and through the second and much of the third year of life, boys and girls grow very rapidly. However, their growth rates constantly slow down during those years, with further braking of the growth rates between 3 and 5 years of age. From age 5 until adolescent growth begins, most boys and girls gain 3 1/4 to 9 3/4 pounds (1.5–4.4 kilograms) each year, while they grow between 1 1/2 and 2 3/4 inches (3.8–7.0 centimeters) taller each year. Thus, childhood growth can be envisioned as consisting of a phase of rapidly slowing growth followed by a phase coinciding with the early school years in which the growth rates remain constant. When this growth finishes, the average girl is about 9 1/2 years old, and she has reached about 82 1/2 percent of the height that she will have as an adult. The average boy is about 11 1/2 years old when he completes this period of growth, and at that time he has attained about 82 percent of his adult height. Thus, the physical growth that takes place between birth and adolescence usually accounts for slightly more than four-fifths of one's final height. In other words, a person's physical stature as an adult is dictated largely by growth before puberty. This is not true, however, of one's adult weight. At the completion of prepuberty, most boys and girls weigh only slightly more than half (53 or 54 percent) of what they will weigh by the time they reach their eighteenth birthdays.

During adolescence

When adolescent growth begins, its rate is marked by a sustained acceleration, first in height, followed closely by increases in weight. Although on the average growth speeds up in girls when they are about 9 1/2, and in boys at about 11 1/2, the normal age range is quite wide. Some boys and girls begin their growth spurts as much as two years before or after the average time of growth acceleration. Because of their head start, girls are, on the average, taller and heavier than boys for several years after their growth spurt begins. Then, between the ages of 13 and 14, boys catch up, and subsequently become taller and heavier than the girls. An adolescent growth spurt that begins relatively early makes a larger contribution to mature size than one that begins when the boy or girl is older.

After adolescent growth begins, it continues to gain speed for about two years, at which time peak growth rates are reached. On the average, when their growth is most rapid, adolescents grow 3 1/2 to 4 inches (9–10 centimeters) a year, a rate as high as the one that occurred when they were about 2 years old. Then growth begins to slow down. While both boys and girls grow in all about 11 1/2 inches (30 centimeters) from the beginning of the adolescent growth spurt to the eighteenth birthday, the difference between average heights of girls and of boys increases only slightly from 4 1/4 inches (11 centimeters) to 4 3/4 inches (12 centimeters), while the difference in their weights widens from 13 1/4 pounds (6 kilograms) to 24 1/4 pounds (11 kilograms).

Growth patterns

Approximately one-third of the change in height and weight during adolescence takes place during growth speed-up. After the growth rate reaches its greatest speed, it begins slowing, and it is during this period that the adolescent gains the remaining height and weight.

During the early stages of adolescent growth, the bones in the arms and legs increase most rapidly in length. Later, the bones of the spine—which influence the length of the trunk—grow more rapidly. As growth proceeds, the width of the shoulders and the pelvis increases, and during adolescence the proportion of shoulder width to pelvic width also changes: in boys, the shoulders become relatively broader than the pelvis, while in girls the reverse is true.

Each bone has a growth center called an **epiphysis,** which is responsible for increasing the length of the bone during childhood and adolescence. As sexual maturation progresses during adolescence, the sex hormones—generally categorized as androgens and estrogens and produced in both boys and girls—gradually alter the potential of the growth centers to increase bone length, and then eventually shut the centers down. As this occurs, the growth rate slows down and finally stops.

Even though the bones involved in growth are distributed throughout the body, it is possible to determine the extent to which growth has progressed by taking an X ray of the bones in the hand and wrist. A specialist, by studying the growth centers revealed by the X ray, can determine the adolescent's skeletal age, or "bone age." It is then possible to estimate with some accuracy the amount of additional height the adolescent can expect to acquire before growth stops. Boys and girls who are worried about the possibility of being either too short or too tall may be reassured by such a checkup. In some cases, treatment might be indicated to influence the growth pattern.

Weight change

On learning that they almost double their body weights between the onset of the growth spurt and age eighteen, adolescents might wonder what changes are responsible for such an impressive gain. A useful way of understanding growth in weight is to compare changes in the amount of **lean body mass** with changes in the amount of **adipose tissue** (fat) in the body. Lean body mass includes all parts of the body *except* the fat cells and their contents. Thus the vital organs, including the brain and spinal cord, the heart and lungs, the liver and both kidneys, the endocrine organs, as well as the skeleton and the skin, all go to make up lean body mass. Adipose tissue—fat— serves as the body's major storage site for energy that is not needed immediately for growth or physical activity. Every component of lean body mass grows larger during adolescence, and, in boys, lean body mass increases more rapidly than it does in girls. For example, the amounts of lean body mass typically found in adolescent boys and girls having the same heights can be compared at 12, 15, and 18 years of age. At 12, the amount of lean body mass per inch of height is about the same in both sexes; at 15, boys have somewhat more lean body mass per unit of height; and by age 18, boys have about 40 percent more lean body mass per inch of height than girls. Of all the changes in lean body mass, the increase in muscle mass is the most impressive. Between 11 and 17 years of age the amount of muscle in a boy doubles, and it increases at least 50 percent in girls. On completion of adolescent growth, muscle represents about 42 percent of body weight in girls and 52 percent in boys.

In girls, there is also usually an increase in the amount of fat. When their growth spurts begin, boys and girls have similar proportions of adipose tissue, averaging between 14 percent and 16 percent of total body weight. As adolescent growth progresses, the proportion of the body consisting of adipose tissue changes. In boys, the amount of fat remains about the same or increases slightly, and because of the increased lean body mass, the proportion of body weight made up by fat actually decreases. Only 9 or 10 percent of the body weight of many boys consists of adipose tissue when they reach 17 or 18 years of age. Among girls, the amount of fat in the body usually increases considerably during adolescent growth, often outrunning the relative increase in lean body mass. As a result the proportion of body weight made up of adipose tissue usually increases to more than 20 percent. While these changes are typical, the normal range of body composition in adolescent boys and girls is quite wide, with some girls having small proportions of body fat and some boys having amounts that resemble those seen typically in girls.

Sexual Maturation

While impressive increases in physical size are some of the most important physical changes adolescents experience, they are accompanied by another equally visible set of changes. These result in the transformation of a sexually immature child into a reproductively capable adult. Our understanding of the process through which sexual maturation occurs has deepened considerably during the last few years, and it stands as one of the most fascinating chapters in human biology.

Between birth and the beginning of adolescence, sexual maturity does not occur because the body is not programmed for it. For sexual maturation to begin, and to be maintained, the pituitary gland must first release into the bloodstream quantities of stimulating agents—**gonadotropins** —which, when they reach the ovaries in girls or testes in boys, trigger the chain of events that eventually leads to sexual maturation. The gonadotropins are manufactured in the pituitary gland under the supervision of control centers located in the brain.

Gonadotropins

There are two gonadotropins: **follicle-stimulating hormone** and **luteinizing hormone.** The gonadotropins are usually called by their initials, FSH and LH. In girls, FSH stimulates the development of follicles within the ovaries. A follicle contains a developing ovum, or egg, as well as cells that produce estrogen when they are stimulated by LH. In boys, FSH stimulates the growth and development of the seminiferous tubules in the testes that produce sperm, and LH provokes other testicular cells, called Leydig cells, to produce androgen. The androgen produced by the Leydig cells encourages the development of the seminiferous tubules that produce sperm and has other effects on more distant parts of the body.

During childhood, the pituitary releases FSH and LH at levels that are too low for sexual maturation to begin. At puberty, changes within the brain make possible the manufacture and release of increasing amounts of FSH and LH by the pituitary. At the earliest stage of puberty, increased gonadotropin release begins shortly after one goes to sleep, but stops during the day when a boy or girl is awake. In midadolescence, increased gonadotropin release goes on during sleep but also occurs when a boy or girl is awake, a pattern that is maintained after sexual maturity is attained.

Ovarian and testicular growth

As the pituitary releases increased amounts of gonadotropins, the ovaries and the testes respond by growing more rapidly and by producing larger amounts of estrogen or androgen. Gradually, the effects of the hormones on the body become apparent.

During the first year of a boy's sexual maturation, his testes enlarge, while the rest of his genitals and his body remain visibly unchanged. At the completion of this first phase of development, sperm begin to be produced, the testes continue to increase in size, and their growth is accompanied by more rapid growth of the penis and the rest of the body. As the testes and the penis grow, sexual hair usually begins to appear. The sexual hair that develops first is pubic hair. It appears initially near the base of the penis, and it is characterized by being somewhat longer and more darkly pigmented than the fine downy hair previously present there. Unlike more mature pubic hair, which is curly, that which appears in early adolescence tends to be straight. As sexual maturation advances, the penis and testes continue to grow in size, the distribution of pubic hair spreads, and the pubic hair resembles more and more that of the adult in quantity, coarseness, and curliness. During adolescence, sexual hair also appears under the arms and on the face. Facial hair begins to grow above the upper lip, then on the chin and along the jawline, and eventually develops on the neck. A deepening in the tone of the voice usually accompanies these changes. Sometimes during adolescence, but often not until the early years of adult life, an increase in body hair also occurs.

Among girls, the growth of the ovaries is of course not noticeable from the outside, and the first conclusive evidence that a major change in ovarian function has occurred is the response of the immature breasts to the increased amounts of estrogen produced by the ovaries. One breast can begin to develop somewhat earlier than the other, or both breasts may begin to develop at the same time. Breast development begins with the appearance of a small amount of new breast tissue located immediately beneath the **areola**, the only portion of the breast visible during childhood and having a slightly different color and texture from the surrounding skin. As breast development begins, a girl becomes aware that the areolar surfaces protrude slightly, and she can feel rather firm breast tissue that was not there earlier. As estrogen continues to be secreted by the ovaries at an increasing rate, the breasts enlarge and eventually assume the shape of mature breasts. At times during breast development, some inequality in the size and shape of the breasts may be evident: these inequalities usually disappear as growth continues and maturity is reached. More obvious discrepancy between the breasts, particularly after maturity, probably ought to be checked by a physician (see p. 169). Sexual maturation in girls is also accompanied by the growth of sexual hair: first, pubic hair, and then underarm hair and some increase in body hair. Small amounts of straight, slightly pigmented pubic hair appear first on the **labia majora** (outer folds of the girl's genitalia). As the hair becomes more mature, the area covered by it increases and the hair spreads toward the groins and onto the inner surfaces of the thighs. In many girls, breast development begins before the growth of pubic hair; in some, breast development and pubic hair growth begin simultaneously; and in others, the appearance of pubic hair precedes breast development. By the time a girl has menarche—her first menstrual period—her breasts are quite mature and both pubic and underarm hair are often similar to that present in mature women.

The relationship between physical growth and sexual maturation

Adolescent physical growth and sexual maturation do not occur as independent phenomena: they are closely related processes that overlap to a considerable extent. In girls, androgens produced by the adrenal glands before sexual maturation gets underway are probably responsible for the speed-up in the rate of physical growth, as the latter often begins before there is any evidence of breast development. As the rate of physical growth continues to accelerate, breast development passes through its early stages, and by the time many girls have reached their peak growth rates, their breasts are moderately well developed. Subsequently, as the growth rate slows, and as nearly mature breast development is achieved, the first menstrual period occurs. On the *average,* girls have menarche just before they are 13 years old. They grow about three inches

(7–8 centimeters) between the time of menarche and the time at which they are fully grown. Girls who grow and mature normally at relatively early ages can expect to have menarche earlier—near their tenth birthdays—and to grow more than an average amount following menarche, while later-maturing girls—those who have menarche at age 15—make smaller than average gains in height after menarche.

Among boys, the relationship between sexual maturation and physical growth begins with testicular growth preceding more rapid physical growth by about one year. Following this first stage of sexual maturation, the testes produce enough androgen to stimulate physical growth to a noticeable extent, and the latter is accompanied by more rapid growth of the penis and the appearance of pubic hair. Most boys do not reach their peak growth rates until they have attained fairly advanced degrees of sexual maturation, and some do not reach their most rapid growth until they are nearly mature. In view of this pattern, a boy whose sexual maturation is in its early stages can be fairly confident of more physical growth.

Menarche

The first menstrual period of adolescent girls occurs toward the end of the processes of sexual maturation and physical growth. Estrogen produced by the ovaries stimulates the development of the **endometrium,** the tissue that lines the cavity of the uterus. Under the estrogen stimulation, the endometrium thickens and it also relies upon receiving constant estrogen support in order to remain intact. Following a prolonged period of estrogen stimulation, a menstrual period is likely to occur if the estrogen levels drop for several days. The first menstrual period is not always a sign that a girl is reproductively mature, and for a year or more thereafter, ovulation may not occur during many menstrual cycles. (No girl should take this state of affairs as any sort of insurance against becoming pregnant, however. Ovulation may in fact occur, and if it does, she can be impregnated.) As girls become increasingly mature, ovulation occurs more frequently, and the mechanism that determines menstruation also changes. Ovulation—which consists of the release of an ovum (an egg) from a follicle—usually takes place about fourteen days before the onset of a menstrual period. Ovulation occurs after the ovaries secrete relatively large amounts of estrogen, which triggers a unique response by the brain's control centers and the pituitary gland. The response consists of the release of large quantities of gonadotropins, particularly LH—which is responsible for producing ovulation. After an ovum is released, the follicle assumes a new physical form and biological function. The transformed follicle becomes a **corpus luteum,** and it produces not only estrogen, but also a hormone called progesterone. The progesterone allows further development of the endometrium, preparing it for the possible implantation of a fertilized ovum, and pregnancy. When pregnancy does not occur, the function of the corpus luteum ceases, and the blood levels of estrogen and progesterone decrease. This change precedes, by two to three days, the beginning of a menstrual period. When the endometrium that has developed, initially in response to estrogen and subsequently to a combination of estrogen and progesterone, is cast off from the uterus in response to the decrease in both hormones, a menstrual period occurs.

At the time of menarche, and for several years thereafter, some fairly wide variations in the frequency, duration, and the intensity of menstrual flow can be expected. Normally maturing girls can have periods as frequently as every three to three and a half weeks, or as infrequently as every two to three months. Some menstrual periods last only a day or so, while others may last as long as seven to nine days; menstrual flow may be heavy or scant. Customarily, menstrual periods following cycles in which ovulation does not take place tend to be free of discomfort, while periods following ovulatory cycles are more likely to be accompanied by cramps or other discomfort during the first day or so of the period.

A *menstrual record*

To be able to understand the pattern of one's own menstrual cycles, it is very useful for an adolescent to keep a permanent record of the dates on which each menstrual period begins and ends. The length of a menstrual cycle equals the number of days from the first day of a period to the first day of the next period. An adolescent might consider her menstrual pattern as irregular, for example, because one period began toward the end of October, none occurred during November, and the next period started in early December. Then, the following period came in mid-January. Yet if the adolescent had timed the length of each cycle, she would have found that they are quite similar, and the pattern regular and nothing to be concerned about. In addition to encouraging an understanding of one's own inner timetable, a menstrual record can provide very helpful information to a physician if any menstrual or reproductive problems do develop.

Masturbation

As adolescents grow into larger and more sexually mature people, their sexual interests increase. These are expressed in a number of ways, one of which is masturbation. As is true with so many developmental issues during adolescence, there is no predictable time at which masturbation begins or increases, either in frequency or in importance, and some adolescents engage in masturbatory activity to a greater extent than others.

As a sexual activity, masturbation includes emotional and physical components. The direct stimulation of the genitalia is usually produced by manipulation of the penis or the clitoris, and this activity generally begins in early childhood when boys and girls discover that the feeling produced is pleasurable. With the sexual maturation occurring during adolescence, masturbation changes to an activity that is increasingly prompted by, or linked with, sexual thoughts, as well as a desire to relieve tension. In addition, masturbation in adolescent girls is normally accompanied by an appreciable degree of moistening and lubrication of the genitalia, and by ejaculation in boys, both of which attest further to the adolescents' greater sexual maturity. In both sexes, orgasm becomes an intense and enjoyable sexual experience. Most adolescents are aware that there is a formidable body of folklore attempting to discourage masturbation and to make adolescents feel guilty about it. The myths about masturbation producing mental illness, blindness, or loss of physical strength are just that —myths. *No* adolescent should fear that masturbation will result in these or any other physical or psychological consequences. A further discussion of the psychological aspects of masturbation will be found on p. 47.

General Factors
in Adolescent Health

As adolescent growth and sexual maturation proceed, three general factors—nutrition, exercise, and sleep—play important roles. Adequate nutrition is especially important to adolescents who need energy for the growth, activity, and operation of a rapidly enlarging body. Exercise complements the growth process, influences nutritional demands, and provides important social and psychological challenges. Sleep is closely linked with the process of sexual maturation. One sleep disturbance, called **enuresis** (bed-wetting), often a holdover from childhood, is included here in the discussion of sleep (see p. 33).

Nutrition

Considering the physical changes and the amount of growth that occur during adolescence, it should come as no surprise that the adolescent's nutritional requirements differ from those of the younger child. At every age, the body requires a basic level of nutrition to keep it operating, to sustain life, and to maintain physical size when the only activity consists of rest and sleep. It needs a higher level to meet demands for activities other than rest or sleep. And it needs a still higher level of nutrition to supply the energy critical to normal growth.

At times of intense growth in the first two years of life and during adolescence, nutritional demands are thus relatively higher than at other times during childhood. Unfortunately, the supply required for growth tends to be the first to be scanted in case of diet deficiencies; life-sustaining requirements and those demanded by basic activity are met first. Nutritional requirements vary considerably from one adolescent to another: physical size directly influences the amount of basic nutrition required, physical activity varies tremendously among adolescents, and the intensity of physical growth is not always the same. The demands for nutrition in a relatively small, slowly growing, physically inactive adolescent are bound to fall short of those made by someone whose body is larger, growing rapidly, and constantly engaged in strenuous physical activity.

Major nutrients

Protein   Adolescents must depend on constant supplies of protein from the food they eat because there is no substantial storage of extra protein in the body. Protein is vital to the growth of new tissue and the repair of existing tissues. It is obtained from the digestive tract in the form of amino acids, which are used as building blocks by the body to construct or reconstruct proteins needed throughout the system. While some amino acids can be made by the adolescent's body, nine of them—called essential amino acids—cannot be. They must be obtained from the diet. Foods that supply protein include animal meats, poultry, seafood, dairy products, and eggs, as well as nuts, grains, and beans. In comparison with other sources of protein, the protein present in vegetables often contains a smaller amount of the essential amino acids. Each day, most adolescents consume between 0.45 and 0.9 grams of protein per pound (1–2 grams per kilogram) of body weight, an amount which is a little above the recommended daily allowance.

Carbohydrates constitute an important part of an adolescent's nutrition because they provide the major source of energy for the brain and because—in the form of sugar—they make things taste better. Unlike some of the amino acids that cannot be manufactured within the body, carbohydrates can be produced in the body through the metabolism of protein and fat. Carbohydrates are especially plentiful in fruits, and are also found in beans, corn, peas, and potatoes. They are present to a lesser extent in other vegetables. Additional valuable sources of carbohydrates include milk, nuts, and grains. Sugar is pure carbohydrate. Following any necessary digestion, carbohydrates are absorbed from the intestines and transported to the liver for storage and distribution to the body.

Fat is a component of many tissues in the body, and the consumption of fat provides the body with a concentrated form of energy and also assists with the absorption of several vitamins from the intestinal tract. The amount of fat in the diet is one—but certainly not the only—factor that influences the level of cholesterol and triglycerides in the bloodstream. Fruits (apart from avocadoes and olives) contain little fat. Among vegetables, soybeans contain some fat, and most members of the nut family contain appreciable amounts, as does chocolate. Butter, margarine, lard, olive oil, and other cooking oils consist almost entirely of fat. Egg yolk contains fat, while the egg white does not. Dairy products, for the most part, contain fat, and animal meats contain more fat than most forms of seafood.

Nutrient combinations in the diet When one considers the immense number of available foods, it is surprising that adolescent diets tend to be so similar. Of the total amount of

25

nutriment consumed each day, many adolescents choose 10 to 15 percent in the form of protein, with the remainder nearly evenly divided between carbohydrate and fat. In general, girls consume between 2,000 and 2,500 calories each day during their adolescent years, and boys consume between 2,500 and 3,000 calories. For any given adolescent, calorie intake tends to parallel the growth spurt, and greater intake usually occurs when growth is rapid than when it is moving at a slower rate. After the growth spurt is over, boys tend to require somewhat larger amounts of energy for basic requirements than girls, a fact that reflects the difference in the amount of muscle present in the mature male and female body.

It should also be stated that there is no "perfect" diet: personal and family preferences, ethnic influences, local and seasonal availability of certain foods, and economic factors all dictate food choices to a considerable extent. For general palatability, and to meet the recommended requirements for energy, vitamins, and minerals, a somewhat balanced diet makes sense. It is not always possible to achieve dietary balance each day, but over the course of a week, several dietary goals can be set. One goal is to have green or yellow vegetables in the diet four to seven times each week. Another is to include fruits and foods with whole grains as parts of each day's diet. Protein, from milk or other dairy products, meat, poultry or eggs, and fish, should be in each meal.

It seems advisable, on the basis of information currently available about the prevention of atherosclerosis, for adolescents to drink low-fat (skimmed) milk, to keep their egg consumption at 4 eggs (or fewer) per week, and to make use of polyunsaturated fats whenever possible. Fish provides polyunsaturated fats, as do cooking and salad oils and margarine spreads made with vegetable oils. Thus, the intake of butter and other products made from more highly saturated fats can be reduced. In comparison with most animal meats, poultry contains less fat, so that eating chicken or turkey occasionally can also reduce the total intake of fat.

In addition to the major energy-supplying nutrients, the diet should also provide vitamins and minerals. These do not supply energy but are needed for the body to function normally.

Vitamins

Among the important vitamins, some are most often called by letters and others are given full names. They include vitamin A, thiamine, riboflavin, vitamins B_6, B_{12}, C, D, and E, folacin, niacin, pantothenic acid, biotin, and vitamin K. In the following discussion, each of these vitamins is described briefly: after its name, the recommended daily allowance of the vitamin is given in parentheses; then its use in the body; and its main dietary sources. In the recommended daily allowances, the following abbreviations are used: mg., for milligram—one thousandth of a gram; and μg., for microgram—one millionth of a gram.

Vitamin A (800–1,000 retinol equivalents) is incorporated in the pigment of the retinas of the eyes. A lack of it causes night blindness—the inability to see in dim light. It is also important in maintaining the tissues that cover the body: the skin, the surfaces of the eyes, and the lining of the nose, the mouth, and the gastrointestinal tract. Natural sources of vitamin A, and of a precursor from which vitamin A can be made in the body, include tomatoes and many yellow and green fruits and vegetables; dairy products containing milk fat, such as whole milk, butter, and cheese; and egg yolk and liver. **Thiamine** (1.1–1.4 mg.) takes part in several metabolic processes in the body. Fortunately, meats, liver, milk, and whole grains, as well as some vegetables, contain appreciable quantities of thiamine, and its general availability makes deficiency very uncommon. **Riboflavin** (1.3–1.7 mg.) resembles thiamine in both its function in the body and in its broad availability in milk, vegetables, meats, and grains. **Vitamin B_6** (1.8–2.0 mg.), also known as pyridoxine, is present in meat, liver, corn, whole grains, soybeans, and peanuts, and it plays a role in the metabolism of other nutrients. Shortages are again unlikely. **Vitamin B$_{12}$** (3 μg.) influences the production of red blood cells and the function of the central nervous system. Adequate amounts of B$_{12}$ prevent the development of a serious but rare condition known as pernicious anemia. The main sources of vitamin B$_{12}$ include meat, milk, and eggs. **Vitamin C** (50–60 mg.), or ascorbic acid, is important in the formation of connective tissues and in the utilization of other nutrients, particularly iron. A deficiency of ascorbic acid is the cause of an illness called scurvy. In recent years ascorbic acid has been much discussed as an agent which might reduce the frequency of common colds, although the theory remains unproved. Abundant natural supplies of vitamin C are found in many fresh fruits and vegetables, especially citrus fruits. **Vitamin D** (10 μg. cholecalciferol), which is also considered a hormone, helps to regulate the process of bone and tooth formation. Vitamin D deficiency produces a bone disease called rickets in growing children and adolescents, and a problem called osteomalacia in bones in which growth has ceased. Vitamin D is produced in the skin by the action of the ultraviolet light present in sunshine, and it also is available from numerous foodstuffs: egg yolk; seafoods such as herring, salmon, tuna, sardines; and, most importantly, milk fortified with vitamin D. **Vitamin E** (8–10 alpha-tocopherol equivalents) is less well understood than many other vitamins. The vitamin appears to be incorporated in many membranes in the body, and a deficiency of it has been associated with anemia in premature infants. Dietary sources include various vegetable oils, butter, and eggs. **Folacin** (400 μg.) is important in metabolism, and when it is lacking in sufficient quantity, the bone marrow fails to form enough new red blood cells. The most abundant natural source of folacin is green vegetables. **Niacin** (14–18 niacin equivalents), **pantothenic acid** (4–7 mg.), and **biotin** (100–200 μg.) are also required for metabolic processes in the body. Niacin is available from meats, fish, green vegetables, and whole grains; pantothenic acid is present in most foods that find their way into the diet; and biotin is found in liver, chocolate, egg yolk, and peanuts.

Vitamin K (50–100 μg.) is one of several factors that regulate the ability of the body to control bleeding, and it is present in many green vegetables and in milk.

Reasonably balanced diets usually include adequate, or more than adequate, amounts of each of these vitamins. Taking vitamin supplements is in most cases quite unnecessary. While there do not appear to be specific undesirable side effects from the use of more than the recommended amounts of most vitamins—the body generally gets rid of them—it should be remembered that whenever the intake of either vitamin A or vitamin D exceeds its current requirements, the surplus is stored in the body. Excesses of either of these vitamins can produce unpleasant, and sometimes serious, consequences.

Minerals

Good nutrition also includes a group of diverse minerals required by the body. As with vitamins, most adolescents receive adequate amounts of almost all of these from food. The only frequent exception is iron. Iron is vitally important in the body for the normal production of hemoglobin, the major and most important component of red blood cells. Iron is also needed for the growth of muscle and as a constituent of various enzymes. During phases of rapid growth, the body's demands for iron are particularly high, and occasionally the diet doesn't furnish enough. During adolescence, girls require increased supplies of iron for muscle growth and for an increase in the total amount of hemoglobin present in the bloodstream. In addition, menstruation creates another continuing demand for iron. As boys grow, their demand for iron for both muscle growth and for an increase in the amount of hemoglobin in the body is even greater than that of girls. Consequently, throughout the adolescent years, boys and girls require an intake of about 18 milligrams of iron per day. Eggs, whole grains, meat, liver, lentils, peas, soybeans, and nuts provide useful sources of dietary iron. However, iron supplements are sometimes necessary.

Exercise

No matter what it consists of, from heavy labor or walking to competitive sports, exercise provides a chance to test and to improve one's strength and endurance, and at the same time to gain some pleasure and relaxation. Exercise provides adolescents with the satisfaction of having a body that is in good shape. Long-term participation in sports usually focuses on improving not only one's competitive prospects, but also endurance, strength, and fitness. Regular conditioning exercise increases muscular size and strength, reduces the body's percentage of fat, and makes the heart and lungs do a better job of taking oxygen into the body: it leads to a special sense of well-being frequently noted by athletes who are in good condition. "Good condition" can even be measured: as the degree of physical fitness increases, the amount of oxygen that can be taken into the body, and used by it during exercise, also increases; and the heart beats slower during stressful exercise. So far as general health is concerned, exercise helps avoid overweight and protects against the development of atherosclerosis. The psychological advantages (and disadvantages) of exercise are discussed on p. 84.

Several useful guidelines can be followed by adolescents whose interests lead them to engage in competitive athletics. In general, if they suffer unusual physical symptoms during exercise, they should have these evaluated by a physician and, if necessary, treated. While engaging in competitive sports, a yearly physical examination is wise. It provides an opportunity to check for problems that might not be evident and might make it advisable to change the form of competitive sport or the degree of participation. It isn't usually necessary to place limits on physical activity and competitive athletics for adolescents, but limits may be recommended when an increased work load on the heart might have an undesirable effect. Such problems usually involve impediments to blood circulation from the heart to the lungs or through the body, either because of physical obstructions or increases in blood pressure. Some orthopedic problems, discussed later in this book (see p. 165), may require sensible limitations on activity. Adolescents with acute medical problems may need to restrict physical activity during their convalescence, a principle that also applies to patients who are healing after surgery. Some adolescents who have seizure disorders, asthma, and diabetes mellitus may need to have some adjustments made in their activity or in their therapeutic programs so that they can participate in sports without undesirable side effects. In addition to preliminary medical screening, a sound competitive sports program should include an emphasis on good conditioning and avoidance of injury, skilled coaching, adequate protective gear, player safety, and access to good training and medical care. In contact sports that are associated with frequent injuries—particularly football and wrestling—the use of protective equipment is very important. In addition, competing athletes should be matched according to their size, strength, and athletic skill. This process makes participation fairer and more enjoyable for all athletes, and also makes it safer. Matching of competitors becomes especially important when girls compete with boys in sports.

Sleep

A casual consideration of the process known as sleep might lead to a hasty conclusion that sleep represents a daily void during which nothing happens. As we are now beginning to understand the process, it is clear that quite the opposite is true. In its simplest terms, sleep affords many adolescents with an escape from life's pressures. One of the most marked differences in sleep behavior between childhood and adolescence is the way a child who likes to get up early in the morning and is ready to go to bed fairly early in the evening becomes an adolescent who appears to have difficulty getting up in the morning (except when absolutely necessary) and who prefers to delay bedtime interminably. Staying up late can become an adventure, an opportunity for quiet, or a chance to reflect on the day's activities and to contemplate plans for the next day. Staying up also provides time for sociability with friends and family members. Thus, getting up late and staying up late seems very much a part of growing up. During the day, adolescents occasionally take naps, and they are more apt than younger children to acknowledge feeling sleepy during the day. It is certainly not unusual for adolescents to feel overwhelmingly sleepy during classes in school. They may find it, in fact, almost impossible to remain awake.

Adolescents seldom have difficulty falling asleep rapidly. However, there may occasionally be a delay in the onset of sleep. This can usually be attributed to excitement or worry about things that have happened during the day, to planning for events that lie ahead, thinking about relationships with friends, or replaying conversations from the day and mulling over how they might be conducted in the future. In the presence of such pre-sleep activity, an adolescent may well lie awake for a while after turning off the light before actually falling asleep.

Earlier in this section, we noted that the earliest stage of sexual maturation is characterized by an increase in gonadotropin secretion accompanying sleep. Luteinizing hormone particularly is secreted during non-rapid eye movement (non-REM) sleep and its secretion stops when rapid eye movement (REM) sleep begins. These two forms of sleep differ: during REM sleep, in addition to movement of the eyes, there are also movements of other muscles and a somewhat heightened level of vital signs such as the heart and respiratory rates; non-REM sleep is deeper and is accompanied by fewer body movements. Growth hormone, essential to the process of physical growth, is released during sleep and also during the waking hours in adolescents.

Dreaming continues during adolescence, and as they begin to think more and more about themselves, adolescents become interested in the contents and the possible meanings of their dreams. They often think of dreams as secrets to be kept or to be shared only occasionally with an interested and trusted friend.

Nocturnal emission

A striking phenomenon that occurs with dreaming during the adolescence of boys is the appearance of "wet dreams," or nocturnal emissions. They are quite normal. Nocturnal emissions are usually closely associated with dreams that have a definite sexual content, although they can occur in connection with dreams that seem less clearly sexual. Wet dreams may produce two contrasting feelings in the boy: on the one hand, pleasure; on the other, upset over being roused suddenly from sleep. The ejaculate produced in a nocturnal emission consists of sperm from the testes contained in fluid produced by the prostate gland. Although nocturnal emissions can be expected to occur in any adolescent male, some have them more frequently than others.

Enuresis

Enuresis, or bed-wetting, does not usually begin during adolescence, but any discussion of the events that accompany sleep would be incomplete without its being mentioned. The term enuresis refers to the involuntary passage of urine during sleep. Enuresis is more common in boys than in girls, and it may go on throughout childhood. Other family members frequently have had the same problem. In some boys and girls enuresis occurs every night, while in others it happens intermittently. Bed-wetting may take place as a child or adolescent shifts from one stage of sleep to another, or it may occur during very sound sleep. In contrast to nocturnal emissions in boys, many who have enuresis do not wake up even though their beds are soaking wet and cannot recall what happened.

Enuresis is generally regarded as a sleep-associated problem, and when other factors that might contribute to bed-wetting have been excluded, treatment is focused upon measures that change the sleep pattern, or that allow the adolescent to respond more quickly to the urge to urinate by waking and going to the bathroom. When enuresis begins during adolescence, factors that either increase the volume of urine in the bladder or irritate the lower urinary tract must be eliminated first. In diabetes mellitus, the loss of glucose in the urine necessitates the passage of increased amounts of water (see p. 203). In another much less common problem called diabetes insipidus, a pituitary hormone known as antidiuretic hormone is not produced in sufficient quantity to control properly the excretion of water by the kidneys. Both of these conditions can be identified quickly and easily by laboratory tests of urine specimens: diabetes mellitus can be identified by the presence of sugar and, sometimes, other diagnostic substances in the urine, as well as by increased blood glucose levels; diabetes insipidus is a possibility when the urine cannot be concentrated above a certain level. Tests to detect infections in the urinary tract can also be carried out easily. The urine is examined for the presence of white blood cells and bacteria, and a specimen is cultured to determine whether bacteria are present in the urine, what kind they are, and what form of treatment might be indicated (see p. 236).

Children who have wet their beds for many years often tolerate it (as do their parents) with the hope that it will disappear eventually. Indeed in many instances it does. However, when adolescence is reached, and boys or girls continue bed-wetting, they may very well wish to have help in controlling the problem. Some adolescents appear to have bladders that are sensitive to relatively small volumes of urine: a record of the number of times each day that they pass their urine, as well as the volume passed each time, may furnish a clue to this possibility. For these adolescents, some increase in the capacity of the bladder to hold urine may be produced by a deliberate effort to urinate less frequently and to accumulate a larger volume of urine before going to the toilet. The number of times each day that urination is necessary will diminish, and less enuresis may occur at night. Other helpful measures can include the use of medication that either alters the sleep pattern, or improves the bladder capacity or the ability of the bladder to retain urine during sleep. Two medications that are effective when taken at bedtime are ephedrine and imipramine. Another approach involves the use of an alarm system: as a small amount of urine is passed during sleep, it triggers an alarm bell or buzzer that promptly rouses the adolescent. Using this system, the adolescent learns to respond quickly to the need to urinate and is eventually able to hold the urine during sleep or to wake up before wetting the bed. Because of the variety of treatments that are available, no child or adolescent should have to suffer from enuresis.

Dental health

When good preventive dental habits begin during infancy and continue throughout childhood, they provide the adolescent with an established pattern of good dental care for life. In fact, so much of one's dental health depends on preventive measures that these should be discussed first. We will then follow with some comments about therapeutic dentistry.

Preventive measures

Most of the measures that maintain dental health and prevent dental problems rely on the early and continued use of fluoride and toothbrushes, and on the wise use of mouth guards during activities that may endanger the teeth. So remarkably effective and safe is fluoride in preventing dental cavities (caries) that when the water supply does not contain enough to do the job, it makes sense to have the child's physician prescribe a proper daily dose. Because the permanent teeth gradually build up their protective coating of enamel all the way through late childhood and early adolescence, consistent use of fluoride is recommended until all the permanent teeth (except the wisdom teeth) have come in.

Regular toothbrushing and the use of dental floss or tape to clean the surfaces between the teeth are especially vital in preventive dental care. In addition to removing obvious food particles from the teeth, these measures prevent or reduce **dental plaque,** the term for bacterial accumulations on the surfaces of the teeth. Dental plaque encourages cavities at most ages and may also lead to inflammation and deterioration in the gums, especially during adolescence and adulthood.

Adolescents who enjoy contact sports like football and hockey, in which tooth injury is a risk, should be sure to include a mouth guard in their protective gear. A mouth guard protects not only the teeth but also the lips and tongue from injury by the teeth.

Therapeutic measures

Therapeutic dentistry for adolescents focuses on cleaning—mainly the removal of dental plaque—the filling of cavities, the correction of a "bad bite" (**malocclusion**), and the management of gum problems. Plaque removal by a dental hygienist is a preventive measure, but it is important because plaque cannot be completely removed by the adolescent alone, even with regular brushing. Timely dental attention also ensures that cavities will be recognized and filled before they become large. With the use of suitable anesthetics, filling cavities should be a nearly painless procedure.

Malocclusion refers to a variety of changes in the customary relationships of the teeth, particularly that of the first permanent molars. It often develops when the teeth simply do not fit neatly into the limited amount of space available for them on one or both jaws. Crowded together, the teeth gradually turn from their normal positions, assuming positions that make the malocclusion still worse. Also, when a "baby" tooth is lost early, the neighboring teeth tend to encroach upon the vacant space; then when the permanent tooth erupts, there may not be enough room for it. In addition to the fact that malocclusion may be unattractive, and prevents the teeth from doing their job very well, crowded teeth are more difficult to clean thoroughly and thus more likely to acquire plaque. This will lead to cavities and gum problems.

Orthodontia is frequently associated with adolescence, but it should begin earlier. Orthodontic management employs measures—braces, extraction, and so forth—aimed at creating a satisfactory arrangement of teeth in adulthood. It may involve preserving sufficient space for permanent teeth when a deciduous ("baby") tooth is lost prematurely; creating space for the majority of the permanent teeth (by, for example, selective removal of the first permanent premolars at the right time); and designing braces to move the permanent teeth into positions that reduce malocclusion and improve facial appearance. It is not always easy, incidentally, to judge the cosmetic effect that orthodontic treatment has on facial appearance in adolescence, because of the large changes, particularly in the growth of the lower jaw, that normally occur during this period of life.

The wisdom teeth, which usually arrive at the end of adolescence or in the early adult years, seldom interfere with orthodontic care. Occasionally they erupt early, cause pain and other symptoms, and warrant dental attention.

During the adolescent years, disorders may begin to appear in the **periodontium.** The periodontal tissues consist of the gums that surround the teeth and the deeper gum and jaw structures that support all of the teeth. Of these disorders, inflammation of the gums, called "gingivitis," is the most common. Its signs are a darkening of the light pink color of the normal gums, a swelling in the gums, and a tendency for the gums to bleed after little provocation. The gums are usually not painful. More serious changes, called periodontitis, can follow gingivitis. This may result in loss of support for the teeth, and eventually loss of the teeth themselves. In fact, during the adult years, more healthy teeth are lost because of periodontitis than from dental caries. Both of these conditions should be treated by a dental specialist. The gingivitis discussed above develops and progresses gradually, whereas other gum inflammations—such as Vincent's infection or "trench mouth"—appear suddenly and involve painful ulcerations of the gums. They too merit prompt attention from a dentist.

Social Issues

Friends

Importance of peers

The more scientists study children's peer patterns, the more they have been impressed by how early such patterns begin and how important they are for development in general and for self-esteem in particular.

While peers and friends are important at every age, they are especially significant for adolescents. Except for the first part of infancy, adolescence is the time of life when the most rapid growth and development occur. Everyone needs help sorting out these changes. And although before and after adolescence the child usually feels fairly comfortable using parents to answer questions and give advice, this practice is less likely during adolescence.

Rapid growth makes teenagers especially fearful about whether or not all is going normally. Bodily growth is very individual, and the greatest changes occur in those parts that differentiate sex. Changes that are too much, too little, too soon, or too late may all evoke concern. To obtain some sort of perspective, adolescents form groups to bolster one another. One way that they have found to minimize these bodily worries is to make themselves all look as much alike as possible. The conformity is not confined to the same sex, but crosses between sexes in such things as jackets, jeans, haircuts, and boots. Young adolescents have always had a psychological investment in the idea of unisex fashion. When you are not sure whether or not your sexual development is going to turn out the way you and society expect, there is something reassuring about the notion that it does not really matter. By the middle teens, however, the sexual confidence of most adolescents is greater, and individual identity begins to become increasingly important.

Peer influences

A child grows up learning right from wrong mainly from parents. Peer influence is of course present but less important prior to adolescence. With the beginning of adolescence, the son or daughter must separate enough emotionally from the parents to become an autonomous adult. To become an adult necessarily means putting away childish points of view. Most teenagers believe that their parents are not objective enough to be relied on to help modify what are chiefly parental values and viewpoints in the first place. The influence of peers increasingly replaces that of parents during early adolescence. This does not mean that parents' past and present values are not still influential, but their relative importance is usually reduced.

Since the whole adolescent peer group is undergoing these great changes, turning to one another for insight is much like the blind leading the blind. While peers seldom have trouble assuring each other that past values should change, it is more difficult to agree about what should take their place. The early adolescent's attention span is legendarily brief. This is partly due to hormonal changes and the upsurge of sexual and aggressive drives, but it is also due to the social pressure to be something different without really knowing what, how, or why. Reluctant to remain young and dependent, many teenagers will pretend to be more mature than they are. They must try on many faces in order to find their own. But so much physical, attitudinal, and emotional change can be dealt with alone only for a relatively short time, and in order to feel secure, the young adolescent must find stability outside of the home. The peer culture provides this. The peer group agrees on the "normal" way to act, to think, and to dress. Once agreed upon, everyone who wants acceptance within that particular group must conform. Lack of conformity is dealt with harshly, because it dares to throw doubt on the normality or correctness of the group and, by extension, the individual group members. This protection from such doubt, after all, was a major reason why the group was formed in the first place.

Adolescents are not a monolithic group, although they may sometimes seem so to the beleaguered parent. Adolescents may generally agree that their generation knows more than the preceding one, but individual collections of teenagers do not necessarily agree with one another. Cliques are stronger during adolescence than at any other time in life. Which group speaks for normality? Obviously each person believes or wishes to believe that it is his or her own. From this perspective each adolescent may conclude that those in other groups are not "normal" but too snobbish or boorish or brainy or dumb or weird or straight or whatever. To a large extent during early adolescence, a person's group becomes both a stamp of normality and an assurance of acceptance. As adolescence proceeds and the teenager develops a surer identity, groups may remain important, but in a less emphatic way.

Secrets

Children in general are fascinated by secrets. To the younger child, adults have multitudinous secrets. Children not only want to have secrets of their own, but often feel they *need* them. Parents seem to know everything, so in order to obtain some privacy and the beginning of a self-identity, young children become interested in secret codes and clubs. "KEEP OUT—THIS MEANS YOU" signs are familiar to most of us. As children grow older and learn more about themselves, they have more to keep secret. By early adolescence, boys also have secrets to keep from girls, as girls do from boys. The chief secrets at this time of life are sexual. A best friend is often chosen as confidant, since the secrets are too personal to spread around. Long hours are spent with the best friend. It may become difficult for other members of the family to use the phone.

With time, sets of best friends often join together. It is a sign of maturity for the early adolescent to expand trusting relationships from a single best friend to a group of friends. It is a risky step, however, in terms of self-esteem. Popularity is based on the recognition and positive judgment of peers, but because of the importance of personal secrets, the beginning of a clique may prove stormy. Aesop noted long ago that a doubtful friend is worse than a certain enemy, and when there is a group of insecure people sharing secrets, there is a tremendous temptation to enhance one's reputation at the expense of somebody else's.

Where there are secrets there are rumors. Rumor-spreading by adolescents in a locker room, on a playground, or at a slumber party is often as skillful and malicious as it was at the Medici court. Reputations at this age are made and broken with the same great speed that secrets are shared, distorted, and betrayed. It is because of the fragility of self-esteem and the difficulty of knowing who one is, at this age, that exposure of personal secrets causes so much heartache and depression. As the teenager's self-concept becomes more stable during later adolescence, secrets and rumors become both less important and less hurtful.

Romance

In our culture it is assumed that girls are more romantic than boys. Since "romance" is a difficult word to define, this assumption may well be a bias. Inherent in the concept of romance is heroic adventure, and such is the stuff that adolescent boys' daydreams are made of. All vital people are romantic to a degree, but toddlerhood and adolescence seem to be periods of life when romance naturally flourishes most. For the toddler, the romance is directed quite obviously toward the parents, although in different ways depending on which parent is involved. For the adolescent, romance toward the parents would obviously be incestuous and is therefore taboo and unacceptable. After all, an important social task of adolescence is for the person to learn how first to attract and then to be intimate sexually with someone outside of the family.

Romance is much more a state of mind than a deed. By the end of primary school, reading preferences are usually changing to favor exploits of remarkable success, sentimental love, or extravagant derring-do. Fantasies during the day may preempt schoolwork or distract attention from other daily tasks. Fantasies present after going to bed may put off sleep for hours, a not unusual occurrence for the early adolescent. These are the romantic fantasies that often become translated into the secrets discussed in the previous section. A chief benefit of fantasy is that anything is possible, and for this age the motto might be that nothing succeeds like excess. For some adolescents, however, this benefit becomes a liability. They become intimidated by the strength of their fantasies, and instead of being propelled by them into action, they draw back from them into greater passivity.

Because of their biological head start, girls tend to become interested in boys before boys are ready to reciprocate. Boys are often frightened by the girls' interest, perhaps because they are at some unconscious level aware that their maturity is not sufficient. They may protect themselves by deprecating females in general. To belittle a problem (whether it be a something or a somebody) to the point of reassuring oneself that it can be ignored is a rather common, if not terribly successful, psychological defense strategy. In adolescents we see it used frequently.

Boys' romantic fantasies commonly involve physical prowess. Athletics often represent the heroics of adolescents. They fantasize besting other men, both their peers and their elders. As with the knights of old, the adulation and possession of women often lie behind the dreams of victory over men. Many an adolescent athlete uses the thought of impressing an admired female as stimulus for excelling, whether or not she is physically present or even aware of his infatuation. Proving one's mark against other men is a rite present in many societies to show that a youth is ready to take his place as a sexually mature male.

As adolescents actually begin to engage in encounters with the other sex, romantic fantasies tend to decrease. To a certain extent, however, romantic fantasies are normal and useful throughout life, both as a way to provide spice when one is feeling bored and to anticipate situations one hopes will occur. They can also represent emotional growth through elaboration and experimentation with feelings and thought.

Parents' view

It may be very difficult for you as a parent to see your child growing up and your own influence waning. There may be a feeling of emptiness and even abandonment. It is often an additional hurt to see whom you are losing influence to. It is difficult enough to see adults taking your place, but it is still harder to witness children asking for and accepting advice from peers who seem to be even less responsible than one's offspring. Peer influence is, regrettably, often greater than peers' knowledge.

It is important and proper for parents to know who their

adolescent's friends are and where they go together. It is also a parent's right, if you have a strong opinion about it, to let the child know what you like or don't like about a particular acquaintance. It is generally prudent, however, to comment as infrequently as possible, since a parental character reference may provoke an opposite conclusion from the child. Since adolescence is the age of delinquency, a parent may have understandable concern about bad companions. The impact of bad companions is difficult to put into perspective, since bad companions are almost always defined as someone else's offspring. Bad companions are probably as often a result as they are a cause of delinquency. Separating an adolescent from a group of delinquent adolescents is, however, usually well worth the effort and may reduce or stop delinquent behavior.

Parents are accustomed to keeping secrets from their children, both to protect them from things that would frighten them and to avoid the necessity of answering bothersome follow-up questions. Now in early adolescence parents find it is their child rather than they who is the chief holder of secrets. Many of these are about their friends. Even when the presence of secrets is recognized as a normal part of the separation process, it is most tempting to wheedle and pry into the offspring's secrets. Such temptation should usually be resisted, however, since prying tends to encourage lying.

By banding together into peer groups, adolescents use each other as justification for behavior. When told to come in at eleven o'clock, the adolescent can assert, "But everyone comes in at midnight." If the adolescent gets a poor grade, the story is that "everyone" did poorly on that test. If clothing or hairstyle are questioned, again "everyone" does it this way. Such solidarity is very strengthening for the adolescent, but difficult for the parent to take. A parent is on the safest ground by not constantly attacking the group's wisdom or foibles. As with the boy who cried wolf, too frequent complaints or predictions of catastrophic consequences soon are ignored altogether. A stand should be reserved for those issues in which the parent has either very strong moral conviction or that involve physical danger. In these instances it is one's duty to say what is expected and why. The less often a parent makes a judgmental statement, the more likely it is to have weight. Before a value judgment statement is made, parents should be sure how they feel and whether they agree with each other. A declaration that is halfhearted or that is belittled by one parent will have little impact and is better avoided.

Although friends are extremely important influences during adolescence and parents are increasingly ignored, parental views past and present remain very influential. When hostility does not become so pronounced as to cause a complete break in the parent-child bond, the adolescent usually will return somewhat to parental values during late adolescence or early adulthood.

Sexuality

Menstruation

Menstruation is discussed in the preceding section on sexual maturation (see pp. 19–21), but there are a few psychological issues that should be mentioned here. How a girl responds to menstruation depends not only on its timing and on her formal preparation, but on her personal view of herself. This, of course, comes much from identification with her mother's views of what it means to be woman. If the adolescent does not like herself and thinks of herself as a bad person, she may regard menstruation as an expression of her inadequacy. She will want to deny it and to hide its presence from others. On the other hand, if she thinks well of herself, she will expect and experience menstruation as an expression of her maturity and ability to be a woman. Girls who do not like being female or who resent having not been born male may find menstruation an unwanted confirmation of their disappointment. For these girls, menstruation can disrupt their lives. Other girls look forward to womanhood and find the regular monthly cycle to be an organizing event. While they had been buffeted by all the social and biological uncertainties of early adolescence, having a period every month gives them something to be sure of about themselves.

Masturbation

Is masturbation a normal activity? Yes, it is. Masturbation may be seen with toddlers. It occurs somewhat less commonly during primary school, but during adolescence, it is practiced by almost all boys and the majority of girls. Indeed, the general popularity of pornographic books and magazines attests to the popularity of masturbation at all ages.

Masturbation has always bothered people more than it should. There are a number of reasons why this is so. First, there seems to be a common human belief that anything that feels very good *must* be bad. Second, the strength of masturbation fantasies and body feelings may cause the fear of losing control. After all, at the time of orgasm there are involuntary sensations. It is this fear of losing control and of conjuring up forbidden visual fantasies that through the generations has created and reinforced the false ideas that masturbation leads to insanity or to blindness. Fear of injury to the penis or vagina is quite common, and adolescents sometimes still assume that illness or other misfortune is punishment for masturbation. Third, there is a feeling of weakness following orgasm; thus, there is a widely held but false belief that masturbation weakens the body permanently. This is especially disturbing to males who may also be measuring their progress toward masculinity by how strong they are. To deal with this problem, some adolescents stop masturbating before climax, and this is very frustrating. We've even known boys who took up weight lifting in order to compensate for strength believed to be lost through masturbation. Finally, adults themselves are usually still uncomfortable about their own past or present masturbatory conflicts, and because of this, masturbatory activity in their children makes them uncomfortable. This uneasiness is transmitted to the child whose worries are increased.

Because the guilt many adolescents feel about masturbating is pitted against the pressures to relieve their psychological and biological tensions in this manner, a conflict results. To resolve this conflict some adolescents develop rituals to be practiced before going to sleep. These rituals are pacts with themselves that determine through skill, repetition, or luck whether or not masturbation will be allowed that night. Sometimes these rituals become so elaborate as to be true obsessions or compulsions, and insomnia may result.

While masturbation per se is not physically or psychologically harmful, when it occurs to a degree that frightens the adolescent, it may reinforce feelings of passivity and isolation. Real-life sexual experiences cannot usually match masturbation fantasies for controlled perfection. For some adolescents, masturbation becomes an easy alternative to the frightening ordeal of learning to become intimate with someone else, but usually the fear of intimacy precedes this use of masturbation rather than the reverse. For most adolescents, masturbation is a healthy way to try out feelings, actions, and reactions before deciding what to attempt with someone else. Woody Allen makes this point in the movie *Love and Death*. When a beautiful woman compliments him on his prowess as a lover, he answers, "Well, I practice a lot when I'm alone."

Homosexuality

Although more than 90 percent of the population is probably heterosexual, at one time or another almost all adolescents wonder whether they are homosexual. In recent years organizations of homosexuals and certain feminist groups have taken a strong public stand claiming that homosexuality is normal, but most adolescents are more willing to accept its normality in someone else than in themselves. The frequency of jokes about homosexuality and the use as insults by adolescents of slang terms for homosexuality suggest the degree of uneasiness that is present. Some adolescents regard masturbation as seriously wrong because of the assumption that since it is sex with themselves, the very action reveals homosexual leanings. What does seem to be relevant to masturbation in this regard is the gender of the fantasy partner. Homosexuals' fantasies tend to involve members of their own sex exclusively, while heterosexuals' fantasies are most often concerned with members of the other sex. It is not unusual, however, for those adolescents who will become strictly heterosexual to have occasional fantasies or dreams with a homosexual theme. These experiences are often frightening, since the adolescent may believe they are proof of homosexuality. They are not.

Accompanying their concern about being homosexual, many, if not most, adolescents have some experience with homosexuality. This might involve being approached by an adult. Such experiences are more common for boys than for girls. Forceful homosexual attack or rape, although discussed commonly among adolescents, is really quite rare. It is not uncommon, however, for homosexual experimentation to take place between peers during early adolescence. Since friendships at this time are mainly between members of the same sex and are often intense, physical fondling and exploration are not unusual. When they don't last long, such experiences cannot be considered evidence of a homosexual orientation.

That a person is male or female is probably the most basic unit of identification for who and what we are. Both sexes, however, arise from identical undifferentiated areas in the early embryo, and most of us are raised and taught by representatives of both sexes. These experiences lead to a certain amount of bisexuality in everyone. This ambiguity may be especially disquieting to early adolescents, since this is the time of life when they are expected to make an unambiguous sexual choice. Although the great majority of adolescents do not have overt sexual encounters with members of both sexes, other more subtle expressions are often seen. Boys may become very interested in how things grow and may raise animals in a very maternal way. Some may think that women have a better time in life and wish they were girls. The wish of a boy to be a girl is so unacceptable socially, however, that few boys will admit to it. It is more socially acceptable for girls to wish they were boys, and tomboys are usually quite popular. Although some boys resent tomboys, most boys seem to value them for what they consider to be their good taste and for the charm that such girls may convey. These boys find reassurance in girls and women wanting to be like men. By the middle teens, most tomboys begin seeing boys more as potential sexual partners than as asexual playmates. A tomboy-like compromise some girls carry into late adolescence is an inordinate interest in horses. While an active, boyish sport, the more traditionally feminine care and grooming of the horse often appear to be important parts of the experience.

Through the ages most societies have made homosexuality illegal, and, as already stated, most adolescents hope they are not homosexual. Because of personal feelings, negative social stigma, and/or the loss of possible grandchildren, adolescents' parents are usually very definite in wanting their children to be heterosexual. Although the data are incomplete, it seems as though homosexuals *do* have greater adjustment problems than do heterosexuals. Statistics, of course, tend only to include homosexuals who are having trouble and exclude those whose lives are so peaceful as to come to no one's notice. What is not at all clear is how many of the adjustment problems of homosexuals are due to the homosexuality per se and how many to outside pressures from society. Pressure is again greater on boys than girls. Holding hands and kissing, for example, are quite acceptable between girls, but unacceptable between boys. Bill Cosby in a comedy sketch notes how common it is for a woman to ask another to accompany her to the bathroom, and suggests that a very different response would result if a man made the same request of another man.

Prior to adolescence the sexes are quite segregated, each associating with his or her own. This is considered normal, and although tomboys may be allowed to play with boys, grade school boys who play a great deal with girls are commonly tagged as unmanly sissies. Many boys who accept a homosexual orientation during adolescence first question their maleness *prior* to adolescence. Some, but not most, male homosexuals act effeminate. Being effeminate is not the same as being feminine, but strikes most people as an exaggeration or mocking of certain feminine characteristics. Effeminate boys do not always become homosexual, but those who do tend to have their first homosexual experiences earlier (most often in early adolescence or before) than those who are not effeminate. For the latter, the first homosexual experiences most often occur during middle or late adolescence.

Although there is no lack of theories, it is not yet clear why some people prefer to have sexual relations with members of their own sex. There is ample evidence, however, that adolescents who believe they are homosexual cannot change their orientation on demand. Parental coercion will not change sexual orientation, but may very well destroy the parent-adolescent relationship permanently. Adolescents who are uncomfortable with their sexual adjustment, whether homosexual or heterosexual, should seek advice or treatment from their physician or from someone they are referred to by a person whom they trust.

Dating and sex among teenagers

In the earliest stage of adolescence, infatuations and crushes tend to be directed toward those with whom dating is impossible. Movie and television stars are favorites. These movie stars usually are not *too* sexy and frequently seem at least a little ambiguous in their sexuality. From Rudy Vallee and Frank Sinatra to Mick Jagger, the most popular male stars with teenagers are often not what the adolescent girl's father would call a man's man. Female stars who are most popular with young adolescent males tend to be more sweet than sexpots. Besides de-emphasizing blatant sexuality, these stars are ideal for daydreams because they are not possible. The adolescent is not yet ready for the possible. Crushes closer to home tend to be on older teachers, older students, and then, finally, available members of the peer group.

At the beginning of adolescence, girls are usually more in-

51

terested in dating than boys are. At parties girls often find themselves in one room, while the boys are in another. The boys feign lack of interest and, being at the same age less mature than the girls, tend to be more frightened. At this early time there is much talk within same-sex groups about who likes or wishes to date whom, but little gets accomplished. (Some readers will consider dating to be too formal and old-fashioned a term to use in this modern era. It is, however, an undeniable fact that single adolescent males and females do end up together socially in more or less sexual meetings, and this is the way we are using the term here.)

Early contact often occurs with groups of two or three members of one sex arranging to meet a similar size group of the other sex. This meeting might be preceded by whispers and note-passing and is characteristically accompanied by giggling, mild insults, and perhaps some playful shoving and grabbing. There is safety in numbers, since not much that is intimate can be countenanced in public. If things go badly, one can close ranks and together blame the other group.

Interest in sex must come before action. There is an old story about two young teenage boys who went to the top of the Empire State Building. As they surveyed Manhattan below them, one boy remarked, "Wow, this reminds me of sex!" "Why is that?" his friend asked. *"Everything* reminds me of sex," the first boy replied. One of the consequences of early adolescents' preoccupation with sex is that it is a substitute for being occupied with it.

Another protection against the intensity of internal sexual pressures is the young adolescent's focus on the physical rather than the emotional aspects of sex. The boy, for example, may be very intrigued and erotically stimulated by breasts and behinds, but have no capability for, and therefore little interest in, the warmth of a close, sustained relationship.

Some aggression is mixed with sexuality at all ages, but in early adolescence the aggression is often overly strong and frightening. Fear, uncertainty, and inexperience increase the likelihood that aggressive impulses will overpower and disrupt the pleasure of early sexual experiments. For all of these reasons, early sexual pairings are usually carried out in groups. By the middle teens, however, couple dating is more the rule, and group or double dates are increasingly considered to be immature.

Early dating often has more social than sexual significance. Whom one dates or is liked by adds or detracts from one's prestige with peers, and this consideration is often the basis on which choices are made. Since the young adolescent is more knowledgeable about social than about sexual maneuvers, this perspective provides a comfortable initial approach to dating. Liaisons tend to be very temporary and changeable, however, and it is a time of many hurt feelings.

Boy-girl contact between dates and meetings is often conducted via notes, letters, and the telephone. Each of these types of communication is valued because it allows intimacy at a distance. This important combination is also found in styles of dancing. You may have noticed that the more erotic a dance is, the farther apart the participants tend to be. One can write passionately and not have to be there to see whether or not the message is spurned. There is, however, the fact of writing being permanent. This can be a problem if passions are not returned, are betrayed to others, or if the message is kept longer than the passion. More modern and less indelible than the written word is the telephone. As parents know, most adolescents spend seemingly inordinate amounts of time telephoning one another. A major reason for the telephone's popularity is that things can be said and propositions discussed without either party having to disclose his or her body language. With the telephone, an adolescent can work to negotiate growing up without leaving the house.

As adolescents grow older, there is increasing pressure both internally and from the peer group for boys and girls to form more lasting relationships. For some this is easy and natural. Most accomplish it in late adolescence, still others do so in early adulthood, and some not at all.

Doubts, however, as to whether love is an illusion or whether they really feel it toward the wrong sex or whether sex is only a tool for oppression and exploitation or whether it is a subversive scheme to defuse revolutionary ardor or whether there is no such thing as love anyway (et cetera) are commonly experienced by adolescents. Adolescence is a time of so many interests and possibilities. For some teenagers, romance and dating must take a backseat to art or science or politics or something else. Humanitarian feelings, for example, are very important for many adolescents, and some find it safer to love humanity than individual humans.

For adolescents who are dating, there is the eternal question of how far to go sexually. Biological and social pressures are strong, but so are prohibitions that have become very deep-seated while growing up. The classical concerns of venereal disease and illegitimate pregnancy, although less common than in past generations, remain active worries for the unwary and for those who wish to punish themselves for what they believe are sexual misdeeds.

Middle and late adolescents' focus tends to shift from defining their identity in relation to the other sex to exploring the implications of this difference. The biological pressure of the sex drive is enormous; the species depends upon it. It should therefore not surprise as many people as it does that sex play and exploration are commonplace among virtually all normal adolescents. There are many variables involved in such decisions, the adolescent's judgment being the most important but perhaps the hardest to define. Judgment gets better with age, and it has been shown that the younger the adolescents are the more likely it is that they will get into physical, psychological, and social difficulties with sexual intimacy. Although sexual experimentation is necessary to consolidate an adolescent's sexual identity, experience alone is not enough, and practice at anything is helpful only when done in a way in which something useful can be learned. Sex for sex's sake is seldom conducive to useful learning.

Sexual fondling between boys and girls is common during

early and middle adolescence. In itself foreplay is enjoyable and usually not harmful, but it will raise sexual excitement and lead to the question of intercourse. *When* adolescents are ready for intercourse has never been agreed upon, but it depends on the individual's background, maturity, and situation. Since sex without commitment often tends to be emotionally confusing for the participants, the odds for successful intimacy are greatly improved when the relationship has some degree of permanence.

Intercourse demands more closeness, involvement, and responsibility than does foreplay, and no single age can be determined for when a person is ready to accept this responsibility. Waiting until after marriage is a course more often urged than followed. A minority of people marry without first having had intercourse. In retrospect, those who had intercourse before marriage generally believe it was helpful in understanding the relationship better prior to making it legal, while those who waited are inclined to believe that they also made the better choice. Adolescents are influenced by adults' behavior, and the number of unmarried couples living together rose eightfold in the fifteen years from 1960 to 1975. Illegitimacy rates have also risen steadily since 1960. Thirteen percent of all babies born in the United States now are children of unwed women.

The reality of adolescents' sexual urges tends to be ignored by those parents who either have the capacity for a remarkable degree of self-deception or who, consciously or unconsciously, wish not to give sexual knowledge to their children in order that the young people will be beset by problems as punishment for pleasures that the parents fear or resent.

Sexual ability precedes, sometimes by many years, emotional maturity. There are many reasons why adolescents should not have intercourse prior to understanding themselves and the situation. Besides feeling "used," overwhelmed, or upset in a way that may interfere with future close relationships, the possibilities of pregnancy and of venereal disease continue to be real problems. Surveys show that even among married couples, less than half of all pregnancies are planned. Withholding from an adolescent factual information regarding sexual function, including conception, contraception, venereal disease, abortion, pregnancy, birth, and early child care, reduces the likelihood of his or her being able to make a *responsible choice* about intercourse. It is unlikely that these facts will increase an adolescent's desire for intercourse. In fact, odds always favor people making more reasonable choices about their lives when they can weigh the choices on intellectual as well as emotional bases. Such information is sometimes denounced as giving the teenager "ideas," but the hormonal upsurge at puberty provides such "ideas" regardless of the adolescent's level of ignorance.

By the late teens, most adolescents have a clearer understanding of who they are. After trying out a number of identifications, they have sorted out at least the beginning of an identity. When this has occurred, the adolescent is able to shift from the more limited focus of defining his or her own sexual orientation to the broader task of exploring the implications of the choice.

In dating, relationships during this later period tend to be more enduring. Although seldom possible for middle or younger teenagers, older adolescents' better grasp of the concept of time allows them to actively think and talk about how long the relationship is likely to last. It may include discussions of such matters as living together, marriage, and compatibility of educational and career goals. With greater sureness of sexual identity comes less need for aggressiveness in sex or the use of sex for psychological reassurance or the attainment of social status. The expression of tenderness, which is missing earlier in adolescence, becomes possible, and the partner's enjoyment becomes an increasingly important aspect of the sexual relationship.

By the end of adolescence, an individual ideally has established a sexual identity and has developed the capacity for lasting relationships with people outside his or her family.

Marriage

Popular songs notwithstanding, teenage marriages more often than not are unsuccessful. The likelihood of success in a marriage is closely related to whether or not the partners' expectations about the marriage are fulfilled. When expectations are unrealistic, a marriage is unlikely to last. Teenagers who marry are often looking for escape from a stormy home or personal situation. Although often not consciously, they are hoping to obtain a perfect or at least superior parent. The marriage partners, however, all too often match one another in immaturity. With both partners seeking to satisfy their wish for dependency, neither can fulfill the expectations of the other. Disappointment leads to anger and depression. Although statistics are of no value in judging whether a particular marriage will succeed, the age of those marrying is the best demographic predictor of divorce. The divorce rate for teenagers is over 50 percent. For some of these adolescents, the failed marriage represents a failed last hope. Although married persons are less likely to commit suicide than those who are single, for one age group this does not hold true. For 15- to 19-year-olds who are married, the likelihood of suicide is greater than it is for their unmarried peers.

Some teenage marriages are successful and do last. The likelihood of success is much greater when there is support for the marriage from the adolescents' parents and when the relationship prior to marriage has been stable and of long duration.

Parents' view

Parents may be as ambivalent as their adolescent is about the latter's burgeoning sexuality. As noted, an offspring's puberty often occurs at the same time as the parents are beginning to notice that age is affecting their own appearance and endurance. This fact sometimes leads to parental jealousy of or attraction to the adolescent. Such feelings are normally warded off by the parent, but might contribute to the parent avoiding the adolescent. This is more common when parent and child are of different sex. As one father stated, "After I had been away on a trip, my daughter enthusiastically came out of the house to greet me. As I saw her running toward me for a hug, I realized for the first time that she had developed breasts. I suddenly didn't know where to put my hands. I ended up keeping them at my side and kissing her demurely on the forehead. She seemed disappointed, and so was I."

Some parents would agree with George Bernard Shaw that it is too bad youth is wasted on the young. Parents may attempt to revive their own waning sexuality vicariously through an exaggerated interest in and sometimes involvement with their adolescent's friends. There are two psychological routes that lead middle-aged adults to believe that adolescents find them attractive. First, some parents believe that with the wisdom acquired over the years they can succeed romantically with adolescents in a way they could not in their youth. Second, since misremembering for the better becomes increasingly common as one grows older, parents may exaggerate their previous levels of popularity, beauty, and prowess and then believe these still exist. An adolescent is as sensitive to parents trying to share his or her sexual life as the parents were earlier when the then younger child tried to intrude into *their* sex life. Indeed, one often sees in the adolescent's reaction the same combination of resentment and bemusement. An adolescent whose parent acts seductively with his or her friends is not only embarrassed directly, but often loses peer status for having such a foolish father or mother. Another parental emotion may be jealousy. Mothers may be kidded about resenting their sons' girlfriends, but it is also not unusual, for example, that although a girl's first boyfriend is the smartest student in class, he is seen by her father as something akin to the village idiot.

For most parents, memories of adolescent dating and sexuality are composed of a strong mixture of nostalgia plus relief that it is over. Although they survived, there is great uneasiness about witnessing it again in their children. Even once removed, desires and hurts are reborn, and it often takes effort not to impose old burdens on a new generation by expecting them to fulfill wishes that are not their own.

The best chance parents have to influence their child's adolescent sexuality comes before the tensions of adolescence set in. Sex education begins during the first year of life with the way the child is treated in terms of consistency, sexual identification, tenderness, affection, and so forth. Later the child notices the parents' relationships to each other and to adults of the same and different sex outside of the family. Such sex education is continuous whether or not a family believes in sex education. Learning is chiefly through observing one's parents and is most powerful when the parents act in a manner consistent with what is taught and expected. When parents teach one set of standards and live another, what is learned from the parents' life is what usually registers with the child.

Parental rules for their adolescent regarding sexuality cannot be standardized. For example, what language should be allowed a 14-year-old or how late a 16-year-old should be allowed to stay out on a date is as variable as the individual family. While every family has its own style, society does advocate certain general rules and expectations for adolescent sexual adjustment. When parents notice either that their adolescent is transgressing these rules or is not meeting these expectations, it is wise to wonder why. Most parents do not *think* about these issues, but only react to them. Rather than being overwhelmed, it often helps to break a concern down into manageable pieces. Parents should as often as possible include the adolescent in discussing their concern. One of three decisions is likely in a given situation, but the method of consideration may prove as or more important than the particular decision reached. One decision is that although outside the societal norm, the way the adolescent is progressing is how the family wishes it to be. A second possible decision is for the family to try to change things. A third alternative is for the family to seek help from an outside person or agency. A final possibility, although more a fact of life than a decision, is that the parents disagree with the adolescent as to whether his or her behavior is acceptable and that they wish the adolescent to change in a way he or she finds unnecessary and/or repugnant. Options possible here include agreement by the adolescent to see a person of his or her choice to obtain a third opinion or by the parents to obtain counseling with or without the adolescent for help in understanding and working with the stalemated situation.

Siblings

Age

Adolescents often get along most smoothly with siblings who are more than a few years different in age. Much older brothers and sisters are usually viewed as models who more or less successfully navigated growing up and out of the family. This impression usually prevails whether or not the older sibling has actually performed this passage with success.

Infants, toddlers, and young school-age brothers or sisters tend to be viewed with detachment. Having arrived so late in the adolescent's life, the newcomer is often not regarded by the older sibling as a true member of the family. An adolescent girl, however, especially in a small family, may show affection in the style of a second mother to a much younger sibling. The adolescent boy, although also affectionate at times, is more likely to be somewhat patronizing, almost as though he would rather not be reminded that he was ever so unsophisticated and immature as his hopeless little brother or sister.

When adolescent siblings' ages are within a few years of one another, jealousies commonly cause problems. The younger often resents the privileges of the older and wants to be treated equally, in spite of the age difference. Older siblings often claim that the younger sibling is given privileges earlier than they were, and they resent it. In addition, older adolescents often believe their younger siblings' spying and prying are an attempt to learn their secrets and to "catch-up" unfairly by obtaining additional privileges.

Teasing and fighting

While sibling rivalry and fighting are experienced in most families, these problems are often most difficult during early adolescence. Insecurity secondary to rapid growth and social expectations makes siblings of this age group both vulnerable to attack and disposed to fight back when attacked. The result may be constant teasing and bickering.

One large subject of teasing is physical looks and changes. Mention, even without derisive comment, of the formation of a sister's breasts or the cracking of a brother's voice may be heard by the older sibling as teasing from the younger sibling and mark the beginning of a bitter argument. Pimples are the source of embarrassment for a great number of adolescents, who are extremely sensitive to remarks and even to glances. Younger siblings are usually rather less eager to tease about pimples than about other physical manifestations of puberty. Such restraint is usually less a matter of etiquette than the fact that the younger siblings may realize that pimples can strike anyone, themselves included. The horror of the possibility of a pocked face may be great enough to bring out sympathy even from where it is thought not to exist, in the preadolescent brother.

Overweight, however, is another matter. Overweight is the most common health concern of adolescents, and in our culture being fat is a severe stigma. In addition, there are a number of vicious cycles involved with being overweight. First, inactive adolescents tend to gain weight, and people who are overweight tend to be inactive. Second, inactive adolescents tend to be unpopular, unpopularity tends to lead to isolation and sadness, and eating is a common response to loneliness and sadness. Therefore, fatness is fair game. Also, since it is generally believed that weight can be controlled, teasing can be rationalized as being constructive rather than destructive. Teasing usually continues over a long period only when it is believed to be deserved. The two most common rationalizations in this regard are that the teasing is for the person's own good—to encourage him or her to change so as not to be so easily teased—or that the teasing is only fair retaliation for previous slights or injustices perpetrated by the person teased.

Besides physical looks and changes, the second most common focus for sibling teasing is on sociosexual issues. Kidding of adolescents by younger siblings about boyfriends, girlfriends, and dating has been incorporated in radio and television plots since family shows were first created. Younger brothers, perhaps because males are more anxious than girls about sexual performance and because boys are expected to be more aggressive sexually than girls, tend to do more teasing about sociosexual issues than do younger sisters.

At times teasing becomes a physical interchange. Such encounters may be loud, but are seldom violent and usually take the form of shoving or tussling. These experiences are often important, especially when the siblings are male and female. Parental reasoning seldom does much to stop it because the participants are so gratified by it. In the same manner as divorced couples who love to fight because it is a legitimate way of remaining close, adolescent siblings who fight obtain similar benefits. Since the touching and feeling experienced in the fighting are done in the name of hatred and anger, neither the stimulation nor the pleasure it gives need be acknowledged.

Since it takes two interested parties to keep it going, and most adolescents mellow with age, sibling teasing and fighting usually tapers off in frequency when one child reaches middle or late adolescence.

Positive reactions

While the emphasis so far has been chiefly on difficulties between siblings, there are many positive aspects as well. Affection between siblings is frequently used as a model for affectionate feelings with peers. The experiences of older siblings are often used for learning by younger adolescents who by what they see and hear have an easier time facing and mastering the same tasks. Adolescent siblings also often use each other for support at home and together are sometimes able to get parents to alter rules that one of them alone would not have the influence to change.

Parents' view

Most parents become aware of sibling rivalry at the time of the birth of their second child. The ferocity of rivalrous actions usually decreases after the toddler years, and parents find it disheartening when the problem intensifies again with adolescence, especially since the children are now too large to control or separate easily.

The chief ingredient in sibling rivalry is jealousy. This emotion cannot be totally avoided in any achievement-oriented society and must be expected. It is obvious that the more pressure placed on children to excel the more likely it is that jealousy will become a problem. It is one of the prices of ambition. Jealousy is the emotion of those who feel they are failing to come up to some mark; therefore it follows that taunts, teasing, and fighting are usually started by siblings who feel inferior or who feel they need a boost to their self-esteem.

Jealousy, however, is a very inefficient emotion. Dwelling on the success of others is a constant reminder of one's own inferior position, and the energy consumed is unavailable to further oneself in a real sense. Pushing someone else down does not necessarily, as with a teeter-totter, elevate oneself, even though that is what the teaser hopes and expects.

What are parents to do? First, the fewer comparisons made the better. Even when compared favorably to peers, adolescents realize they are reduced to being part of a network of intra- and interfamilial competitions to determine parental ratings of success. It is better for parents to approve or disapprove without relating the adolescent's performance to that of siblings, cousins, or neighbors. The rest of the world offers plenty of comparison feedback to children, and home should be one place where everyone is judged individually.

Second, the more time and attention parents can give adolescents the less they will have to fight each other to gain what they feel is enough. Some adolescents find a powerful incentive for trouble when they learn that while they are quiet they are ignored but when they "act up" they are successful in getting attention.

Finally, parents should as much as possible avoid intruding into sibling arguments. There are, of course, times when one cannot stand the aggravation any longer or when there is the fear that someone will get hurt, but in general parental intervention in sibling disagreements is not helpful and often makes matters worse rather than better. Except when obvious, trying to determine fault is usually a mistake, since it continues to pit sibling against sibling. This approach not only encourages lying, but underlines the determination that one sibling is right or good and the other wrong or bad. Such a conclusion is likely to be used as a basis for further jealousy and fighting. In any case, it is rare that a parent *can* be sure which adolescent "started it" or is "right." Too often parents try to act as Solomon when it cannot be done, and it is a good rule not to attempt the impossible.

School

Meaning of changes in mental ability

As with physical growth, the spurt in thinking ability that takes place during adolescence is second in magnitude only to that which occurs in infancy.

Advances in the intellectual ability to conceptualize begin around age 11 or 12 and are usually relatively stable by the age of 15 or 16. The major change is the ability to think logically about abstract concepts. During the latter part of grade school, the child learns to think logically about sets of concrete objects or groups of similar structures, such as numbers, and to classify them. During the teens, an adolescent learns to detach logical considerations from the objects themselves and also to manipulate mentally concepts that are not tied to objects or to any kind of classification. In short, what this maturation allows is the reasoning of hypotheses, even when the ideal or theory is abstract and doesn't connect to things and issues already known. The shift from being able to think only in concrete terms, or how things are, to abstract terms, or how things might be, gives rise to many of the characteristics usually considered typical for adolescence. Adolescents often go overboard with their newly found mental ability. They revel in switching the focus of an issue, especially when confronted with a problem or a complaint, from what has already happened or is likely to happen to what might have happened or what should happen. It is obvious that arguments conducted at two levels of abstraction can never reach a mutually acceptable conclusion. It is this fact that has led some parents to the belief that there is nothing wrong with teenagers that reasoning with them will not aggravate!

It is not unusual for some adolescents to become preoccupied with ideal abstractions and with utopian planning. In this way adolescents act as a conscience for their elders and as a source of alternative thinking for old problems. On the other hand, such thinking is usually less practical than the adolescent believes (although often *more* practical than older adults believe). Because of this, adolescents' solutions to political and moral problems are often impractically direct and do not take into account the emotions of people who might resist the change. Only during late adolescence or early adulthood do most people begin to develop the ability to keep in mind simultaneously the practical and the theoretical, how things are and how they should be.

A second important maturational surge that occurs in conceptual thinking during adolescence is the development of a sense of time. Children and early adolescents are remarkably unable to think clearly about their past or to plan in terms of the future. They are almost exclusively oriented to the present. Life after high school, college, age 30, or, almost certainly, age 40 may seem to them either implausible, undesirable, or both. Not being able to formulate their own future, adolescents can seldom be as enthusiastic as their teachers and parents about preparing for it. As one adolescent said in trying to understand his parents' intense interest in what would become of him later, "I guess the future is not what it used to be."

Once adolescents are able to grasp the concept of the flow of time, they can break out of the constraints of the perpetual present and become capable of projecting their present actions and plans into the future. Adults often call this capacity responsibility. There is a thorn on the rose, however, since with this gift comes the suspicion of one's mortality, and with this suspicion often comes the beginning of terror. This is the reason that preoccupation with the idea of death is not unusual during late adolescence.

Scholastic pressures

It was noted by educators in the past that the simultaneous stresses produced by the biological upheaval of puberty and having to adjust to coping with a multitude of different teachers was too difficult for many students and disrupted their scholastic progress. Junior high (now often called middle school) was originally intended to ease the pupil from the single teacher orientation common in grade school to the different teacher for each subject approach in high school. What actually has occurred is that the multiple teacher approach now begins earlier and has become even more common in primary schools. Although specialization has some advantages academically, it harms the work of a fairly large group of students, because even in early adolescence they still need the support of a close personal tie with one teacher.

Some studies have found that adolescents ranked school and studying as their most important area of conflict. Although educational and vocational goals must be determined at this time, adolescents often do not know what they want to be, a problem again related to their difficulty in grasping a sense of time. Those pupils who do do well may be teased by their peers as being "brains," while nonacademic students may be berated or ignored by the school staff. Not enough attention is given in most schools to the recognition and encouragement of work competence. There is a substantial number of students in every high school who are not academically oriented, but who are capable of being aided to join the work force successfully before or following graduation. For example, a recent follow-up study of "hyperactive" primary school children showed they were rated very low by high school teachers, but still later, as young adults, they received work ratings from their employers that were no lower than the average rating for all other employees on that job.

In the more academic high school tracks, there may be not only intense competition but much cheating to further class standing. The recent increase in the number of those of adolescent age has made places in prestigious schools especially difficult to attain. As the adolescent population decreases in size, which it is now beginning to do, competition will also lessen. It would be helpful if more facilities became available for the adolescent who wishes a chiefly technical rather than a chiefly scholastic education. The constant lengthening of education, especially when puberty is arriving earlier and earlier, has forced many adolescents to remain in school long after they wish to and are able to do something else.

For some adolescents the pressures of school are too great. Some students are truant because they wish to do something else. These students are then often suspended or expelled, a punishment philosophically akin to locking up a drunkard in a brewery. In fact, only about 5 percent of the more than a million suspensions from school each year are for what can be considered truly dangerous behavior. Other adolescents may stay away from school not because they wish to be elsewhere, but because they are afraid to leave home. This type of school avoidance is frequently a sign of quite serious psychological difficulty (see p. 242).

Teachers

Adolescents spend almost as many of their waking hours at school with teachers as they do at home. Since adolescents are in the process of distancing themselves emotionally from their parents, teachers often become important parent substitutes. Some surveys show that the majority of adolescent students are critical of teachers, complaining that they are boring or lacking in humor. It seems that although some students are aware at the time of the powerful positive effect a teacher is having, more often it is only after a number of years that a teacher's influence is fully recognized.

Not surprisingly, most teachers prefer pupils who are quiet and do not make trouble. Girls fill this ideal more often than boys. In general, teachers tend to reward pupils who are most like what they are or wish they were. Thus, the adolescents who are most likely to be positively influenced by teachers are those who are involved enough in some aspect of school life to inspire a teacher's interest. Students who are not involved or who seem by their behavior to belittle teachers' beliefs are usually belittled in return. This is unfortunate since the latter category of students is the one most in need of help. One of the most basic tenets of human nature, however, is that people treat others in the manner they feel they are being treated. By the mid to late teens, many adolescents can understand this truth, and the realization contributes to closer relationships with teachers and to an improvement in school adjustment.

Gym

In a number of surveys, boys stated that athletic coaches were the teachers who most often treated them as individuals. Gym gives students an opportunity to win recognition in school through nonacademic achievement. Since school is a powerful social as well as educational institution, it is important that there are a variety of ways to succeed. Schools, however, may become imbalanced in their emphasis, and this causes students unnecessary difficulty.

In some schools only academic excellence is recognized, and physical skill is either ignored or belittled. In these places the assumption seems to be that all pupils should be good students. Given the known distribution of intelligence in the population, this is a foolish expectation. Many adolescents in truth have modest or poor academic ability, and, no matter how hard they are pushed, 50 percent of students will always be in the lower half of the class. When gym and athletics are not provided and supported, the adolescents who would otherwise participate are likely to seek success in different sorts of physical endeavors, including delinquency. On the other hand, students not interested in sports may be ridiculed in schools overbalanced in favor of athletics. Such ridicule may question the male students' masculinity and create problems of sexual identity. Excessive emphasis on sports may also interfere with or discourage the pursuit of academic excellence, both in terms of student support and of hiring a scholastically rigorous faculty.

Especially in early adolescence, students may dread or avoid gym because of their fear of locker room nudity and showers. The physical and especially the sexual changes of puberty cause much self-consciousness. Some students who develop early feel proud, but others may believe that their precocity in some way signals to others their impure interest in sex. Some girls feel ashamed to be noticed menstruating, although this is less frequent than in the past. The locker room and shower may also be experienced as torment by those who mature late. Lack of the body hair, breasts, or enlarged penises possessed by most of their peers can cause embarrassment. Even for the majority who are developing physically at the usual rate, the nudity of the locker room experience may give rise to fears of unflattering sexual comparisons, ridicule, or of homosexual advances, urges, and horseplay.

These fears lead some students to hate gym and others to avoid it. While some uneasiness about gym is common and should not be considered abnormal, students who become incapacitated by their fear or who cannot be consoled with extra privacy and the staff's reassurances deserve further attention. Although it may seem easier to release these students from gym with the hope that all will be well, statistics show that their feelings of uneasiness about their bodies and about sex following such segregation from peers often become more rather than less serious.

Social considerations

The socialization impact of school life is tremendous for the adolescent. Because the rapid changes in body, mind, and family foster insecurity, the importance of the peer group and of feeling accepted or not accepted are greater during adolescence than at any other time of life. Since at least during early adolescence the concept of future is still vague, most students place more emphasis on present social acceptance than on academic achievement that might lead to a higher social or economic standing in the future. Although social position and popularity often do change after high school, a surprisingly large number of adults have difficulty adjusting to these changes, up or down, and continue to think basically of themselves as they were perceived in those first social ratings of junior high or high school. Indeed, adults who return years later to high school reunions often realize to their dismay or horror that the old social order is immediately resumed, even though subsequent achievements may have varied greatly.

Many schools' student populations break down into five major types. There are, of course, students who fit none of the types and others who belong to more than one group, but in general there are those students whose strength is academic, those whose strength is athletic, those whose strength is social standing, those who are group misfits, and those who are individual misfits. Students in each of the first three categories tend to believe that their strength is what the school is all about. The social prestige group is the one of the three that is least influenced by the students' own ability, being based largely on parental achievement, and there is usually the most overlap between the social and athletic groups. Of the two misfit types, the group misfits may express their loneliness through disruptive behavior and threatened or actual violence, while the individual misfits are usually quiet in their loneliness. When ability is present, this quietness may, however, lead to creativity in some field of art or science.

By late adolescence fewer students are in the category of individual misfits. With greater maturity and opportunity, they tend to find one another and coalesce into small groups of two, three, or four. Also, by this time academic pursuits and college aspirations have become more real. Some adolescents who had looked down upon the hardworking students now feel envy of the scholarships, prestigious school acceptances, or other post-high school arrangements of those who had planned ahead more carefully. Some adolescents influential in high school but without obvious opportunities following graduation may be struck with the sad realization that the best of their lives already lies behind them.

Parents' view

Education is the most common way in this country for children to improve on their parents' economic and social status. Teachers are the most powerful rivals to parents in terms of influence on their child's personality development. Add to these forces the leftover feelings of uneasiness about school that most adults still carry with them as parents, and it becomes clear why parents may have very strong and mixed feelings about their adolescent's school experience.

Parents of adolescents are often uneasy about whether or not they are doing a good job and feel sensitive about this concern. They may look to the school either to blame teachers rather than themselves for problems their adolescent is having or to expect the school to find solutions for problems already present. This is especially true in junior high school. This is the age when puberty is beginning, when school groupings enhance rebellion and delinquency, and when anger is especially explosive. Although schools are seldom perfect places, too much is often expected from them. Impossible expectations lead to inevitable failure and school becomes an easy target for parental criticism.

Parents' views of the school are not only determined by whether the school is good at what it is doing, but also by whether or not the goals of the school coincide with those of the parent. Some parents do not believe in education, and some feel competitive intellectually with their offspring. Parents may also feel competitive with a teacher, since as part of the process of distancing themselves from their parents, adolescents may make a point of frequently comparing the parent unfavorably to one or more teachers. As a result, some parents accuse their adolescent of acting uppity, or they belittle learning and academic accomplishment. This parental approach tends to be successful in discouraging the adolescent from learning, although for some students parental disapproval stimulates rebellion in the form of even more dedicated study.

On the other side, most parents want their adolescents to succeed in school. In addition, it is natural for parents to feel some of that success as their own. But herein lies a danger. It is very easy for parents to view children's accomplishments and failures as payments for their labor of parenthood. In this view, an adolescent's studying, grades, SAT scores, and such are experienced more as equivalents of the *parent's* worth than of the adolescent's ability.

Such illogic can cause much mischief. When a student does poorly, the parent may feel both a failure and unappreciated. It is a matter not of the adolescent having let himself or herself down, but of having let the *parent* down. In such cases, the parent's anger and punishment almost always get in the way of focusing on how to help the student improve.

Adolescents who do well scholastically are often a great joy for parents, but even with success there are some potential pitfalls. One is that the students may come to believe that their worth in the family is based solely or mainly on their grades. Such a belief creates emotional pressure to excel that may turn gradually into resentment and rebellion. Another potential problem is that the glow of reflected success can be addicting. When children begin to do well, all parents enjoy the feeling, but some parents, as with other addicts, need and begin to demand more success to obtain the same level of pleasure. Here too, adolescents may begin to be pushed primarily for the parent's need and perhaps beyond their realistic level of ability. Some of those adolescents who are considered "geniuses" by their parents note the incongruity of also being expected to follow their parents' plans for using this ability. They know, of course, that a hallmark of genius is *not* to do what others think and say.

The most reasonable attitude for parents to take regarding their adolescent's schooling is to provide support in obtaining the best education their child can attain. This does not automatically mean the best grades or admission to the best colleges, but an understanding with the school of what the student's capacities are and encouragement to reach them. Such counseling often leads to continued academic work, but it may also lead at times to technical school or to departure from conventional school for on-the-job training.

Clothing

Styles

Clothes fulfill a number of important functions, including protection, decoration, modesty, and communication. Decoration or style may be the most important. Charles Darwin wrote of giving red cloth to naked natives in the damp and chilly climate of Tierra del Fuego only to find that instead of wrapping the cloth around themselves for warmth, they tore it into strips to use as body ornaments. Clothes often act as a sort of portable territory to express either how the wearers feel about themselves or how they want others to feel about them.

Probably the most basic way of categorizing human beings is to identify them as male or female. It is interesting to see that at puberty, when physical sex differentiation finally becomes generally apparent, clothing is traditionally at its most ambiguous in proclaiming its wearer's gender. It is as though the adolescent needs a little more time for identity consolidation before "coming out" completely. A recent additional force toward unisex dressing is the feminist argument that a woman has the right to dress as comfortably as possible, and that traditional men's clothing is more comfortable than traditional women's clothing. Since men seem to agree and show no movement to dress as women do, pants and shirts remain standard dress for a large proportion of adolescents of both sexes.

A second tradition in adolescent dress is that it must not be traditional. It must distinguish adolescent from parent. Whether the zoot suit, the bobby-sock look, or the unisex approach, the style is seen by the adolescent as fresh and distinctive compared to the stodgy dress of the older generation. Another at least apparent generational difference in clothes regards cleanliness and neatness versus dirtiness and sloppiness. The word "apparent" is used because although young adolescents are often dirty and sloppy, as they grow older they may well become very careful about their dress. Even when the style looks sloppy, it may be sloppy in the most studied way. Clothing styles that appear haphazard to the average adult may be in keeping with a very meticulous code known within the peer group. For example, small variations in a general style often characterize different cliques and groups within a city or even within a single school.

Adolescents' clothing must not only be different from that of the older generation, but it must also be different from whatever used to be stylish, often meaning the fashion of a year or less ago. The adolescent need to be different while being the same encourages the clothing fads for which teenagers are notorious. Given the importance adolescents place on not feeling left out, manufacturers have a relatively easy time promoting what is "in" for that moment. Some teenagers obtain high peer status solely by keeping track of what style has become so popular that it must be replaced with something else.

Clothing styles also express class and ethnic distinctions. Socioeconomic class differences in clothing have become less marked in recent generations. A trend begun in the 1960s among adolescents gave status to what was formerly regarded as working-class clothing. With periodic modifications this trend continues, encouraging upper- and middle-class youths to "dress down" more than it inspires lower- and middle-class adolescents to "dress up." This trend will probably also pass and greater stratification will again appear. Since, however, the need to look alike is greater for adolescents than adults, teenagers will in their own way always be more slavish to style than their parents, and less inclined to tie fashion to socioeconomic status.

With the returning importance of cultural identity, many adolescents, especially from the black, Puerto Rican, American Indian, and Oriental communities, enjoy retaining or rediscovering clothing styles that reflect their heritage and proclaim that they have not been assimilated into the white melting pot. Except for the cultures mentioned, the wearing of ethnic clothing has generally decreased in this country during this century. Usually young offspring of immigrant parents strongly wish to blend in with other youth as closely as possible. Adherence to accepted clothing styles is the quickest and easiest way to achieve this.

In terms of age, younger adolescents are more likely than older adolescents to wear either overly modest, immodest, or outrageous clothing. By the late teens, clothing usually becomes less trendy and more similar to that popular with young adults. Indeed, it becomes increasingly important *not* to dress like a teenager.

Clothing as personal communication

Clothing not only represents the adolescent's own particular group, but is also used to reflect more personal attributes. Being our second skin, clothing reflects our feelings. It is common knowledge among adolescents that when friends begin dressing sloppily or only in dark colors, this means they are "down," depressed, or going through a period of low self-esteem. On the other hand, when an adolescent is feeling especially good, he or she may prefer bright or flamboyant clothes. Adolescents will often have certain clothes that they keep to be worn only in particular moods. Such designated clothes tend to reinforce the mood and if worn in anticipation, may even bring it on.

Personal self-expression through clothing is used not only to communicate about oneself to oneself. Clothing is one of the best ways to transmit feelings nonverbally to others. Revealing clothes, for example, may be worn to express potential sexuality or to attract or excite someone else. On a date with someone the adolescent doesn't like, clothing may also be chosen to discourage advances.

Clothing may be used to express potential aggression. For example, for decades leather, whether jacket or boots, and metal studs proclaimed the wearer dangerous and to be avoided. Some persons in such dress are violent, but many more wear it simply as a means of intimidating others, or to avoid challenges and to be left alone.

There are other body coverings besides clothes that are important to teenagers and used in much the same way. Not long ago cosmetics were considered a significant part of dressing up, but this has not been so true recently. When cosmetic fads do occur, such as using a special type of eye shadow or lipstick, they usually come and go quickly.

Hairstyling is another important extension of clothing. It

too can convey information about the wearer's sex, age, ethnic background, group affiliation, and attitude toward him or herself. Adolescents usually wear their hair differently from adults, and, as with clothes, certain subcultures of adolescents display very distinctive—some would say bizarre—hairstyles.

Shoes and glasses also go through fads and can be used by adolescents for personal expression as well as for practical purposes. High heels are sometimes favored by girls, and in some places boots or elevated shoes are worn by males to accentuate their height and sense of masculinity. Sunglasses serve a similar purpose and are favored by some adolescent males as a means of simultaneously preventing outsiders from reading emotions (especially fear) in their eyes, and at the same time presenting a mysteriously threatening image. (The same ploy was popular with chiefs of state from emerging nations during the 1960s.) Once adolescents become more comfortable with themselves, they can allow others to see them without the protective mask. (The same thing happened with the chiefs of state.)

In addition, the inappropriateness of wearing sunglasses while not in the sun attracts attention, a state of affairs valued by some adolescents. Based on the examples of Hollywood movie stars, the wearers hope to give the impression that their faces are worth hiding.

Parents' view

Each generation of parents bemoans the foolish clothing fads of teenagers. At the same time, when they look at old photographs, most parents are equally horrified at how bad the clothing and hairstyles were during their own adolescence.

It is crucial for parents to remember how important being accepted is for adolescents and that wearing unstylish clothes almost automatically ostracizes the young person. By definition a popular style is "in," and it matters little how ridiculous the style seems to adults. Clothes may not make the man, but only a fool despises appearances. A reinforcement of this warning comes from the fact that often adults copy adolescent clothes and hairstyles. It is not unusual to find parents wearing a modified version of styles they dismissed as strange a year earlier. In fact, to keep ahead of such imitations is one reason why adolescents change their styles so frequently.

Clothing has provided a generational battleground for a long time. Adolescents are sometimes considered "no good" because of how they dress or cut their hair. At various times in this country's history, dress codes have been used to exclude adolescents from school, jobs, home, and even from their right to vote. Considering the variety of things the generations have to fight about, disagreements over clothes are often substitutes for more substantial topics. Also, since clothes are superficial and changeable by nature, the great amount of anger and righteous indignation expressed over them should be recognized as foolish in itself and almost always representing other problems.

The cost of fad clothes *can* become a family problem. When a fashion is new, it is almost always expensive. Once it becomes mass-produced and cheap, it is often on its way out of style and therefore won't be worn long. Either way, parents may argue that the clothes are impractical, while the teenager believes they are a social necessity. This problem is greatly eased when the adolescent earns the money to buy his or her clothes, and parents agree not to forbid or ridicule clothes just because they seem ridiculous. When the disagreement is over decency rather than strangeness, community acceptability is a good standard to follow. By community acceptability we mean that the style is used by at least 20 or 30 percent of the students in the class or school. Obviously standards vary from community to community as well as from year to year, and parents may wish their adolescent was copying the practice of a different community or a different group. As a rule of thumb, however, this approach to arguments about clothes is as good as any and better than most.

Driving

When to start?

Obviously, there is nothing magically maturing about a certain birthday, but when an adolescent can begin to drive legally is determined in most states by age and some sort of examination.

Physical prowess is a relatively minor issue for driving competence. As with sex, physical ability almost always precedes emotional capability. Some parents teach their teenagers the techniques of starting, steering, and shifting the gears of the family car before the child can drive legally. While this may help instill driving confidence, there are some dangers. A double message comes across to the adolescent. The law tells the teenager that he or she is not old enough to drive, while the parental teaching implies that there's no reason not to start right now. Parents should realize that once they understand the techniques it is often difficult for adolescents to wait for the legal age before trying out their skills on the road. Parents should make very plain by word and action that their children should not drive illegally. Blurring the point may place the teenager in jeopardy with the law. It may also place him or her in extreme danger of having an accident, and it tends to set the tone for disobeying traffic rules, which in turn increases the likelihood of future lawbreaking and/or injury.

The best indicator of driving responsibility is the adolescent's history of responsibility in other matters. When the teenager can be trusted to follow rules and is generally reliable, it is likely that these same traits will control his or her behavior while driving. On the other hand, traits that suggest an adolescent will not be a safe, responsible driver include untrustworthiness, impulsiveness, the reckless use of drugs and alcohol, and a tendency to lash out when angry. When these latter traits exist, it is better for parents to refuse to allow their child to drive or to obtain a license. It is a fact that driving accidents are the main cause of death during adolescence.

How to start?

The parents' own approach to driving serves as their adolescent's basic training, and this informal driver education takes place throughout childhood. The child notices the techniques of steering and shifting, but what is more important is that he or she notices and incorporates attitudes. The most influential of these in terms of safety include how carefully, rapidly, and courteously the parent drives.

In terms of formal training, most schools or communities now have excellent driver education courses. These can also be obtained privately. Although a family member can teach road skills to the new driver effectively and it will often work well, there are advantages to having the teacher be someone outside of the family. Driver and teacher tend to be less nervous when unrelated, because the situation can more easily be kept on an objective rather than a personal basis. Previous experiences, such as the teacher's own bad habits and past mistakes, are unknown and thus do not complicate the situation when the teacher is not part of the family. An outside teacher is also not tainted by any current family bickering that might be going on. Finally, some adolescents would rather have their competence as drivers come from an outside, "official" source rather than trust the rating of a parent or older sibling, which is perhaps more demanding, and certainly more subjective.

Meanings of a car

A car is a large, powerful, dangerous machine that does one's bidding. As such it represents many things.

Becoming a driver is an important privilege shared with adults; it is a major rite in the transition between childhood and adulthood. Associated with this issue for many boys is the car as a representation of masculinity. Ships and countries may be feminine, but advertisements make clear that automobiles are masculine. Just as some girls clean and preen and give much loving attention to that antique mode of transportation, the horse, many boys do the same things to a car. They find strength and beauty in a car, and the large amounts of time spent on it are experienced as though spent on themselves.

Girls are usually less interested in cars than boys. Boys are under more peer pressure to start driving early and to prove their prowess and courage by driving dangerously. Dares, taunts, and bravado in the pursuit of acting manly kill and maim many young men each year. A boy's predisposition to race and to show off are reflected in the much higher accident rates and dramatically higher insurance rates for boys than for girls.

When an adolescent obtains his or her driver's license, it not only gives status among peers but also represents access to power and freedom. Power comes not only from racing and other show-off stunts, but also through severing an important tie to parents. Once they are able to drive, adolescents no longer need to rely so much on parents, older siblings, or friends for transportation. They can more easily go where they want when they want to. The car may be used as part of a job. In addition, its use as a mode of escape is often highly valued. When pressures build up, drivers can put distance between themselves and things that or people who bother them. Having control over a powerful machine is often soothing and strengthening to the sense of self-esteem. Although the ability to get away can be a source of great satisfaction and an opportunity to calm down, it is not a final answer to problems, and driving while emotional is dangerous for the driver and others. Driving while angry is second only to driving while drinking or drugged as a cause of adolescent traffic fatalities.

Driving also serves as an aid to sexual freedom. A driver's license means that adolescents need not be driven by parents or by others on dates. A parked car is also where adolescent sexual experimentation often takes place. A car is more private than a parent's house and is usually safer than an outside meeting place. Parking for romance may take place on a street, parkway, or driveway, and drive-in movies have always catered chiefly to adolescents.

Car costs

There are many expenses associated with an adolescent beginning to drive. Insurance premiums, especially when the adolescent is male, are often doubled or tripled for a family that does not already have a teenage driver. Insurance companies have discovered that adolescents who have good grades and who have successfully completed a driver education course have fewer accidents. Because of this, adolescents with these advantages are often entitled to somewhat lower than top rates for insurance. Parents ought to check with various insurers to discover what discount their adolescent might qualify for.

Some adolescents want to own their own cars. Occasionally this is a necessity due to work or other duties, but it is usually a luxury urged by peer pressure. Besides cost, the first question is whether or not the adolescent is a safe driver. This determination requires observation of the adolescent driving the family car for a sufficient period of time. As for cost, some parents buy old cars for their offspring, and the teenagers learn much from fixing them up by themselves. Some adolescents help pay part or all of the added insurance premium. In general, a car bought and serviced by the adolescent teaches responsibility in a way a car bought and maintained by parents cannot. Such a commitment on the part of the adolescent for something wanted provides the opportunity of working for a goal and of feeling the self-satisfaction of aiding the move toward independence in a positive way.

Alcohol, drugs, and driving

Drinking when driving is a great killer of American youth, and the problem is becoming more serious.

The annual number of deaths of adolescent drivers has risen

considerably in recent years. This increase is due to a large extent to the widespread lowering of the legal age for drinking liquor from 21 to 18 years. On an empty stomach, most persons' blood alcohol level reaches 150 mg. percent following either the consumption of eight ounces of whiskey or approximately a full gallon of beer. This blood alcohol level has been shown to make a driver thirty-three times more likely to have an accident than a driver with no alcohol in the blood. The generally accepted level at which drivers are considered legally intoxicated is 100 mg. percent.

Drunken driving is a major cause of traffic fatalities at every age, but it is an especially serious problem for adolescents. The number of adolescents involved in traffic accidents and fatalities has risen in every state that has lowered the legal age for drinking, and this increase is not limited only to those legally old enough to drink. The increase generally reaches down to age 15. What has occurred is that since 18-year-olds are often still in high school, they buy alcohol for younger friends who then drive and are injured or killed. Some states are raising the age limit to 19 or even higher, thus more effectively removing the availability of liquor from the high school environment.

Drugs other than alcohol also impair driving. Amphetamines ("speed") often increase risk-taking; barbiturates or "downers" slow reaction time; and hallucinogens distort perception. The drug second in popularity to alcohol with adolescents is marijuana. Marijuana does not encourage risk-taking as much as alcohol does, but it impairs perception and attention sufficiently to increase the likelihood of driving errors. In practice, two or more drugs are often taken together and when this is the case, they work together to destroy the driver's natural skills.

Parents' view

Driving is the most likely way in which one's adolescent child will die. It has been said that it is a good thing that the state rather than mothers issues driving licenses, since many mothers never would, especially to the oldest child in the family.

As noted earlier, the parents' view of driving is expressed to their children through their own driving habits for years before the adolescent is ready to take the wheel. What one does is always more influential than what one says, but what is said is also important. What should be emphasized are the dangers of recklessness and of driving under the influence of alcohol or other drugs. Adolescents should be taught to be aware of the effects of drugs and the signs of intoxication. They should be told not to be ashamed to admit to them or afraid to point them out in others. No one should drive when affected. It should be made clear that these dangers are not only present for the driver, but for all the passengers as well.

When parents know that certain of their offspring's friends are dangerous drivers, they should urge their adolescent not to ride with them. It is also prudent to take away driving privileges when an adolescent abuses them. This teaches responsibility as well as protects the child, car, and others.

Sports

Age and sex considerations

Before adolescence, boys and girls are similar in physical potential for sports. Boys are not, for example, inherently stronger than girls until the onset of puberty. With the influx of male hormones, however, boys do become stronger than girls. A boy's muscular strength usually doubles between the ages of 12 and 16.

Within the same sex, athletic performance is also relatively similar before puberty. This changes, and the unpredictable timing of the growth spurt is only one factor that causes increased variability in athletic performance during the teen years. There is a common belief that rapid growth causes clumsiness, but this has never been proved. It is likely that clumsiness following changes in size, especially when the changes are early, is less due to anatomical problems than to lack of practice following embarrassed withdrawal from physical endeavors. Those young people who want to grow to play basketball, for example, and who keep up their practice show no coordination problems associated with a spurt in height.

In general, physical endurance, stamina, and skill increase throughout adolescence. The most notable exception is swimming: the fastest times are often produced by athletes in mid-adolescence.

Women's athletics have been gaining in recognition, recompense, and popularity. School funds must now be used for women's as well as men's athletic programs. Although some concern remains, the fear that a woman cannot be both athletic and feminine is declining under the impact of the many exceptions seen regularly on television. With the greater involvement of women in athletics has grown the myth that women are more easily injured than men. Careful studies, however, have shown that well-trained women athletes are no more prone to injury than well-trained men. As coaching for women's sports improves, injuries will become even rarer.

Dangers in sports

It is difficult to think of any dangers inherent in sports, but as with all things, there is danger in excess. Excesses may be injurious physically, emotionally, or morally.

The early adolescent may be pushed too hard physically, before he or she has the strength or the ability to adapt to the demand. For example, the heart will enlarge to adapt to increased need, but in the early teens this compensation often does not take place. Another potential problem is that some adolescents develop asthma with exercise, and they should not be pushed into sickness. It is interesting that swimmers do not usually suffer from exercise asthma. In fact, asthmatics have been Olympic gold medalists.

Although usually not a problem in high school athletics, drugs such as amphetamines ("speed") and steroids are sometimes given or taken to improve performance. This can have a damaging effect on the adolescent's body and mind.

Emotional difficulties can occur when sports become all-important in the adolescent's life. When self-esteem becomes irrevocably tied to athletic success, generally there are problems. If the adolescent is not sufficiently skillful to be a consistent winner in increasingly difficult competition, there is often the feeling of being a failure as a person. Even the adolescent who is successful and becomes a recognized star may be forced to pay a high price. Devotion to the practice necessary to succeed may exclude other experiences and accomplishments. Even the future may be influenced. For example, we know a number of people who trained so long and hard as competitive swimmers in their adolescence that they cannot enjoy swimming for pleasure as adults.

Moral dangers arise when young people are exposed to adults whose philosophy is to win at any cost. Bad as well as good sportsmanship can be taught and become the model for a future life-style.

Advantages of sports

Sports, whether organized or not, provide a healthy way to become acquainted with one's body, to build camaraderie, to find an outlet for energy and aggression that could otherwise be used in mischievous or dangerous ways, and to develop physical habits that can be helpful throughout life.

Athletics can provide a means for achieving success. For some adolescents it is only one of several areas of accomplishment, but for others it is the main thing that sustains their self-esteem through this developmental period. Girls as well as boys are buoyed by the realization that they can improve their bodies and are in control of them rather than simply at their mercy. This is even more vividly illustrated when the emphasis is on competing against oneself, against one's own past performance.

It is necessary to stress that not only organized or competitive sports are advantageous for adolescents. Any systematic use of the body—skiing, hiking, cycling—provides exercise, discipline, and self-awareness, all traits that can prove valuable in life.

Most sports require attention to rules. This can be useful at an age when rebellion against rules is often prevalent in other areas of the athlete's life. Some people maintain that athletes use less tobacco, alcohol, and other drugs than non-athletes. This theory is unproved, but experience suggests it is most likely true when the adolescent participates in a sport requiring prolonged exertion and is aware of the effects of these drugs on performance. A final and very important contribution of athletics is that they encourage activity rather than passivity.

Impact of athletics on the adolescent's future

Studies show that adolescents who participate in sports in school are more likely than non-athletes to exercise in later life. It is not, however, necessary to have participated in competitive sports to set a pattern for exercise. For example, it has been shown that adolescents who have physical education programs in their schools are more likely to exercise as adults than those who do not. What seems to be learned is that there are alternatives to physical passivity and that physical fitness tends to make a person feel better.

Ongoing exercise in adult life is related to good health and to a lower rate of heart attacks. Almost half of adult Americans do not engage in physical activity for the purpose of exercise and, paradoxically, surveys show that those adults who do not exercise regularly are more likely to state they are sure they exercise enough than are those who do exercise regularly. In any case, it does seem that an involvement in sports during adolescence is helpful in later life. This is true even though most of the activities named by the President's Council on Physical Fitness as providing the best all-around exercise for adults (jogging, bicycling, swimming, skating, handball, and squash) are not normally included in school programs for adolescents.

Parents' view

The parents' pattern of physical fitness is an important model and will in part determine whether their offspring's emphasis will be on competition, fitness, both, or on no sport at all. Most parents enjoy their adolescent's athletic endeavors, whether the achievements are great or small, and attending athletic contests that include a member can be a very enjoyable family outing. It may even become an important family tradition.

As always, there is the danger of parents becoming too involved or not involved enough. A balance is the obvious ideal.

Some parents are against girls' participating or believe that sports interfere with a job or with academic work. Other parents keep their children out of sports because of unrealistic fears of injuries. A realistic view of just how dangerous a given sport is may be obtained from a physician, the coach, or from parents of adolescents who have already participated in it for a while.

On the other hand, some parents overemphasize athletics. This usually shows up in their tendency to push the adolescent to practice to the exclusion of a more well-rounded life. It is usually obvious in such cases that the parent has attached his or her self-esteem to the adolescent's athletic destiny, and the overinvolvement is at least as much for the sake of the parent as for the child.

Hobbies

Reasons for hobbies

Hobbies are not new phenomena that develop during adolescence. Many primary school children collect things or acquire very strong interests that they study with boundless enthusiasm. Indeed, during early adolescence it is not unusual for established hobbies to be given up or interrupted rather than started. It is as though there are too many new things happening for the young adolescent to concentrate on a hobby. More common are sequential hobbies where a vivid interest in one thing consumes the young person briefly, burns out, and is replaced by a passionate concern with something else, leaving basement or closet stuffed with half-completed projects.

As the adolescent grows older, however, a hobby may offer a comfortably peaceful alternative to the constant changes he or she must otherwise face. One way of categorizing hobbies is whether they involve chiefly doing something, making something, or learning something, although for many hobbies all three factors are present to some degree.

Sports are good examples of hobbies in which doing something is primary. Although activity itself may be a crucial pleasure in this type of hobby, the doing something need not be strenuous. For example, although the adolescent athlete may obtain great satisfaction from actively developing and experiencing his or her body, the teenage fisherman may obtain equal satisfaction and pleasure from the activity of sitting still for hours watching a bobber float next to a lily pad. Although the one adolescent is kinetic and the other static, both are actively doing something that functions as a barrier against other all-too-insistent parts of life. Escape is commonly an important ingredient in all hobbies.

Adolescents may "work" harder physically or mentally at a hobby than they would allow themselves to be pushed by a teacher at school, yet the result is refreshment rather than fatigue. Since the effort is made voluntarily, it is not "work." In rare cases, an adolescent becomes obsessed and *has* to perform the "something" of the hobby, or at least a caricature of it. When this occurs, the hobby becomes a compulsion, and play becomes work.

Many hobbies are chiefly involved with making something. This can take various forms, but one of the most popular for adolescent boys is to work on a means of transportation: a bicycle, motorcycle, car, or boat. It is as if they are building the status and power that will allow them to get away, literally and figuratively, from childhood and family. Cooking is a popular hobby for some adolescents, especially girls, and it too mostly involves making something. Gardening and the raising of animals are hobbies shared by both sexes. Here one helps life to be made and nurtured, and these hobbies are a socially accepted way that boys can experience some of the power and joy experienced mainly by females. Hobbies involving the arts depend on another type of creativity. Many adolescents use the forms of poetry and the short story to make a literary world in which they can express their deepest and strongest emotions. Finally, as shown by the many marvelous adolescent musicians, it is clear that the something that is made in a hobby need not always be seen or touched.

The third category of hobbies is that in which the chief benefit is the knowledge gained in their pursuit. Some obvious examples here would be adolescents who delve into the study of an ancient civilization or who spend great amounts of time with their chemistry sets. These adolescents may not have begun the hobby in order to learn. In fact, one advantage of a hobby is that what one does and learns will not be tested without the initiation of the hobbyist. Learning, however, is sometimes an unforeseen accomplishment. For example, a beer can collector may come to learn the states of the Union; and to fully understand gear ratios and a car's transmission, an adolescent will have to master some mathematics.

Knowledge obtained within the safety of a hobby sometimes leads an adolescent to take a greater interest in learning in general. Such closet scholars may also take a special delight in knowing more about their areas of interest than do their teachers or parents. This satisfaction in reversing the roles of who is more knowledgeable is especially gratifying for the average or below-average student. When such students are encouraged to share officially their expertise with peers in school, self-esteem is enhanced and interest in general learning is usually furthered.

Avocations and vocations

By definition, hobbies are leisure-time activities, but, espe-cially during adolescence, they often bring out hidden inter-ests and talents in ways that help the teenager choose a voca-tion. Because of this, parents are often tempted to push their offspring toward hobbies associated with a vocation they favor. The gift of a stethoscope to a toddler or a microscope to a 6-year-old is not all that unusual, and such "help" in finding an appropriate hobby for an adolescent may be equally unsubtle and unsuitable. Adult pressure not only changes a hobby into work, but usually is also not successful. Although, for example, some adolescents who love to draw buildings become ar-chitects and some chemistry set fanatics become chemical engineers, most often the interest precedes the hobby rather than being caused by it.

More often, instead of leading to a specific vocation, a hobby is beneficial in nonspecific ways. It teaches adolescents about themselves. As already noted, in hobbies adolescents may learn without "working" at learning. In this process they may realize they possess an attention span far greater than they or their teachers had heretofore been aware. Learning that one can process information, follow instructions, and see things through is crucial in developing the confidence needed in finding and mastering employment. Hobbies may also demon-strate to the adolescent that while he or she may have trouble with academic schoolwork, it is possible at the same time to have many other skills. Today about five million adolescents of high school age are enrolled in public vocational schools, and the increase of employer participation in vocational education has allowed many youths to make the transition smoothly from hobby to training to work.

Parents' view

Most parents are pleased with their adolescent's interest in hobbies as long as it does not get in the way of schoolwork or things that must be done around the house.

Sequential hobbies, however, can pose a number of problems and concerns for parents. First, hobbies can involve very expensive lessons and equipment, and a constant turnover of interests can be unrealistic for a family budget. For example, some young adolescents constantly change musical instruments, while others obtain extensive athletic equipment only to lose interest and request more for another sport. Second, sequential hobbies can fill closets if not rooms with once loved but now rejected paraphernalia. To clear the mess, parents usually want it sold or given away, while the adolescent is more often reluctant, believing it "might come in handy one day." Third, some parents worry that hobbies keep their child from doing something more useful. Obviously, some hobbies are more productive and creative than others, but hobbies are leisure-time activities and leisure time is needed at all ages. Conflict is most likely to come when parents believe their adolescent is spending too much time on a hobby. While this is a very legitimate concern, it is important to weigh what actually will take its place if hobby time is curtailed. Often what replaces it is inactivity or less desirable activity rather than increased work at home, school, or job.

Sequential hobbies are less frequently found with older adolescents, but at this age persons may want to take time off from work or school. This is the well-known moratorium or "time out" that Erik Erikson has written about. In general, a moratorium involving travel or immersion in a special interest or hobby will eventually aid the adolescent in settling down to a productive life. On the other hand, taking months or years off without any plans for how the time is to be spent is much less likely to lead to adjustment.

Religion

Typical reactions

When their parents are religious, usually the young adolescents are also religious, but less so than their parents would like them to be. When asked, these adolescents typically say they believe in God and do not mind going to church or synagogue but do not like going as often as their parents wish them to. Dressing up and sitting still are aspects of religious services about which young adolescents often complain. For this age group, the concept of God learned in childhood is still quite strong, but with the developing ability for abstract thinking, Bible stories and their old explanations may no longer seem so clear. Adolescents whose faith remains but not their understanding may become argumentative, but when handled sensitively will find new, less simple understandings. Those whose faith ends with their lack of understanding do not argue.

It is common for religious faith to be relatively unimportant in the lives of adolescents during their final years of high school. During this time, social events and contacts may be the most important aspects of the adolescents' ties with their temples or churches. This relative religious indifference typically continues when adolescents leave home for work or college, although some youths return to religion at this time, finding in it a strength associated with their lost parents and childhood.

Religious fervor

For some, adolescence is the time of peak religious experience. Throughout history evangelical movements have been bolstered to a large degree by enthusiastic teenaged converts. Such fervor is, however, a mixed blessing. A revival movement marked by a large number of adolescents is usually unacceptable to adults, and without the interest of adults it is unable to sustain itself.

93

Even outside of the revival movement, strong religious conviction is a keystone for some adolescents' development. They either use their religious conviction to exclude themselves from the academic and social activities common to their peers or use it to sustain a single-mindedness in obtaining a goal. It is not unusual, as examples of the latter, to listen to an interview with a promising ballerina, a chess champion, or a world-class swimming star and hear him or her credit religious conviction for the ability to sustain the self-deprivation required in order to attain a high level of skill. Indeed, adolescence is the most popular age for the development of religious asceticism, and this may lead either to enhanced self-awareness, to solid achievement, or to sterile withdrawal.

Transition to adulthood

In the past when society was more closely tied to religious practice, a specific religious ceremony would often mark the turning point from childhood to adulthood. When the adolescent was converted, bar or bat mitzvahed, baptized, or confirmed, then he or she was considered no longer a boy or a girl, but a man or a woman. The service was very important in terms of identity formation. One day the person was officially a child and the next an adult. As the secular landmarks of finishing school and earning a living have more and more replaced the religious rites of passage, the demarcation between child and adult has become less definite and more prolonged. This is one of the changes that helped develop what we now call the stage of adolescence.

Religious enthusiasm or at least confirmation of the parents' stated beliefs has traditionally allowed entry into the world of adults. It was considered a sign of maturity and a reason for acceptance, even by those adults who were not especially religious themselves. Religious enthusiasm can also, however, be used as a way to prolong adolescence or to reject acceptance by the adult world.

Adolescents are very aware of the hypocrisy often connected to religion. Throughout their childhoods they may have been forced to attend religious services, while their parents did not. They may have heard their parents worship one way, but act in a completely different way toward family, friends, and business associates during the rest of the week. They may have also been aware that the appearance of religious faith is flaunted in politics, especially presidential politics, while there is seldom palpable evidence that the religious convictions espoused are converted into national or international approaches to policy. It is therefore very common for adolescents to drop out of religion, although they often return to the religion of their parents shortly after they themselves become parents.

While some adolescents express their separateness from their parents by rejecting their parents' religion, others express rebellion and independence not through an absence of religion but through the way they express their religious beliefs. Most religions are personal, and therefore religiosity is difficult to measure. Adolescents who choose a religion different from that of their parents or who emphasize a different aspect of the family religion can easily consider themselves as more religious than their parents. The parents may be accused of not having the correct faith or a strong enough faith. The adolescent becomes the religious parent of the parents.

Some adolescents become interested in Eastern religions, transcendental meditation, and other beliefs emphasizing contemplation. Adherence to this life-style may be used as a rebuke of parental achievement and an excuse for not entering the competitive world of adults.

Adolescents who become religious zealots illustrate a different approach to a similar child-parent outcome. Throughout history there have been sects catering mainly to adolescents. These groups generally combine a charismatic male leader, rejection of the values of conventional adult society, an intense combination of asceticism and excess, and the conviction that only initiates understand the meaning of life. Usually, at least three-quarters of the members are female. Parental and family values are denigrated, and obedience to the leader is absolute. Such groups provide adolescents with an unchallengeable rationale for separating from their families while maintaining a connection to a protecting, all-knowing parental figure who provides them with a religious task. This task transcends the cultural expectation to enter the work force and to form conventional social and sexual relationships. Such groups are often so rule-bound that they do not allow the adolescents to think for themselves or to explore different approaches to adult life. Although such authoritarianism outside of the home may seem liberating and comforting, too often participants never grow beyond the need to follow a leader. Such sects seldom last for more than five or ten years, new ones are always forming, and habitual participants usually find a new leader who offers a similar structure, although the new beliefs may be very different.

Occasionally adolescent religious rebellion goes beyond ideological confrontation. Commonly this never gets beyond the stage of an adult's arm being grabbed on a street corner in order that the evangelical adolescent can make an impassioned plea or thrust a pamphlet into the hand. Occasionally, however, religious belief is used as a reason for harming adults whom one envies. A well-publicized example is the Manson murder cult, and the Salem witch trials represent an occasion when adolescents' zeal turned their parents' own religion against them in a most deadly way.

More recently, the November 1978 suicide-murder of over 900 members of the Reverend Jim Jones's People's Temple in Guyana has triggered increasing concern with the control that religious cults exert over their members. While the First Amendment to the Constitution provides for freedom of religion, it is becoming clearer to many people that this right is no more important than the rights of cult members to be protected from physical and emotional coercion. Indeed, our Founding Fathers' interest was as much in freedom *from* religion as in freedom *for* religion. Important questions include whether parents have the right legally to demand the return of a child kept *incommunicado* in a religious commune and/ or to "de-program" an adolescent who is believed to be brain-washed. Because these issues are highly charged emotionally, they will not be easy to solve legally.

Parents' view

Religion is a sustaining force in the lives of many adults. Not only are the religious concepts important per se, but also the continuity with one's forebears that they represent. Accept-ance or rejection of one's belief system by one's children is understandably often experienced as personal acceptance or rejection.

In many families there is a generational tradition that begins with religious training during childhood, continues with a fall-ing away from faith during adolescence, and progresses to a resumption of religious affiliation at the time of parenthood. The latter seems based not only on the wish for moral assist-ance in the task of child-rearing, but also on a wish to please the child's grandparents and be assisted in a difficult task by the comfort of a known and socially accepted approach to moral teachings. Just at the time that new parents are intro-ducing their young children to religion, they may be so ab-sorbed with personal advancement and security that their religious affiliation is more in form than practice. By middle life, however, many adults go through a period of self-assess-ment and conclude that they are not as self-sufficient as they had wished. Especially for those with a religious background, such a discovery may increase the importance and meaning of religion at the same time that their now adolescent children are at a peak of needing to feel self-sufficient and without the need of parents or parental religion.

Parents often wonder how hard they should push religious training, especially when their children become adolescents. As with other types of training, what has been done before adolescence will usually be more important to the outcome than what is done during this period. The best measure of how much to stress religious training for a young child is the level of the parents' own beliefs. Parents who do not have true religious beliefs themselves, but who force their children to obtain unwanted instruction, often find that as the children grow older, they follow what the parents do rather than what they say. In addition, adolescents may rightly brand the parents as hypocritical and then hold this up as the main reason for their giving up the parents' religion.

Parents who do have religious feelings usually have no doubt about wanting to give their children instruction. Again, this should be consistent with the level of the parents' own beliefs. Younger children usually accept such training as natural, since what they learn at church or temple is reinforced by life at home. During adolescence, these offspring may turn away from religion as part of rebellion. Without the complaint of hypocrisy, however, usually there is less vigor or bitterness present than in the church-schooled adolescents of nonreligious parents. Many, if not most, of the children of religious parents who turn away as adolescents return again in their twenties or thirties to the faith of their parents.

Adolescent dating of those of a different faith is a major issue for some parents. While it is clear why parents wish their children to remain in their faith and bring up grandchildren that way as well, it is also clear that haranguing is not very persuasive. It is reasonable and important that parents make known to their children the reasons why they are against interfaith marriages, if that is the case, but repeated questioning or other types of harassment seem to drive more adolescents away from the fold than persuade them to remain.

Parents who are atheists or agnostics sometimes become quite concerned when their adolescent becomes interested in religion. Interest may be stirred through pamphlets, television, or schoolmates. As in the religious families, how the adolescent acts toward religion will depend greatly on the model presented by the parents. Those parents who are clear as to why they are not religious, who have a clear set of secular values, and who are not defensive or prone to attack religion compulsively are likely to raise children who feel the same way. As an expression of rebellion, however, some adolescents from nonreligious families choose religious conversion as a way to show their separateness. This may be especially appalling to parents whose refusal to adhere to a faith represents for them radicalism, rationalism, or an important distinction between them and their own parents. For example, we once heard an outraged and incredulous woman complain that her adolescent son had "become religious in spite of the fact that we disproved all that rubbish twenty years ago." Clearly one important aspect of religious faith is that it does not have to follow logic.

Employment

Work in the home and neighborhood

Most grade school children do tasks around the house, and many of them are paid in the form of an allowance. At the time of adolescence, with a new interest in clothes, food, and social obligations, teenagers often look around the neighborhood for ways of making money. This may have begun earlier with the youngster clipping coupons in comic book ads promising fantastic profits to youthful door-to-door sales personnel who specialize in greeting cards, cosmetics, and magazine subscriptions. While some young adolescents may join the mail-order work force, the strength and responsibility that develop during the teens allow a more diversified approach to neighborhood employment.

At the age of 11 or 12, paper routes become a job opportunity in most cities. A paper route is the most common first job outside of the home for boys, and girls also have recently begun to deliver papers. With the advent of employment outside of the home, the adolescent faces the problem of balancing the time needed for work against the time wanted for play. One often hears spirited debate among seventh graders as to whether a morning or afternoon paper route is better. The protagonists' positions usually depend on whether they prefer sleeping in the morning to athletics in the afternoon. (The weight of the papers is also an important, but usually secondary, debating point in deciding which paper to deliver.) Besides teaching an appreciation of the time required to deliver the papers, a paper route compels a carrier to learn to deliver the papers on time and in the right place. Probably, however, the key lesson learned by delivering papers is that nothing is earned until the money is collected. This is often the most difficult part of the job, and the young adolescent must develop persistence and overcome the shyness with adults that is common at this age. In order not to lose money, the carrier must collect at least as much as he or she owes the company for the papers. Anything over this is profit.

Baby-sitting is a common money-making job, especially for adolescent girls. Responsibility for taking care of younger children often begins in the home with younger siblings. Full responsibility without an adult present usually takes place first for short periods during the day. It is interesting, however, how often neighbors will ask a girl to baby-sit for their children before her own parents have allowed her to stay alone with her younger siblings at home. This may be because parents "know too much," but more often is probably because adolescents do act more mature with neighbors' children than with siblings for whom they have much stronger and often rivalrous feelings. Depending on the baby-sitter and the situation, many early adolescents can do a responsible job at night by the age of 12 or 13. Some do it earlier. Sometimes young adolescents first accompany a parent, older sibling, or experienced friend for on-the-job training to see how a baby-sitter should act. It is always important that the adolescent have a way to reach a responsible adult in case of trouble.

Group sitting, when two or more adolescents sit together in order to provide mutual support and comfort, can be helpful, especially during first jobs. Once familiarity with sitting occurs, however, multiple sitters are likely to provide distraction rather than support, and the employing parents are likely to find that more means less in terms of the sitters' attention to their child. As baby-sitters grow older, visiting friends become an increasing hazard and are usually best banned.

Baby-sitting performance depends most on interest and experience. There is an increasing awareness that boys can also take care of younger children, and that there is certainly no biological reason why boys cannot baby-sit as competently as girls. Baby-sitting is an especially useful job for both sexes, since it teaches adolescents responsibility not only to employers—the parents, who are their elders—but also to younger, demanding, dependent children. This latter role is a rarity for most adolescents and provides an experience that allows them a sympathetic understanding of the task of being a parent at a time when such an understanding is not one to which they are naturally inclined.

Other common neighborhood jobs include lawn mowing and sidewalk shoveling. This type of work is traditionally done by boys, although especially with power mowers it may be within the physical capacity of girls as well. The greatest lesson learned with such jobs is usually the importance of commitment. To be responsible and successful, the lawn must be cut on schedule and the shoveling must be done after every snowfall, regardless of how inconvenient the timing is or how many other more exciting activities present themselves.

Summer jobs

Many adolescents earn money by working during the summer. In early adolescence such work may consist of neighborhood chores, but around the age of 16 more formal jobs become common. Unless obtained completely on the initiative of the parent, finding work will teach the adolescent something about planning and the law of supply and demand. For example, the novice job hunter will discover that looking for work may be more fun when done with one or more peers, but the chance of finding work is greater when done alone. Competition for grades in school may seem abstract to some adolescents, but competing in a tight summer job market demonstrates clearly that planning and preparation may make the difference between working and not working. Such summer experiences frequently persuade some previously lethargic students to apply themselves more diligently to fall studies.

Work in factories, on construction projects, and at camps are popular summer jobs for teenagers. One advantage to summer work is that it often mixes adolescents with adults from heterogeneous social and economic backgrounds. There has been an increased effort to hire disadvantaged youths in government-sponsored construction, neighborhood redevelopment, and even office and clerical jobs. Adolescents from upper-middle-class homes frequently find summer jobs with blue-collar workers. Daily experience with people from different social and ethnic settings tends to break down stereotypes and teaches the teenager that persons from different backgrounds are not really so smart or dumb or frightening or different as they seemed in the abstract.

There is also much to be learned from working under the command of an adult who is neither a family member nor a teacher. Complaints and reprimands tend to be less tender or personal than the adolescent is accustomed to. Not only is censure apt to be more harsh on the job, but also fairness is usually less evident than in school. A summer job provides the adolescent with an opportunity to experience and survive in a new type of competitive milieu.

A job not only teaches the teenager the difficulties of working under and with adults, but also many positive things as well. The situation of being a peer with adults occurs in many summer jobs, and for most teenagers this is unique. Forming even short-lived friendships with adults as relatively equal co-workers can give adolescents a feeling of acceptance that is very important in developing a sense of self-esteem.

Family employment

Adolescents who work for members of their families have a special experience. Although such employment may also occur in a store, factory, or office, the problems of getting a job and keeping it are quite different. There is much less of a feeling of being on one's own, although much can be learned and earned. Discipline is also likely to be influenced. Although at times family members make it a point to be especially strict with a child or young relative, this is usually not the case, and even when it is, nonfamily employees are usually wise enough not to follow suit.

Working for family is easier in many ways than working for strangers, but it is also influenced by whatever negative family feelings are present. One can never, for example, avoid home problems through work or vice versa. While family employment for an adolescent may be all that can be found or is insisted on for other reasons—as a means of evaluating the extent of the young person's interest and aptitude for the family business, for instance—it seldom offers the sense of accomplishment won by successfully obtaining and surviving in an outside job on one's own.

Parents' view

Most parents are very eager to see their adolescent work. They realize that employability will eventually be the single most important factor, at least for males, in whether or not their child will grow up to be an adult who can function successfully without them. With an increasing percentage of women entering the work force, the development of an adolescent girl's ability to gain and maintain employment is now more widely recognized by parents. A woman without work skills is very much at a disadvantage, even if she marries early, because her options for self-reliability are drastically curtailed.

An adolescent's first full-time job has important implications for the family. The initial question is whether or not parents and adolescent agree on the step. For the high-school-aged student, a full-time job usually means quitting school or having a difficult time keeping up with schoolwork. Parents may believe that the adolescent is jeopardizing his or her future earning ability by taking a full-time job. In some cases the family needs the extra money, and a decision must be made as to how much of the salary should go toward family expenses. Sometimes an older sibling in a large family, especially in a single-parent family, must put off his or her education until the younger siblings have completed their basic schooling.

Another important implication of an adolescent's full-time job is the independence it affords. When he or she remains at home paying room and board, there is the question of how much autonomy there should be. The basic rules of the home must clearly continue to be obeyed, but the teenager is usually allowed much more latitude in regard to personal life outside the house.

Frequently the acquisition of a full-time job coincides with or heralds the adolescent's decision to move out. For some parents this is a disappointment—since the money may be needed by the family or the parents may believe the teenager is not yet mature enough to live on his or her own. Many other parents, however, are pleased when their adolescents can separate and are financially independent. Whether or not parents believe their employed teenagers should move away, most states have laws that designate adolescents who are under age 18 but who support themselves and live apart from their parents as "emancipated minors." These adolescents are considered adults in all legal matters.

Adolescents who are neither in school nor employed and who still live at home can pose a major problem for parents. Vocational aptitude testing can often be helpful for teenagers who drop out of school and who do not know what they want to do or could succeed in doing. Those adolescents who are afraid to work because of the independence it represents should have psychological counseling.

Parental Issues

Rebellion

Because disengagement from parents is a major developmental task of adolescence, parental influence plays a prominent part in whatever teenagers choose to do or not do. It is in recognition of this importance that specific issues facing parents are emphasized throughout this book.

Even when adolescents are rebelling against their parents, the fact that the parents are taken as those against whom teenagers choose to measure themselves proclaims the primacy of the position parents continue to hold. A true-life example is the mother who every morning is asked by her teenage daughter to help her pick out her clothes and every morning is told how horrible her taste is, even though those precise clothes may have been the girl's choice a few mornings before or will be a few mornings later. This mother is actually performing an important if thankless task. By making a suggestion, the mother provides something tangible the daughter can be against and use as a basis for making her own choice.

If the girl were not getting something out of the confrontation, she would tell her mother to stay away in the morning. Her opportunity to begin every day feeling right by proclaiming her mother wrong is too gratifying to give up just because it is illogical.

Is adolescent rebellion inevitable?

Psychiatric studies have for years detailed the predictable rebellion of adolescents. Art and entertainment use adolescent rebellion as a popular theme. Sometimes the rebellion is portrayed as justified, while at other times the adolescent is pictured as a rebel without a cause. A perfect example of the latter sort is voiced in *The Wild One,* a movie about a motorcycle gang. When the young Marlon Brando is asked what he is rebelling against, he answers disdainfully, "What have you got?"

Parents of teenagers tend to commiserate with one another about the rebellious attitudes of their offspring. Children may be good for one's old age, goes the classic joke, but it's too bad that they bring it on so soon. In fact, Mother Nature does seem prudent in giving parents twelve years to develop love for their children before turning them into teenagers.

There seems to be a common thread tying together psychological problems in the adolescent, family discord, and rebellion. Recent studies of large numbers of adolescents demonstrate that for many families teenage rebellion is not an especially serious or disruptive force, although minor parent-adolescent disagreements over how strict parents should be are common. It is obvious that adolescence is a stressful time, and adolescents do report considerably more feelings of sadness, misery, and self-depreciation than their parents recognize. However, it is only when these feelings become especially strong, or when family discord makes the necessary parental support unavailable, or when both these conditions are present, that severe rebellion is likely to occur. While some studies suggest that adolescent rebellion and adult creativity often go together, it is clear that one is not the cause of the other. Less positive factors than creativity are usually involved. It is also clear that although some people believe only rebellious adolescents can become interesting adults, there is little hard data on this subject. We do know that adolescents must at least to a certain extent separate themselves psychologically from their parents if they are truly to become adults. The timetable and explosiveness of this process varies greatly, and the fact that the process *is* accomplished is in the long run more important than the individual path taken to attain the goal.

Parental factors affecting rebellion

One important factor in rebellion is age. Around the ages of 12, 13, and 14, rebellion over seemingly small and insignificant issues is common in most families. Minor delinquent behavior is also most common at this age. As teenagers grow older, arguments become less frequent, although when at age 16 the adolescent learns to drive, there are often disagreements about the use of a car. By the end of adolescence, rebellion is seldom much of a problem, since the truly rebellious teenager has already had ample opportunity to strike out on his or her own. In some cases, however, there is the extremely difficult problem of the older adolescent who combines being rebellious with the refusal to leave home and rebel elsewhere. This problem will be discussed more fully later.

Another important factor affecting rebellion is the parents' tolerance of independence. To many parents, the only acceptable form of "independence" is for the adolescent to do independently what the parent wants him or her to do. This notion is a contradiction in terms and may aggravate rebellion in homes in which it is used.

Independence is best granted gradually. When there is little discipline throughout childhood and the adolescent has had no model for self-discipline, the newfound aggressive and sexual tendencies may well up totally out of control. Discipline cannot be successfully begun in the home during adolescence. It has to have started earlier. If this has not been the case and self-control is lacking to the point of lawbreaking or other publicly unacceptable behavior, society is likely eventually to label the youth as delinquent and attempt to discipline him or her. The label of delinquent often becomes a self-fulfilling prophecy. While such teenagers rebel because they believe they can and should do whatever they wish, other adolescent rebellion stems from *too* strict an upbringing. These children continue to be supervised closely by parents even in matters that adolescents are capable of monitoring themselves. Because of such inappropriate control, the teenagers' powers of self-discipline are stifled and they tend always to look to outside authority for instructions about what is right and wrong. This defect in self-discipline may not be a problem when the teenager remains in a close and familiar environment where the parental values are never questioned, but difficulties may occur when he or she is exposed to other, more open and free life-styles. Once outside their parents' influence, as for example at college, these adolescents may surprise everyone by a show of uncharacteristic, boisterous behavior. Their naïveté may lead to inadvertent rule-breaking as well as to bewilderment at being reprimanded.

If independence is indeed best gained gradually, how can this be managed? Certainly rules should be kept to a minimum throughout childhood. Too many rules are confusing and as with the boy who cried wolf, the child cannot really be sure which rules are the important ones and which are "just because I say so." This does not mean there should be no rules. Such a lack will scare the child, since rules provide needed structure and a feeling of being cared for. When children do not have enough rules, they often misbehave in order to communicate their need for more guidance.

What rules are best stressed are usually those dealing with safety and with the basic moral beliefs of the parents. Rules that are not agreed to and supported by both parents are usually not very binding, and it is important that parents agree on rules before they lay them down. A good general rule about rules is not to give any that you know will not be followed. The linguistic root from which the word discipline comes means "to teach," and the object of discipline should be self-discipline. Rules aid discipline by being unchangeable. By adolescence, however, children are less likely to follow rules just because they are there. This is why a relatively few, well-thought-out rules act as a deterrent to rebellion. If parental rules make sense and are dropped or modified as the adolescent becomes more mature and capable, independence proceeds gradually. The adolescent is neither stifled nor forced to explode through rebellion. Such a parental stance on rule modification provides adolescents with opportunities to make mistakes as well as to grow in responsibility. The freedom to make some errors can at times give rise to parental guilt, as when a parent blames himself or herself for not enforcing rules that would have prevented the errors from occurring. This sort of guilt, however, is not realistic when parent and teenager have discussed the various transfers of responsibility and the dangers inherent in them. It is important to remember that every experience is profitable if you allow it to be, and that it is not easy to know what is enough until you allow yourself to know what is more than enough. Adolescence is a key period for experimenting with various quantities and mixtures of independence.

The development of stable values of responsibility becomes increasingly important during the latter part of adolescence and early adulthood. Whether these values are chiefly ethical, religious, or both, they are a needed psychological anchor. Since being human is a random and arbitrary business, everybody needs personal truths to believe in to keep life from being too random and too arbitrary to handle.

Adolescent factors affecting rebellion

Problem adolescents are usually not trying to *create* problems but to *solve* them. In general, young adolescents love their parents, but they must also work on the developmental task of separating from them. This conflict is a major reason behind adolescent instability. In addition, the mix of strong feelings of love and hate enhance the likelihood of misunderstanding. It is a fact that strong emotions, whether positive or negative, hamper one's ability to understand one's feelings accurately. This is a reason why parents can often understand neighbors' children better than their own and vice versa.

Difficulty with communication is usually high on the list when parents and adolescents describe mutual problems. The ability to think abstractly that is first possible during early adolescence allows for the questioning of family rules and beliefs which had been accepted unquestioningly before. This stage is somewhat comparable to the endless "why" questions heard from advanced toddlers. Like the toddler's, many of the early adolescent's questions are difficult to answer because the adult has not thought about them for years. But with the adolescent's questions, the parent must face the truth that his or her personal answers are based on faith or tradition rather than reason. Security lies in the perpetuation of the familiar, and few of us enjoy having the familiar questioned.

Adolescence is usually a confusing time. Because emotions often outreach the teenager's ability to explain them, adolescents don't often communicate accurately with words, even though they demand that adults around them do so. Also, since separation from parents is a goal in adolescence, communication is sometimes blurred purposely. This may involve not only lying (we once heard a mother say she was sure her teenage son really respected the truth since he used it so sparingly) but frequently slang, which can effectively eliminate adult understanding. The critical aspect of communication is after all not the saying of things but having the things heard and understood. Sometimes the adolescent does not want to be understood because he or she is sure that the parents will not approve unless there is a misunderstanding of the true intent. At other times, the adolescent might be ashamed of an accurate explanation and therefore misrepresent the facts. Some teenagers gain much support from telling parents their problems, but for others the belief is that although confessions may be good for one's soul, they are very bad for one's reputation. Reputation and self-esteem are often synonomous; therefore, when self-esteem is precarious, accuracy is sometimes sacrificed.

Adolescents are often aware that they are torn between wanting to be different or special while at the same time wanting to be normal, "like everybody else." This may make communicating with adults especially difficult. For example, facts are often of limited help in adult-adolescent discussions of rebellious behavior. Irrational acts and theories are individualistic; thus, if the adolescent should resort to facts, he or she would no longer be a special individual but just like everybody else. Being like everybody else may be what was being fought in the first place. This difficulty in communication with adolescents does not mean that the parent should avoid facts in dealing with rebellious behavior. Facts are necessary points of reference and help keep a discussion from becoming too theoretical and hypothetical, but it is important to remember that "facts" are often one-dimensional and also an event may involve a number of varying "facts" depending on the viewer's perspective. For example, it may be a fact that a boy would rather be at a neighbor's than at home to eat supper, but such a fact usually also expresses other current issues.

Types of rebellion

As we have already emphasized, adolescence is not a monolithic stage but a broad period during which individuals vary in maturity from childish to adult. It is also true that some adolescents have more need to break away violently from parents than do others. When adolescence passes most smoothly, the teenager increasingly is offered and accepts independence, and separation occurs, but with little rebellion. At the other end of the spectrum, some adolescents are always fighting with their parents. They question and resent every parental act. Such adolescents may realize they are acting illogically, since they disagree no matter which side of an argument the parents speak on, but the arguments are the ties that allow the adolescents to feel as though they are independent, while simultaneously remaining dependent. These arguments differ from those that aid independence in that nothing is usually settled, and nothing is ever learned. Parents and their adolescents can, on the other hand, have intense arguments that are very constructive. Such arguments are not just for the sake of argument, but each side tries to learn the motives and reasons of the other. In such arguments, the "losing" side may not be happy about the outcome, but something will be learned about freedom, fairness, safety, caring, and so on. Something is also learned about the concept of parent-child independence, if only the realization that both sides can survive a hard fight.

Adolescents tend to see things as right or wrong and often cannot understand the parents' wish or ability to moderate. It is much simpler for them either to be sure of being right or not to take a stand at all. The watchword of the latter and less common stance is "nothing ventured, nothing lost." The former and more common approach is to assume that one's parents are consistently wrong. Crisis is a time for opportunity as well as danger, and a negative adolescent is not uncommon or necessarily pathological. Adolescents generally begin by defining themselves not by what they want, but by what they do not want. As a matter of fact, people of all ages tend to be more ready to try to rectify what is bad than to initiate what is good. During the latter part of adolescence, teenagers generally will develop goals they favor as well as those they oppose.

The impact of other important adults

It has already been noted that teachers, club leaders, religious advisers, neighbors, and other adults are frequently chosen as **parent substitutes.** Studies show that such individuals can provide important stability for adolescents who feel the need to separate from their parents but are not independent enough to do so without adult guidance. Parental values remain the most powerful long-term influence on adolescents, and it is important that actual parents do not become destructively jealous of these pseudoparents. It is difficult for a parent after raising an adolescent for over a decade to have him or her turn to someone else for guidance and perhaps also to make frequent and pointed comparisons, always to one's own disadvantage.

It is impossible in such circumstances for a parent not to feel some jealousy. Such parental jealousy can follow two courses that prove destructive. In one the parents feel compelled to attack the other adult with such strength that the adolescent must put up a defense with equal vigor. As with battling a tar baby, the harder the parents fight the more they lose. A second course that can be destructive is to try to mimic the approach of the other adult. It adds injury to insult for parents to change their morals, views, and style in order to fit in with the younger generation, only to find themselves ridiculed more rather than less. Very often the other adult was followed as an alternative to the parents not because of what was advocated, but because it was *different* from what the adolescent's parents advocated. No matter how much the parents change, they will still be wrong because the point of the dispute was not style or content, but *the need to be independent.*

The best approach to such situations is for the parents not to seem jealous. To do this, parents may have to get rid of their hurt feelings by attacking the rival when they are alone with one another. This can be cathartic, good fun, and do away with the need to do so in front of the offspring. Of course, while it is not wise to seem to be attacking the other adult out of jealousy, it is more important for parents not to abdicate their beliefs. If there are differences that are important to the parents, those differences should be noted in as straightforward and nonrepetitious a manner as possible. When parental values are sound, adolescents seldom stray from them for long to follow truly unrealistic practices.

Parents must realize that the jealousy they feel toward an adult to whom their teenager turns may not be based on the views the person holds, but on the fact that this person has, at least temporarily, usurped the parents' place in the life of their child. It is often true that the other adult's views and morals are actually quite similar to those of the parents. Since, if anything, jealousy will be more severe when there are not obvious weaknesses to attack, parents must be especially careful not to attack standards they believe in just because they are voiced by another. When this *is* done, the adolescent usually not only recognizes the jealousy, but points it out in a way that weakens parental credibility. Since parental credibility is in relatively short supply during the teenage years, it is a shame to lose any unnecessarily.

One-parent families

More than 10 percent of white families and 40 percent of black families are headed by one parent today. With the increase in divorce rates, the single-parent family is becoming more common. Although the great majority of one-parent families are headed by women, men are increasingly retaining custody of their children. Writings on one-parent families are often contradictory. Because virtually every family is different, investigators approach the situation the way the blind men approach an elephant, and come up with many different conclusions. Some of the important variables include the age of the child when the separation took place, the circumstances of the separation, the quality of the presence (or the fact of the absence) of the other parent, the stability of the remaining parent, and how good the available family and community support services are.

It is usually better for the adolescent to have no contact with a second parent than to have a disputatious relationship. The latter is more likely when a divorce takes place during adolescence than when it took place earlier. Occasionally, teenagers whose parents divorced years ago and who are in the custody of the other-sex parent may decide they wish to change custody to the like-sex parent. It is not unusual during early adolescence for all teenagers to doubt that their parents are really their parents, and the adolescent in a one-parent family frequently idealizes the absent parent. This is, of course, part of the usual adolescent process of effecting separation from the caretaking parent. Although a judge will often allow an adolescent from the age of 12 or 13 years on to live with whichever parent he or she prefers, switches should not be performed precipitately. When the teenager advocates a switch, it may be useful to have a trial period before any legal action is taken.

When divorces take place in families with adolescent children, custody is usually based on the adolescent's wishes. There is often much hostility expressed by the children toward both parents for placing them in the impossible or at least difficult position of having to choose. Even when the adolescent is placed with the chosen parent, that parent may be surprised during the first year by being deluged with anger. This anger may be so strong because it represents anger felt toward that parent and *also* toward the absent parent. In short, the available parent gets it for both.

When a parent dies during a child's adolescence, the dead parent is usually idealized. The adolescent may take on some of the dead parent's traits or mannerisms. Less obvious may be anger at the dead parent for abandoning the adolescent at a time when guidance and support are especially needed. This reaction is most strong when the parent died through an avoidable accident or an illness that was aggravated by poor self-care. Again, because the adolescent may feel guilt about such anger and because the dead parent is not available for its direct expression, this anger may be expressed toward the remaining parent. Although displaced anger of this type seldom persists beyond the first year, it is an extremely difficult additional burden for the grief-stricken parent. This and other expressions of mourning are not unusual, although an adolescent is more likely than an adult to refuse to show sadness openly.

Although single parents have difficulty knowing quite how to act as a model for an adolescent child of the other sex, it seems that the most important factor is how the parent relates in general to members of the other sex. For mothers with adolescent sons, for example, the mother's general attitude toward males is much more important than any special effort she could make to increase her son's masculinity. If she judges men fairly and interacts reasonably with them, the son not only will feel it is all right to mature into manhood but will feel that he can search the community for older males to use as direct models. Some single parents, however, are so angry with the child's other parent that they believe all members of that sex are bad. This attitude is sure to be noticed by the adolescent, and although homosexuality is not as common as once thought in adolescents raised by the other-sex parent, it is not easy to make the transition to be an adult woman or adult man when one knows that to do so is to become a bitch or a bastard.

The impact of "losing" one's child to adulthood

Many of the problems that face parents and adolescents may be due to the necessarily long childhood of human beings. We have capacious brains, but it takes a terribly long time to learn how to use them properly, especially as more and more of our daily lives are controlled by technology. As the average time of training and education is lengthened, children remain dependent on their parents longer and longer. It may be civilized to have a long childhood, but it increases sibling jealousies and parent-child detachment problems.

A lengthening of childhood coupled with an older average age for beginning a family has made parents of adolescents older than was the case in past generations. As a result, parents' advancing age is thrust on them both by what their adolescent tells them about it and by what is happening to their own parents. It is an uncomfortable sandwich to be the middle of. Only parents who have inexhaustible supplies of denial can ignore the fact that their looks are fading at the very time their adolescent's appearance is blossoming. At the same time, it is not unusual for parents to become aware for the first time that their own parents are getting old enough to require support. It is dispiriting to realize that your parents are turning more to you for support than you can turn to them. Parents' own parents may also begin to become physically infirm about this time, and this experience cannot help but serve as an unwelcome reminder of one's own mortality. To comprehend much more fully that one is really going to die is a phenomenon of middle age. It is a harrowing developmental step under the best of circumstances, but may be made more difficult by simultaneously having one's children grow up and leave home.

There has been quite a bit said and written about the so-called "empty nest syndrome." Mothers who have had little involvement outside the home may feel they gave their lives for children who are not turning out well or at least are leaving home, which from the mother's point of view is not a triumph. Parents may note a rather hollow echo from the dreams that as new parents they had for their children, from dreams they had while the children were growing, and from the dreams their adolescents now have for their own lives. Such dreams, of course, are nature's way of keeping the generations moving along. If adolescents could know the future and the problems that will beset them, rather than be bathed in the belief that they can do anything, each new generation would not begin the work at the bottom of the career ladder so willingly.

All of these factors suggest that parents of adolescents and young adults are a pretty sad and bedraggled lot. Some are, but statistics reveal that the "empty nest syndrome" is largely a myth and that parenting adolescents is not as difficult for most as is parenting younger children. For example, divorce rates decrease with age, and there is no rise in divorce rates for couples during the empty nest period. In addition, most general population surveys of satisfaction with life show that parents believe their lives are happier after their children have left home and that parents are more often dissatisfied with the job of raising young children than with coping with adolescents.

By the time adolescents are ready to leave home, they have usually mellowed somewhat from the time of their early teens, and parent-child disagreements are more accurately symbolized by the separate but peaceful mixture of water and oil than the earlier explosive mixture of water and phosphorus. Mark Twain once noted that when he was 14 his father was so ignorant he could hardly stand to have him around, but when he got to be 21, he was astonished at how much the old man had learned in just seven years. One rule of thumb for knowing when adolescence is over may be said to be when young persons can publicly feel good about something while knowing it also pleases their parents.

Parents, too, tend to become more mellow with age. Part of this comes with the realization that one does not get everything one hopes for in life, and another part comes from learning that one way you can have more is to desire less. Expectations for one's children have been readjusted. Only recently have developmentalists emphasized the fact that a person does not stop changing and growing at the end of adolescence. It is comforting to know that much developmental progress can occur in adulthood, and that although parents are their children's most important teachers in life, they are not their only or final ones. What parents must do at this latter stage of adolescence is to allow their offspring to live their own lives. In this respect, having parented an adolescent is similar to experiencing an airplane landing. If you can walk away from them, they are successful.

Medical Care

At the doctor's office

Like anyone else, an adolescent goes to a doctor or any other health professional for many reasons—illness, an accident, a problem connected with growth. Many adolescents see their doctors for checkups annually, although in the absence of illness or any symptoms of illness, adolescents who are not involved in competitive sports usually do not require a physical examination every year. Adequate health supervision and screening for inconspicuous problems can usually be accomplished with examinations every two or even three years. In some cases the teenager will go to the same family physician or pediatrician who has been treating him or her since childhood. But in other cases, it will be the adolescent's first visit to a "regular" doctor, usually an internist. The following section describes what typically goes on when an adolescent first goes to a doctor for a specific problem. In many medical centers, of course, clinicians other than physicians are involved in patient care, and an adolescent might well be seen by a nurse practitioner or a physician's associate. But in this discussion, for the sake of simplicity, the health professional referred to will be a male doctor.

The clinical visit aims at accomplishing four closely related tasks. Depending on how much the doctor already knows about the patient's problem, how active the problem is, and whether treatment is doing it any good, one or more of these four tasks may take precedence. They are: 1) taking the patient's history; 2) performing a physical examination; 3) organizing the information gathered from the history and the physical examination into a useful form; and 4) planning additional diagnostic procedures (if needed) and setting forth effective treatment.

Patient's history

To develop a patient's history, the doctor puts down a description, chronologically arranged, of the pertinent physical, social, and psychological changes that have occurred since the patient was last free of the current problem. The doctor usually asks the patient to describe the problem that's bothering him or her and then asks additional questions designed to bring out specific details and to help the patient clarify the account. While the doctor can help the patient develop the history, it is the patient's own participation—and ability and willingness to remember and relate details—that in the end is most important.

When a doctor has cared for a particular adolescent before, they know each other and a new relationship does not have to be established. When he or she visits a doctor for the first time, they need to get acquainted, and the doctor has to assemble some general information about the adolescent that will give him a sense of the patient as a person—as well as someone with a health problem. This may include an outline of the adolescent's birth history and the early years of childhood, physical growth and general development during childhood, immunizations, and any illnesses and allergies. A good family history also makes the doctor aware of relationships within the adolescent's family, and of how healthy other family members are. As the adolescent grows, additional information is added to this basic fund of information so that the doctor is always aware of everything contributing to health and illness in the adolescent's life. In the process of getting to know their patients, clinicians are also interested in learning something about their patients' special interests and future plans, as well as their social, academic, and athletic activities, and their employment.

The physical examination

Once the adolescent and the doctor have had an opportunity to discuss the problem, the stage is set to continue the evaluation, usually by means of a physical examination. During adolescence, the physical examination provides the doctor and patient with useful information about physical growth and sexual maturation, as well as about specific clinical problems. The physical examination itself is similar to that given to a child, but during the examination, the doctor pays particular attention to growth and sexual maturation.

The description that follows is that of a fairly complete physical examination. Obviously, an adolescent will not receive this complete a physical examination each time a problem arises, but it is described here so he or she will know what to expect.

The examination might begin with the clinician checking the patient's general appearance and mood. Whether he or she appears tired and ill, unhappy or cheerful, or well and full of energy gives the doctor a sense of the patient's current state of well-being. Then the doctor might look at the patient's hands, noting the color of the skin and nail beds, and the shape of the nails; the presence of any skin rash; the general shape of the fingers; and the movement of the joints. In addition, he might take the patient's pulse over one of the arteries in the wrist.

As the physical examination continues, the doctor checks

the appearance of the skin on each part of the body, and skin problems that tend to develop in one area to a greater extent than in other areas are noted in particular. For example, skin rashes caused by contact with chemicals or plants are frequently on the hands or other exposed surfaces; psoriasis often develops on the outer surfaces of the elbows and knees, while atopic dermatitis is more frequently found on the inner surfaces of the same joints; acne appears on the face, shoulders, back, and chest; some fungal infections develop on the chest, others in the groin or on the genitals; and warts are found on the hands and on the soles of the feet more often than elsewhere.

Another part of the physical examination that is carried out at several body locations is the examination of the lymph nodes. Some are found near the elbow, others under the arms, many in the neck region, and some in the groin.

The examination of the head might follow. The scalp hair, the eyebrows, and face and neck hair are checked, and the eyes, ears, nose, mouth, and throat examined. In examining the eyes, the doctor makes sure each eye can move in various directions; he checks the appearance of the conjunctiva, the cornea, and the lens, and the reactions of the pupil both to stimulation by light and to the act of changing from viewing a distant object to one that is nearer. Then he examines the interior of the eye using an instrument called an ophthalmoscope: directing its light into the eye, the doctor can see the retina, the blood vessels which supply the retina, and the optic nerve which carries visual information from the retina to the brain. He also checks the sharpness of the patient's eyesight.

In examining the ears, the doctor notes the shape and position of the outer ear, and (using a speculum) the appearance of the ear canal and the eardrum. He may check to see if the eardrum moves normally and may perform an audiogram to test hearing. He can examine the inside of the nose with the assistance of a small nasal speculum that permits him to see the nasal septum (the partition that divides the entire nasal space into two approximately equal parts) and the nasal turbinates (rounded folds within the lining of the nose). Examination of the mouth includes inspection of the palate (the "roof" of the mouth), the tongue and the teeth, the lining of the insides of the cheeks, and the surfaces of the gums. He also looks at the throat and any tonsils and adenoids still visible there.

The examination of the neck includes checking any lymph nodes which can be felt in the neck, the position of the larynx (voice box), and the size and shape of the thyroid gland. Either by touching the surface of the neck lightly or by listening with a stethoscope held against the neck, the doctor can feel vibrations or hear the sometimes significant noises coming from within the blood vessels that pass through the neck.

The examination of the chest includes the general appearance of the chest and the state of breast development. Then, by a combination of touching, tapping, and listening, the doctor can examine the lungs and the heart. At this time in the examination, he may count the heart rate, note the rate of breathing, and take the adolescent's blood pressure. A detailed description of the measurement of blood pressure is included in the section on cardiovascular problems (see p. 215).

As the clinician examines the abdomen, he may first listen to it with a stethoscope. He can hear sounds made by the gastrointestinal tract, and he may also hear sounds made within blood vessels. He checks the location, size, and shape of the liver and spleen, notes any discomfort of these organs or others within the abdomen, and looks and feels for unusual masses.

The genital examination of a boy includes a judgment of how mature he is sexually, as well as careful checking of the skin covering the genitals and the testes and their supporting structures within the scrotum. When this part of the examination is performed, it is also practical to check for the presence of a hernia. The pelvic examination in adolescent girls, which is more complex, is discussed separately in the next section.

Now the doctor examines the patient's legs, particularly the skin that covers them, the muscles within, the hip and knee joints, and the feet. Another part of the skeletal system which must be examined is the spine. Its alignment and flexibility are assessed, and the presence of any discomfort noted.

An evaluation of the neurological system focuses on the functions of the cranial nerves, which are the nerves that supply all of the structures within the head and neck with connections to the brain. It is through these nerves that the brain receives impressions of the outside world, via taste, smell, sight, touch, and hearing. The neurological examination also assesses the strength and coordination of various parts of the body, tests numerous reflexes, and appraises the ability of the body to perceive different stimuli. Memory, the ability to solve simple and complex problems, and the written and spoken use of language may also be evaluated, if there seems to be reason for it.

At some point during the examination, the doctor will carefully measure height and weight. This is done to determine the adolescent's rate of growth, to compare his or her physical size with others of the same age and sex, and to assess, approximately, the adolescent's nutritional state.

A doctor usually will not take the patient's body temperature during a physical examination unless, of course, there is some possibility that it might be abnormal.

Pelvic examination

Girls seldom need a pelvic examination before adolescence, and not always then. However, there are conditions in which the clinical information needed for diagnosis and proper treatment can be obtained only by means of a pelvic. The examination is performed most comfortably when the patient lies on her back. The examining table has two supports on which the adolescent can rest her legs, permitting her to be as relaxed as possible and positioning her lower body so the doctor can most readily conduct a thorough examination. It begins with an inspection of the external genitalia—the labia majora and minora, the clitoris, and the outer portion of the vagina. By the use of a small mirror, the adolescent can see what is going on and share in this part of the examination. Then, with a speculum inserted into the vagina, the doctor examines the surfaces of the vagina and the cervix (the lower portion of the uterus, which joins the uppermost portion of the vagina). The doctor first makes sure that the speculum can be placed comfortably within the vagina, then inserts it, and opens it just enough to be able to see the physical structures well. With the use of the mirror, the patient can also see these structures. The adolescent should be comfortable during this part of the pelvic examination, noticing only a feeling of pressure when the speculum is opened up. This portion of the pelvic examination allows the doctor to gather several useful specimens: vaginal secretions, which may be checked for the presence of infection; secretions from the cervix, which are also used to identify the presence of infection; and a specimen of cervical cells, which is used to make a Papanicolaou ("Pap") smear, a test for cancer. In the final portion of the pelvic examination, the clinician examines the internal organs, placing one or two fingers in the vagina and the other hand on the surface of the lower abdomen. He can feel the size, shape, and position of the uterus and the ovaries, and the regions around them and the fallopian tubes.

Organization of the clinical information

The information provided by the adolescent's history together with the physical findings from the examination often allow the doctor to come to a conclusion about the nature of the adolescent's problem. The doctor discusses the conclusion with the patient. This conversation should supply the patient with information about his or her problem, as well as an understanding of any further measures that may have to be taken. These measures might include some laboratory tests or other tests necessary to establish a diagnosis or to gain a more precise understanding of the problem. These additional steps, along with a plan for treatment, make up the fourth portion of the visit.

Planning additional studies and treatment

Any number of laboratory procedures can be used to secure more information about various clinical problems. Sometimes, none is needed. When they *are* indicated, they are often performed on blood and urine specimens. Other laboratory tests analyze samples of spinal fluid or stool. Specimens are also gathered from a variety of body sites for cultures (see p. 128).

Other frequently used diagnostic measures include a wide variety of X ray examinations used in order to pin down more precisely physical changes in the body, or to see how well certain body systems are functioning.

Particularly useful diagnostic studies will be mentioned later in connection with the specific health problems that occur in adolescence. Some of the most commonly used diagnostic studies are outlined briefly in the following sections.

Frequently used blood tests

By the time adolescence begins, almost everyone has had several blood tests performed for one reason or another. Most blood tests can be performed using small quantities of blood. Younger children are often checked for anemia with a few drops of blood obtained by pricking the end of a finger. In adolescents, blood is usually drawn from a vein on the inner surface of the arm near the elbow. Most adolescents are more comfortable if they lie down when their blood is drawn. Using alcohol, the doctor cleans the skin where the needle will be placed, and then wraps a small tourniquet around the upper arm to make the veins swell slightly and simplify the blood-drawing procedure.

Among the most frequent blood studies are the hematocrit, hemoglobin concentration, erythrocyte ("red cell") count, leukocyte ("white cell") count, differential white cell count, and the erythrocyte sedimentation rate. The **hematocrit** value represents the proportion of the circulating blood volume that is made up of red blood cells. The **hemoglobin** concentration is a measurement of the number of grams of hemoglobin that are present in 100 milliliters of blood. The number of red blood cells present in one cubic millimeter of blood establishes the **erythrocyte** count. During adolescence the typical values for the hematocrit, hemoglobin, and erythrocyte counts in boys and girls begin to diverge because of the higher androgen levels in boys, and by the time they are fully grown and sexually mature, boys tend to have higher values for each of these measurements than girls. The major usefulness of the hematocrit, hemoglobin, and erythrocyte counts is in determining the presence of various forms of anemia, some of which are described later in this book (see p. 230). Another test, called a **reticulocyte** count, assesses the rate at which red blood cells are produced by the bone marrow. The **white blood cell** count is the number of white blood cells present in one cubic millimeter of blood, and the **differential** white cell count describes the proportions of the total white cell count made up of different types of white cells. The white blood cell count may be decreased in the presence of some conditions and markedly increased in others. It is particularly affected by many bacterial infections and other illnesses which cause inflammation. The **erythrocyte sedimentation rate** is determined by measuring the speed at which the red cells in blood settle to the bottom of a calibrated glass tube. Rapid sedimenting of the red cells often occurs in the presence of bacterial infections and other illnesses that cause inflammation.

Another blood test measures the number of **platelets** present in the blood. This test is especially useful in cases of abnormal bleeding, because platelets play a vital role in blood clotting. Blood typing is not usually included among the conventional laboratory studies performed on blood specimens.

Other substances present in the blood can be and sometimes are measured in the laboratory. Among them are many minerals, vitamins, enzymes, fats, proteins, glucose, antibodies, medicines, and hormones that are transported in the bloodstream.

Urine tests

The urine test most frequently performed is called a **urinalysis** —literally, an analysis of the urine. In performing a urinalysis the laboratory technician determines how acidic or alkaline the urine is; measures its specific gravity, which reflects its degree of concentration; checks the urine for substances such as protein, sugar, blood, and ketones (metabolic products that appear when fat stored in the body is used extensively for energy); and examines the sediment in the urine microscopically to detect any white or red blood cells or bacteria.

If an adolescent's urinalysis does not appear to be entirely normal, additional tests are available to find out more. One such test is a urine culture. In this test, a specially collected urine specimen is sent to the laboratory to determine whether abnormal amounts of bacteria are present in it. The laboratory also identifies the bacteria that are present and carries out antibiotic sensitivity tests to learn what drugs are most effective in getting rid of them (see p. 226).

Urine is also used for other laboratory studies. A well-known one is a pregnancy test; other tests are used to determine the amounts of various proteins and hormones that are excreted by the kidneys.

Cultures and other laboratory studies

Cultures of specimens from many parts of the body are used to identify the presence of bacteria, viruses, and fungi that cause infections. Perhaps the most frequently performed culture is a so-called throat culture. In this test the throat is thoroughly swabbed with a cotton-tipped stick, and the specimen that is obtained is transferred to a culture plate on which microbes will grow. The culture plate is placed in an incubator and examined after a day or two. Cultures are helpful in checking for, and identifying the cause of, infections anywhere in the body.

Other laboratory studies include examination of the stool for the presence of such diverse substances as blood, increased amount of fat, and various parasites. Examination of the spinal fluid is carried out when an infection of the central nervous system such as meningitis or encephalitis is suspected. The spinal fluid is examined for the presence of white blood cells, for changes in its protein and sugar content, and for bacteria. Sometimes bacteria present in the spinal fluid can be seen and identified immediately with the help of a microscope; or it may be necessary to identify them by means of a laboratory culture.

Tuberculin skin tests

Tuberculin skin tests are used throughout childhood and adolescence to determine whether or not a patient has received a significant exposure to the microorganisms that cause tuberculosis. A small amount of test material is injected into the skin, and the site is examined two or three days later. Any redness or swelling indicates a "positive" test result. If they lack any of the symptoms or physical changes typical of tuberculosis, patients whose tuberculin test results become positive are usually treated with medication for a year.

X rays

Contemporary radiological techniques make clinical diagnosis much simpler and more accurate by revealing both large and very tiny changes in many structures in the body. Many adolescents have X rays taken of the head, chest, and bones, particularly in the course of investigating injuries and infections. Other X ray studies focus on the size and shape of the heart, or the configuration of the gastrointestinal tract, and they are made after the patient swallows "contrast" material, which creates a more vivid outline of the organs under investigation. Occasionally, the understanding of an adolescent's clinical problem benefits from the use of a newer radiological technique, such as a CAT (computerized axial tomography) scan. In this procedure, a whole series of radiological images is obtained from one section of the body. When the information has been processed by a computer, the result is a detailed cross-sectional picture that can reveal important changes that might escape detection under more conventional methods.

Ultrasound examinations

Unlike a radiological examination, an ultrasound examination does not require the use of X ray, but employs instead high-frequency sound waves. The sound waves are reflected by the different structures in the body, and the "echo" thus produced is used to form an image of the tissues being studied. Some organs in the abdomen such as the pancreas, uterus, and ovaries—otherwise hard to "see" with X rays— can be examined with this technique. Ultrasound is also very useful in studying the size and shape of the heart, and the movement of its valves.

Genetic screening

The purpose of genetic screening is to identify the healthy person who carries the trait of a potentially serious hereditary condition. Though he or she is not aware of any signs of the condition, this person can transmit it to a member of the next generation, just as the trait was transmitted to him from one of his parents. Most of the genetically determined conditions whose carriers can be readily identified are conditions that appear only when a child receives a "double dose" of the trait, one from each of his parents. Any adolescent whose genes may carry information controlling the appearance of one of these conditions should be made aware of the possibility and should learn more about the condition—then he or she can decide about having genetic screening. Given this information, mate selection and reproductive decisions can be made on the basis of adequate knowledge, and the next generation can be protected from a major life-threatening illness.

At the present time, three conditions stand out as ones that qualify for consideration by adolescents. The first is **Tay-Sachs disease**. It is a severe illness, causing mental deterioration and blindness and ending in death early in childhood. This disease primarily afflicts Jews, among whom the trait is carried by about one in thirty. A blood test that screens for the Tay-Sachs trait measures the amount of an enzyme, Hexosaminidase A. A second important condition, mostly affecting those of Mediterranean ancestry, is **thalassemia major,** sometimes called Cooley's anemia. The carrier of the trait for this severe form of anemia can be identified by a blood test that measures the level of Hemoglobin A_2. The third condition is **sickle-cell anemia**. Largely afflicting blacks, it is another severe form of anemia whose carriers can be detected by measuring the level of Hemoglobin S in the blood. About 8 percent of blacks carry sickle-cell trait.

Adolescents who would like to have more information about these or other genetic conditions may consult their physicians, a genetics clinic if one is nearby, an ethnic organization involved in genetic screening programs, or the National Genetics Foundation, which is located at 9 West 57th Street, New York, New York 10019.

Immunizations

Immunization is not usually of great importance in adolescence, because the majority of the immunizations required during the first twenty years of life should be received by children before they are 5 or 6. However, some immunizations are given during adolescence, and other shots may be prompted by special circumstances, such as travel or exposure to specific illnesses. Adolescence is also a good time to review one's immunization record, and to be certain of full protection against several easily prevented diseases.

During infancy and early childhood, the immunizations that children receive are of the "active" variety. That is, the immune system of the body responds to the shot (or other immunization) by building up resistance to a specific disease, even if the person is exposed to the organism that causes it. During the first year of life, often at 2, 4, and 6 months of age, infants have immunizations for diphtheria, pertussis (whooping cough), tetanus, and polio. The so-called DPT immunization is given by injection; the polio immunization consists of a fluid that is swallowed. At or after 15 months of age, children receive immunization for measles, mumps, and rubella (German measles). (Measles immunizations may not "take" if given at a younger age.) At 1 1/2 years of age, they receive booster immunizations for DPT and polio. Both the DPT and the polio immunizations are repeated again at about the time children begin to attend school, between 4 and 6 years of age. This immunization program completes the bulk of those required for a lifetime, and the next one that is required routinely will follow in ten years (between 14 and 16 years of age), and consists of an adult diphtheria and tetanus immunization.

When a child or adolescent suffers a contaminated cut or a puncture wound that offers a threat of tetanus infection, a tetanus booster shot is given. Protection continues to be effective for at least ten years. Active immunization, for protection during travel or for other conditions under which specific infections might develop, can be given for many other diseases such as typhoid fever, meningococcal and pneumococcal infections, cholera, smallpox, yellow fever, and rabies. More frequently than for any of these, immunization is given to prevent influenza: the vaccine and recommendations for its use in adolescents change from year to year. "Passive" immunization—the administration by injection of antibodies against specific infective organisms—can also be useful. Such shots are given when a nonimmunized person is exposed to an infected person, and they can prevent or ease the effects of certain diseases, among them rabies, hepatitis, measles, and tetanus.

The shots consist of immune serum globulin containing the specific, effective antibody required. In addition, persons whose own immunological systems do not produce adequate amounts of protective antibody benefit from regular passive immunization.

Physical Problems

We now turn to the discussion of more specific problems of physical health developed by adolescents. No attempt will be made to provide a comprehensive list of *all* the disorders adolescents *might* develop. Instead, this section will concentrate on those health problems that appear only during adolescence, and on problems that are moderately common among adolescents, but not necessarily limited to them.

Problems of body size or shape

During much of adolescence, girls and boys are constantly faced with the need to adjust to an ever-changing body. As they grow taller, gain weight, undergo changes in body composition, and become sexually mature, adolescents seldom seem to remain the same for more than a few weeks at a time. Before they reach adolescence, many boys and girls look at those who are already in adolescence and wonder silently if they will ever be so grown-up; once adolescence begins, however, many find themselves wondering if they will grow enough and whether their growth is normal.

This section discusses the major variations in height and weight found among normal adolescents, and the problems faced by adolescents who are worried about being, or becoming, too tall, too short, too heavy, or too thin. So that adolescents and their parents can compare their heights and weights with those of the population at large, we include two sets of growth charts, one for boys and another for girls. Each set has two charts, one for height and another for weight. By following the the instructions given, you can find out roughly where one adolescent stands in relation to his or her peers, and see whether the degree of growth, in terms of current height and weight, is in any way unusual (see pp. 139–43).

Extremes of body size—those beyond the usual range of expected values—consist of measurements that fall beyond the upper or the lower percentile curves: thus, a very *tall* boy or girl has a height that is greater than the 95th percentile value, while a very *short* adolescent's height falls below the 5th percentile curve. Extreme variations in weight are similar. Since there are general guides for determining variations in body size, each variation can be discussed separately.

Shortness

Like other physical characteristics, shortness tends to be a subjective description, depending on the preference and perspective of the adolescent involved. Adolescents whose heights are well above average may nevertheless think of themselves as being regrettably short, while others who are shorter than average, but somewhat taller than a parent or friend, may not consider themselves short at all. From a statistical standpoint, of course, few adolescents are of average height and there are as many "short" adolescents as there are "tall" ones. Because shortness may be caused by a variety of physical problems, it tends to arouse more concern than tallness among adolescents, their families, and their doctors.

In investigating a case of excessive shortness, one must first take into account the adolescent's family history. Children have a strong tendency to resemble their parents in physical appearance. If, among the adolescent's parents, grandparents, brothers, and sisters, there are some who are relatively short, then it is likely that the adolescent also may be fairly short when preadolescent growth is finished, and at maturity, too. When shortness is determined by hereditary factors, the overall growth pattern of the short child and adolescent is probably quite normal.

Next, the adolescent's growth and state of health during childhood must be considered. Children who have severe congenital heart disease, kidney disease, problems with absorption of nourishment from the gastrointestinal tract, anemia (particularly sickle-cell anemia and Cooley's anemia), chronic infection, severe arthritis, and gastrointestinal diseases such as Crohn's disease (see p. 225) and ulcerative colitis, often have impaired growth during childhood and therefore are shorter when they reach adolescence than they would have been had they not suffered from any health problems. Compared with children whose shortness can be attributed to membership in relatively short families and who are likely to grow normally during childhood, children who have major health problems during this period of their lives grow much less vigorously. During the years before adolescence, most girls and boys grow between 1 1/2 and 2 3/4 inches a year, and gain 3 1/4 to 9 3/4 pounds each year. If in the preadolescent years the growth rate falls below this range, a youngster's physical size shifts toward his becoming shorter and lighter than his peers. This may signal that a health problem is interfering with normal growth. A doctor's evaluation would include a search for anything affecting adequate nutrition or its efficient utilization by the body. He would look for disorders of the kidneys or gastrointestinal tract, as well as endocrine disturbances in which insufficient production of thyroid or growth hormone might be involved. As will be discussed in the next section, a determination of whether sexual maturation is progressing normally would also be included.

When an adolescent is concerned about being short and has no physical problems that might interfere with growth, a doctor can assess the prospects for further growth. The amount is estimated using the adolescent's present height and weight, a judgment of how far the skeleton has matured (based on an X ray of the hand and wrist), and information about the heights of both parents. This evaluation gives the teenager some idea of how much more he or she can expect to grow before maturity.

Tallness

When preadolescent children or early adolescents are taller than many of their peers, it is often taken as a sign of good health, and seldom as a cause for worry about an underlying problem. This view is generally an accurate one, but it should be related to the context of the adolescent's family. Just as short adolescents tend to resemble their parents in physical appearance, adolescents who are tall usually have parents or other family members who are also taller than average. Thus, when an adolescent is extremely tall and other family members are only short to middling, there is a possibility of a health problem associated with tallness. Some concerns of this kind include an overproduction of growth hormone by the pituitary gland, causing gigantism; gonadal dysgenesis in girls, in which tallness is accompanied by failure of sexual maturation; Klinefelter's syndrome in boys who have incomplete sexual development and gynecomastia; Marfan's syndrome in which the arms and legs are unusually long, the lens of the eye dislocates, and the portion of the aorta near the heart dilates; and a metabolic disease called homocystinuria, of which excessive height is one characteristic.

In general, the preadolescent or adolescent who is remarkably taller than most other boys and girls of the same age is in fact very healthy. In times past, tallness, especially in girls, was not as accepted, appreciated, or valued as it is now, and a tall girl was often subjected to criticism and pressure that made her feel that she should not be tall and that her life would be ruined by her stature, in one way or another. As a result of this bias, much clinical effort has gone into figuring out ways to halt or slow the growth of girls destined to be taller than many of their peers. Even though these efforts have been undertaken with the hope that some reduction in mature height might contribute to the girl being happier during her late adolescence and adult life, no particularly convincing evidence has ever been assembled that indicates clearly that tallness is itself a disadvantage.

For the adolescent who is particularly interested, a doctor can estimate, at any time during late childhood or early adolescence, the amount of continuing growth that can be expected. This can help the adolescent decide whether to continue growing without interference or to attempt to shorten one's mature height. The latter process is made more difficult by the fact that any definitive steps that can be taken to alter an adolescent's growth pattern must be taken while further growth is still in view. The growth pattern is changed by giving rather large doses of estrogen to girls, or androgen to boys. During the administration of these hormones, the speed at which the bony epiphyses (the growth center in the bones) mature is accelerated while the rate of growth is slowed considerably. This change in the growth process begins at the start of treatment in girls, and after a brief period of accelerated growth in boys. The earlier in the growth process that treatment is given, the greater the reduction in mature height, as a rule; generally speaking, treatment may reduce mature height by one to three inches.

Just as there are normal adolescents who are shorter than average, there are those whose height is above average: adolescent and adult society certainly has room for both. On reaching maturity, adolescents who decided not to alter their own growth patterns and potentials may find their height, even if it is unusual, to be much more acceptable than they had expected it would be.

USE OF GROWTH CHARTS

The following pages display separate sets of growth charts for the heights and weights of boys and girls who range in age from 2 to 18 years. The charts, developed by the National Center for Health Statistics in collaboration with the Center for Disease Control, show the percentile values at each age for various heights and weights.

After height and weight are measured, without shoes and with minimal clothing, the values can be plotted on these charts by first locating the adolescent's age on the horizontal line at the bottom of the appropriate chart. Then, follow an imaginary line straight up until you reach the adolescent's height or weight measurement, shown on the vertical line at the left-hand side of the chart. Make a mark at that point on the chart. Now notice that seven curving lines run from the lower left hand corner of each chart toward the upper right hand corner: each line represents a percentile value within the population.

As an example, a 14-year-old girl who is 63 inches tall, and who weighs 110 pounds, is at the 50th percentile value for each measurement. Both her height and weight are greater than 49 percent and less than 50 percent of girls her age. In contrast, a 15-1/2-year-old boy who is 69 1/2 inches tall and who weighs 118 pounds, has a height at the 75th percentile, and a weight at the 25th percentile. Considerations of overweight and underweight benefit from comparison of the percentile value obtained for height with that for weight.

Using a number of measurements taken over many years, an adolescent can plot his or her own growth pattern on these charts.

Weight for Age

BOYS FROM 2 TO 18 YEARS

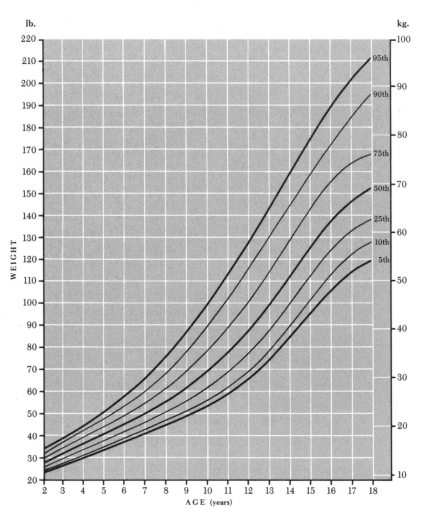

Height for Age

BOYS FROM 2 TO 18 YEARS

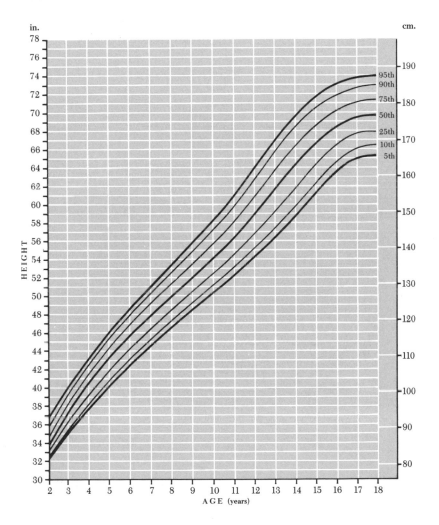

Weight for Age

GIRLS FROM 2 TO 18 YEARS

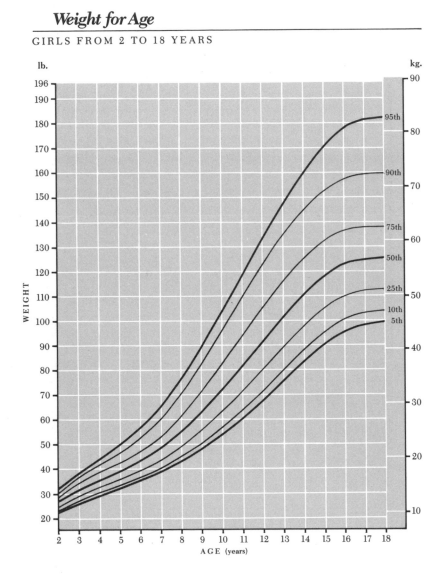

Height for Age

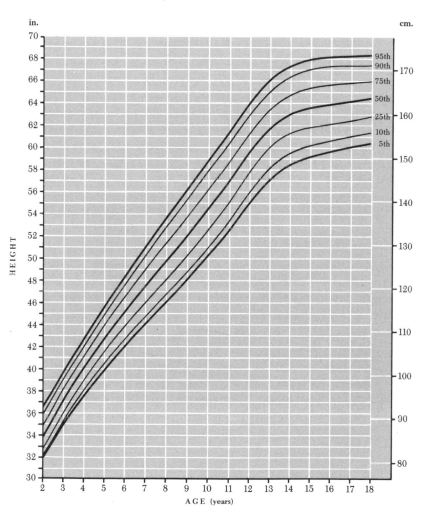

in.

cm.

95th
90th
75th
50th
25th
10th
5th

HEIGHT

AGE (years)

Overweight

An adolescent who has relatively more weight than expected for height may well have more than the average amount of fat. Generally, the average percentage of body weight consisting of fat decreases in boys from 16 percent to about 10 percent during the adolescent growth process. In girls, who also have an average of 16 percent of body weight as fat at the beginning of their growth spurts, the percentage increases to 20 to 24 percent during adolescent growth. When a boy or girl has appreciably more body fat than is typical, obesity begins. Overweight adolescents who have too much fat must be distinguished from others who weigh more than expected and yet have average or even less than average amounts of body fat. Well-trained athletes are often found in the latter group. An adolescent may be considered overweight when he or she has more than an average amount of weight for his or her height, and in absolute terms, this may amount to no more than a few pounds. **Obesity** refers to overweight amounting to at least 20 percent more than expected on the basis of height. As an example, a 14-year-old girl who is 63 inches tall and weighs 110 pounds is at the 50th percentile value for each measurement. She would probably be considered obese if her weight were 132 pounds or more. Another convenient way of measuring excess body fat, used increasingly by doctors and coaches of sports teams, involves a device called a skin-fold caliper. At one or more points on the surface of the body, the skin is pinched into a skin-fold, and the caliper is used to measure its thickness. The measurements obtained are then compared with standards, or used in mathematical equations to calculate the percentage of fat in the entire body.

Obesity is one of the most common health problems in modern society. It occasionally begins during adolescence, but more often makes its appearance earlier in life. Then, during the adolescent years, it becomes more pronounced and people begin to worry about it. Obesity beginning in infancy and the early childhood years is a complex phenomenon that seems to be influenced by several different factors. First among them is the existence of obesity in other members of the family. A child who has no close family member (parent, brother, or sister) who is obese runs very little risk of becoming obese either. In contrast, when both parents are obese, their children have a considerable chance of becoming obese; and a child with only one parent, brother, or sister who is obese has a moderate risk of developing obesity. Besides family pattern, nutritional factors are also important. For a child to become overly fat, he or she must consistently absorb more energy than is necessary to meet the day-to-day basic requirements and those for activity and growth. The excess supply of calories is diverted to storage in the body's fat cells. Physical activity patterns are also important: a very active child consuming a diet that contains more than the average number of calories seldom becomes obese. In contrast, a moderately inactive child promptly begins to accumulate excess energy when he or she eats too much. Eating can become ritualized, and a child can develop a pattern that involves overeating. In addition, food can occupy an important position in a child's life; much activity can become focused on eating. Food may serve not only to satisfy hunger but also as a response to other feelings—boredom, worry, frustration, happiness. Food can be used as a form of self-reward, too.

When children become obese during their early years and continue to be obese through late childhood and into adolescence, they are quite often entirely unaware of what it would be like to be normal. Adolescents already worried about threatening physical changes can be understandably reluctant to get involved in any plan that would actually lead to some reduction in body fat.

Among adults, long-standing obesity is one factor that places them at some increased risk for the development of various heart and circulatory problems, osteoarthritis (particularly involving the knees), and increased levels of cholesterol and triglycerides in the bloodstream. In addition, obesity may bring out an otherwise undetectable tendency toward diabetes mellitus, and obesity is often associated with undesirable increases in blood pressure (see p. 216). None of these problems as a rule poses an immediate risk to the health of an obese adolescent, and because he or she feels well, there may not seem to be any compelling reason to reduce. However, adolescents who are obese might think of it this way. Assuming only a moderate degree of obesity, perhaps twenty-five pounds of excess fat is stored in the body. It is not hard to imagine the discomfort and physical drain involved in wearing a twenty-five-pound body suit twenty-four hours a day, seven days a week. Most adolescents can recognize that it would certainly detract from their ability to perform various physical tasks and would enhance the likelihood of their becoming easily fatigued. Yet because obesity progresses gradually from childhood to adolescence, obese adolescents tend to adjust to the increased work load, and to find it hard to imagine how much differently their bodies would function if the excess weight were removed.

In most instances, obesity is not caused by an underlying "glandular" disturbance. (There are rare cases in which insufficient function of the thyroid gland or overproduction of hormones by the adrenal glands does influence a trend toward obesity, and the usual characteristics of some of these endocrinological problems are discussed later in the book [see section beginning on p. 200].) The obese state does, however, cause many disturbances in the functioning of various glands, which persist until the obesity is adequately treated. Among these disturbances are increases in the blood levels of some amino acids, increased blood levels of insulin, and abnormalities in glucose tolerance.

Reasons for treating obesity   The prevention or treatment of obesity during childhood or adolescence is the best sort of preventive medicine because it can help avoid the complications of obesity that are bound to arise during adulthood. In addition, getting rid of excess weight makes possible more efficient and more enjoyable physical activity. Being able to wear more attractive clothing pleases other adolescents. Contemporary society emphasizes being slim. This may or may not be fair, but it is a fact of modern life. Moreover, the social bias against obese adolescents in general is particularly strong against obese girls. The impact of this bias is felt in the adolescent's social life, and it functions in an unspoken or unconscious manner when adolescents apply for admission to college and seek employment. Because many obese adolescents believe (probably rightly) that their physical appearance interferes with their social lives, their educational and employment opportunities, their physical performance, and their future health, they may regard their obesity as a major handicap. But while wishing to do something about it, they may find it very difficult.

Zeroing in on obesity Anyone browsing through a well-stocked bookstore or perusing the contents of monthly magazines becomes aware of the profusion of books and articles that offer systems for weight loss. These writings often promise easy and rapid—almost magical—ways of treating obesity. Yet despite all this information, many adolescents who contemplate losing weight never try, and among those who try, many fail. It must be stated flatly that long-standing obesity, closely tied to personal eating habits, activity patterns, and family trends, is not a condition to be tackled lightly. Successful weight loss is almost always a difficult and unpleasant task, and one that takes much longer to accomplish than the obese person expects. Like any hard job, the treatment of obesity should not be undertaken casually, but should be approached thoughtfully and reasonably after two essential questions have been answered honestly. The first question that the adolescent needs to ask, and answer, is "Why do I want to lose weight?" Sometimes, only one strong reason answers this question; sometimes there are several. These reasons should be written down, probably kept secret and reviewed—and revised occasionally—during the course of the weight loss. The second question is "How much weight do I want to lose?" Note that the question does not say, "How much weight do I *need* to lose?" Even though a return to normal body composition is ideal and desirable, weight loss is so difficult that some adolescents may decide to lose an appreciable amount of excess weight, and yet not all that they could and ideally should lose. The growth charts on pages 140–3 can give some guidance in finding a weight that is a reasonably good one. Adolescents can locate their heights on one growth chart and then find the approximate weight that would represent the same percentile value on the weight chart. In general, because long-standing obesity is associated with an increase in the amount of lean body mass, the percentile value for ideal weight can be somewhat higher than that for height. As an example, an adolescent whose height is in the 50th percentile might be in good shape with a weight that fell close to the 75th percentile. However the weight goal is chosen, the adolescent subtracts goal weight from current weight, and arrives at the number of pounds that needs to be lost.

This approach to the setting of a weight goal can be used by adolescents who are close to, or at the end of, their physical growth: in practical terms, those who have grown less than an inch in the past year. Another approach is available to young adolescents who, having considerable growth ahead of them, may be fortunate in not yet having acquired large amounts of excess weight. Such adolescents can estimate how much more they can expect to grow during the remainder of their adolescent years, and then choose a weight in keeping with that height. They may be able to do quite nicely by maintaining their current weights while they grow, slimming down automatically as growth continues. Others may need to lose a small or moderate amount of weight, gradually, over the several years in which they will continue to grow.

Once the decision to lose weight has been made and the weight goal set, many adolescents can achieve an average weight loss of one to two pounds per week through the use of a sensible, non-painful food allowance and a reasonable amount of physical activity.

Changes in food allowance   While it is theoretically possible to increase activity to an extent that would cause appreciable weight loss, there is usually not enough time in an adolescent's daily schedule for it, and the use of exercise alone is impractical. The food allowance is the key. The basis for changing one's food allowance is quite simple. To reduce the amount of fat stored in each fat cell in the body, an adolescent must create a **daily energy deficit.**

For example, assume that a boy requires 2,200 calories a day for body operation and repair, physical activity, and growth. At a caloric intake of 2,200 calories a day, his weight remains quite constant. However, if his food allowance is decreased to 1,800 calories a day, then the difference between that amount and the energy he needs for the day is 400 calories, an amount that can be drawn from his body's fat stores. As a pound of stored fat contains about 3,500 calories, a daily caloric deficit of 500 calories permits him to use up the energy contained in a pound of body fat in one week. As the energy deficit increases, the amount drawn from the fat stores increases, and the rate at which he loses weight also increases.

His next step is to figure out the caloric value of the food he eats, in order to be able to arrive at a food allowance that creates a regular energy deficit. When he is ready to begin losing weight, he reviews his reasons, and measures and records his body weight first thing in the morning. Then, for one week, he records in a pocket-sized notebook *all* the foods he eats and *all* the beverages he drinks, day by day. It is very important to record the portion size—in cups, ounces, tablespoons, or teaspoons—as well as the kinds of food and beverage. At the end of the week, he will once again check and record his early morning weight. The next step is to review each day's food intake, one item at a time, using a calorie counter (available in bookstores, drugstores, and many supermarkets). Write down the number of calories contained in each item. For example, an 8-ounce glass of whole milk contains 160 calories; a slice of bread with a teaspoon of butter spread on it contains 78 calories (60 from the bread and 18 from the butter). It will take some time to estimate the caloric value of every bit of food consumed each day during the week, but a total for each day, and an average daily intake for the week, can be calculated quickly as soon as each item is given a caloric value.

Once the average daily intake for the week is known, the dieter compares the weights at the beginning and end of the week. If the weight increased by a pound, it indicates that his average daily intake was about 500 calories greater than that needed to maintain his weight. If the weight did not change, then the food intake was just enough to meet the basic needs of the body and the demands for physical activity. If weight was lost, a caloric deficit existed during the week, and if a pound had been lost, the deficit was about 500 calories per day. Remember this figure: 500 calories a day = one pound a week.

With this information the adolescent can set up a weight-control program. If he or she decides to lose two pounds during a week, which is a sensible amount, the food allowance will have to be changed enough to make that goal possible. For someone who gained weight during the first week, the number of pounds gained should be multiplied by 500, and that value is added to 1,000. For the adolescent whose weight was constant during the week, a value of 1,000 should be used, and for the adolescent who lost weight during the week the number of pounds lost is multiplied by 500 and subtracted from 1,000. In each case, the final number of calories has to be taken away from the average daily food allowance: thus, if the food intake was 2,600 calories a day and the indicated changes amount to 1,000 calories, then the average food allowance for the following week must be reduced to 1,600 calories per day.

As a general guide, a food allowance should not be less than 1,000 or 1,200 calories per day because this is low enough to achieve weight loss, and high enough to avoid doing physical harm. To make definite plans for the first week of the weight-loss program, the dieter uses the projected food allowance as a guide in reducing the average daily caloric allowance. While making certain that adequate protein, such as that provided by six to eight ounces of lean meat, poultry, or fish, and a pint of low-fat (skimmed) milk, is part of the daily food allowance, the adolescent can reduce the use of other foods in any way that seems satisfactory. There is no need to resort to a specific diet of particular foods. In general, a fairly appealing, balanced diet can be worked out if reductions are made proportionately in each food category. If they have an equal number of calories, one type of food is no more fattening than another.

As the diet is put into operation, it is a good idea for the adolescent to continue to record the portions of food and beverages consumed during the day, and to make sure that each day's total intake of calories equals the number in the food allowance set at the beginning of the week. At the end of the second week the adolescent should be particularly interested in seeing how well the plan has worked. If the weight loss has been as great as was expected, no changes are necessary for the following week. If the weight loss is not as great as expected, the adolescent should review the portion sizes and the daily intake to make sure that the goal is being met each day and should consider making a few small adjustments to the food allowance so that weight will be lost somewhat more quickly during the third week. An adolescent should be able to tolerate this approach to weight loss reasonably well over an extended period of time, because it does not require a radical change in diet, provides appealing, nourishing, and satisfying meals, and it avoids what nearly every teenager abhors—hunger.

Changes in activity   As pointed out before, adolescents cannot rely entirely upon extra activity to accomplish a major loss of excess body fat. However, there are advantages to some increase in daily exercise. Activity not only promotes further use of stored energy and makes weight loss easier, but it also improves one's general physical condition. The increase in activity does not have to be drastic; an adolescent should not, for example, assume that exercise means doing large numbers of boring calisthenics. Instead, teenagers can look for opportunities to get just a bit more physical activity each day. Walk or ride a bicycle instead of riding in a car or on a bus; climb stairs rather than take elevators; do some physically active work around home; and take advantage of opportunities to engage in sports at school or in the community—all these are possibilities.

Continuing the program   Once a weight-loss program is underway, and the first few weeks of successful weight loss have been accomplished, it is a good idea to go on monitoring one's food allowance carefully, to be sure that the daily intake does not slowly rise above the ideal amount, permitting the weekly rate of weight loss to slow down. Weighing once a week and recording the weight give an overall view of the success of the program. There may very well be some "bumps" along the road of weight reduction, times when weight loss is temporarily interrupted. Parties, birthday celebrations, and holidays present the dieter with the need to choose between a desire to participate and a desire to go on losing weight. Sometimes adolescents can make up for the slippage by eating even less in the next few days; sometimes they learn they can't, and will have to settle for sticking to the diet instead of enjoying an occasional temporary lapse.

At times when adolescents are under particular pressure or stress, they may feel "more hungry," and find it very difficult not to eat more than their plan calls for. As long as they can anticipate and understand this, adolescents may be able to avoid some extra eating, or to get back on the track quickly if extra eating occurs. Another factor which plays a subtle but important role in a weight-loss program is the way family members—especially—and sometimes friends respond to the adolescent's success in losing weight. Actually, success is not usually evident right away. As much as one-third of the desired weight loss must be accomplished before either the dieter or others become aware of a definite change in physical appearance or in the way clothing fits. This phenomenon tends to make the first part of the weight-loss program the most difficult part, simply because it doesn't seem to be worth the effort. However, after the first third of the weight loss is accomplished, and as the adolescent continues to make progress, the change in physical appearance becomes evident more rapidly. Ironically, family members who have never seen the adolescent looking like this may be made uncomfortable by the change. Furthermore, they may not be entirely certain *why* they are uncomfortable. Their nervousness may actually lead them to slow or arrest the dieter's progress.

Nearing the end of the weight-reduction program   As the adolescent draws nearer to his or her weight goal, it is possible to case up on the food allowance. For example, if an adolescent is approximately four pounds away from the goal, and four weeks of dieting remain, 200 calories could be added to the daily food allowance each week. This approach would allow four pounds to be lost during the four weeks, instead of the usual eight pounds. At the end of the program, it's a good idea to maintain the new food allowance at a constant level for several weeks. If one's weight continues to drop, further weekly additions of 200 calories to the daily food allowance are made until weight remains stable. Likewise, if the weight begins to rise, an appropriate reduction in calories should be made to correct it.

Adolescents who become more physically active during their weight-loss programs find that they are able to increase their food intake considerably once they have reached their goals without regaining the weight they have worked so hard to lose. While the compliments on their appearance are pleasant rewards, adolescents are usually most pleased by the fact that they planned and attained these new, and sometimes unexpected, physical selves all on their own. They have the satisfaction of knowing not only that they can now wear clothes that fit well and are attractive but also that their persistence has served to benefit their future lives and well-being.

Thinness

As is the case with overweight, thinness in adolescence is usually not caused by an illness or any other disorder. It may seem surprising to adolescents who are overweight and who wish to be slim, but many thin teenagers wish they could weigh more. For those who have always been thin, gaining weight is not an easy task. However, most adolescents discover that their bodies fill out considerably during their growth spurts.

For some teenagers, thinness has another meaning and importance. To the wrestler, gymnast, long-distance runner, and to many swimmers, being thin means having the maximum amount of lean body mass and the minimum amount of body fat. Consequently, the "thin" athlete is frequently one whose weight is considerably above average for height but whose body composition reflects a low fat content. Well-trained adolescent boys who participate in such sports tend to have percentages of body fat of 5 to 7 percent, while girls have 10 to 14 percent (as determined by the methods discussed on page 144). Careful long-term physical conditioning, plus attention to diet, can lead the teenager to an ideal physical state, in which the amount of lean body mass remains stable (or increases) as the amount or proportion of fat in the body decreases.

In general, thin, healthy adolescents grow and mature quite normally during childhood and their adolescent years, and do not develop any worrisome physical symptoms or abnormal changes in body function related to their thinness. But when the teenager fails to gain weight normally, or loses weight unexpectedly, an illness may be responsible.

Weight loss

One cause of weight loss is especially common and is familiar to most adolescents from personal experience. In the course of a brief, self-limited illness—a bad cold, flu, sore throat, or gastrointestinal upset—a temporary decrease in appetite is not unusual, and in some cases the body absorbs and uses food less efficiently. Such episodes make a distinct impression. In a week or ten days, the adolescent may well lose three or four pounds. Because the illness does not last any longer, and because the adolescent's health returns quickly, the weight loss can be tolerated and replaced rapidly.

This simple example illustrates several typical and important points about weight loss. First, any condition that reduces a person's desire for food over an extended period of time will have a major impact on weight. In addition, if the adolescent has a health problem that interferes with either the absorption of food or its use by the body, weight loss will occur unless food intake is increased markedly. In most instances of weight loss that continue for more than a week or two, adolescents are often aware of a variety of symptoms such as loss of appetite, nausea, change in gastrointestinal function (vomiting, diarrhea, change in the appearance of bowel movements), pain, or fever. The persistence of these or any other symptoms, and the weight loss, is likely to prompt a visit to a physician. Obtaining professional help makes very good sense, because weight loss that continues for more than a short time is frequently caused by an underlying health problem, and it could be a serious one.

Anorexia nervosa

Another kind of severe weight loss, usually confined to adolescence, is known as anorexia nervosa, and is about six times as common in girls as in boys. A particular pattern clearly distinguishes this illness from practically all other causes of weight loss during adolescence. An adolescent who is slightly overweight makes a decision to lose some weight, and then continues to lose weight even when he or she has reached an inordinate degree of thinness. As the weight loss occurs, the adolescent seems to feel fine, is enthusiastic about his or her success, and does not see any reason to seek professional attention, even when the weight loss becomes severe.

Most adolescent girls who develop this potentially lethal illness do so after menarche, and the onset of anorexia nervosa is frequently preceded by a halt in menstruation. Within a few months, the adolescent decides that she needs to lose weight —perhaps with the hope of improving the appearance of a particular part of her body. She may set a fairly specific weight-loss goal, and she adopts a diet sufficiently limited to reach it. In girls who were still having menstrual periods when they started dieting, the periods cease after some weight loss has been achieved. On reaching the goal, however, she does not seem to be entirely satisfied by her weight loss or the appearance of her body, and even though she is slim, she begins to be obsessed with a need to lose still more weight. She continues to restrict her food intake, performs increased amounts of exercise, and loses a noticeably greater amount of weight. As her body becomes lighter, she often notices changes in the ways in which her body works, although she may attempt to discount their importance. Particularly evident changes reflect the depletion of the body's energy stores. During the initial phase of the illness, adolescents with anorexia nervosa tend to use up most of the energy stored as body fat. As the energy supply hoarded in the fat cells dwindles and dietary intake does not match the body's continuing demand for energy, other sources are drawn upon. Most of these sources consist of energy held by the body in the form of muscle. However, as the muscles are used for energy, they become smaller, less efficient, and more easily fatigued. The adolescent realizes that she cannot perform a variety of physical tasks with her previous ease, confidence, and comfort. She also finds herself becoming increasingly sensitive to cold; even in warm rooms, or in warm clothing, or on summer days, she feels cold. Her skin becomes dry, and small cuts and insect bites heal slowly; increased growth of fine hair appears on her face, trunk, and arms. Her bowel movements also occur less frequently, perhaps only once every week or ten days, and because the production of LH and FSH (see p. 16) is reduced drastically, she continues to have no menstrual periods.

Under these circumstances, an adolescent would appear to need more rest than ever, but instead she does not sleep as long or as soundly as before her weight loss began. At bedtime she may lie awake for a long time; in addition, her sleep may be interrupted during the night for no apparent reason. Then, following a relatively small amount of sleep, she may wake up early and be unable to get back to sleep. During the day most adolescents with anorexia nervosa postpone from one meal to the next eating adequate amounts of food. Yet they do not stay away from food entirely. Many who have anorexia nervosa spend vast amounts of time shopping for food, reading about its preparation, and cooking. They enjoy serving food to others. Most are able to continue their schoolwork and be quite successful at it; they also stay involved in physical activities such as running, dancing, and bicycle riding. Many victims discover that as their weight decreases they become more demanding, less happy, and more irritable than in the past. They also find that their friendships are more difficult to sustain, and they have increased difficulty in getting along at home. As their parents become more concerned about them and exert more pressure on them to eat, the adolescents will not comply; instead of eating, they may hide or surreptitiously discard food.

This description of the progress of an anorexia nervosa case is a composite, based on multiple observations. It does not pretend to answer the questions people ask about why this condition occurs at all, and why it strikes girls so conspicuously. Such questions are not answered easily, but we can take note of certain characteristics of anorexia nervosa patients that are suggestive. It has often been observed that adolescents who develop anorexia nervosa were ideal or perfect children when they were younger, children who caused their parents little difficulty. Looking back, one wonders if they concentrated their efforts as children on pleasing all those around them, while tending not to express, and satisfy, their own needs sufficiently. Perhaps lacking somewhat in the ability to solve personal problems or to manage relationships with others, they arrive at adolescence. Then two intersecting forces appear that seem to influence the onset of the disorder. One consists of a recent or impending change in the adolescent's life—entering a new school, being separated from home and family, becoming aware that serious parental marital difficulty exists. The other is the discovery that one is overweight, or that one's rump (for example) is unacceptably large, the result of which is a decision to lose weight. When these forces intersect, dieting, exercising, and preoccupation with food and weight loss gain ascendancy—perhaps because they provide the adolescent with a challenge to which she can respond actively—and for a long time, they divert attention from the other truly important areas of concern. The marked discrepancy between the incidence of anorexia nervosa in girls and boys is not readily explained. While there is the suspicion that girls, who begin to grow and mature some two years earlier than boys, and who tend to be more interested in dieting and weight control than boys, might be more vulnerable to a problem of this kind, other influences probably also exist.

There is no good reason to assume that anorexia nervosa can be cured or relieved without professional help, and the sooner the adolescent and her parents obtain a comprehensive evaluation of the problem and recommendations for treatment from a physician, the sooner he or she is likely to recover. During treatment it is important for the adolescent to be able to gain an understanding of the psychological issues that are playing roles in the illness.

Problems in reproductive function

In this section, we discuss some of the health concerns arising from the process of sexual maturation. Some of these problems occur so frequently that they can almost be considered a typical part of adolescence, while others represent variations from the usual developmental pattern. The rather common problems in reproductive function that accompany sexual maturation occur primarily in girls, though some problems, such as a failure to complete the maturation process on schedule, can occur with equal frequency in boys.

Menstrual periods

Cessation of periods   Many times a girl's menstrual function begins normally, continues regularly for some time, and then lapses. A month or more passes without another menstrual period and the girl becomes curious about the reason. From a developmental viewpoint, this kind of interruption (called **amenorrhea**) during the first few years following menarche is not at all unusual and does not point to any abnormality or serious underlying problem. When it occurs without any other symptoms, the loss of menstrual function seldom indicates that a girl is ill. Often in early adolescence there are menstrual cycles in which ovulation does not take place, and considerable variation in cycle length is not uncommon. In any event, menstrual function usually resumes in one or two months.

Other conditions may also set the stage for interruption of previously regular periods. Some girls who change their place of residence find that their menstrual function stops for a few months. Girls who go to camp or who travel during summer vacations may stop having periods during their absence from home. Other girls who leave home in September to live at school may notice that their menstrual periods cease for several months, and then begin again when they are home on vacation. The precise reason for these changes in menstrual function is not very clear, but they are common and, in general, should not be a cause for alarm.

Menstrual periods often cease when a girl becomes ill, and then return as she recovers. Sometimes the loss of menstrual function that accompanies illness seems to be associated with weight loss, and sometimes weight loss alone predisposes girls to cessation of menstrual periods. The latter factor is particularly likely when the amount of weight loss is severe (as in anorexia nervosa), or when weight is lost quite rapidly. Thus, someone who goes about losing a great deal of weight, for example, to improve her appearance or to enhance her competitive edge in weight-conscious sports such as gymnastics and cross-country track, might also experience a temporary loss of menstrual function.

In other instances, interrupted menstruation has a more serious basis. Among girls who are sexually active and who do not use contraception, amenorrhea is one of the earliest signs of pregnancy. Ovulation usually occurs about fourteen days before the start of a menstrual period. For example, if a girl ovulates on June 10, her next menstrual period will begin about June 24. When the ovum is fertilized and pregnancy occurs, the menstrual period does not come when it is expected, and other signs of pregnancy usually follow. These include changes in the breasts (increased fullness or slight tenderness), either an increase in appetite or "morning sickness," or a need to get up during the night to empty the bladder. All of these changes, which signify pregnancy, usually begin a few weeks after the missed period; at the time of the missed period itself, the girl may not notice anything at all.

At the earliest stages, the most useful and accurate method of telling whether one is pregnant is a pregnancy test. The test, however, must be done at the correct time. Most of the standard laboratory tests for pregnancy are performed on urine specimens, and they become "positive" twenty-one to twenty-three days following ovulation, or about a week to ten days after the time when the missed menstrual period should have begun. Tests done somewhat later will, of course, be positive when pregnancy has occurred. But tests done too early may be falsely negative and provide the adolescent with misleading information. Newer tests, run on blood specimens, can establish pregnancy even before the first menstrual period is missed. After four to six weeks, pregnancy can be detected by softening of the cervix and enlargement of the uterus, conditions obvious to a doctor during a pelvic examination.

When none of the conditions mentioned so far—illness or weight loss, movement from home, pregnancy—seems to account for a lapse in menstrual function, other possibilities merit consideration. They are reasonably uncommon in adolescents. A decrease in the production of thyroid hormone (see p. 201) can be accompanied by loss of menstrual function; increased androgen production (which may have other effects, such as increasing the growth of male-type hair on the body) is also frequently associated with amenorrhea. Loss of menstrual function also occurs in girls whose pituitary glands produce excessive amounts of a hormone known as **prolactin**. In some girls, overproduction of prolactin also causes **galactorrhea**, the production of a milky secretion from the breasts (see p. 173). Each of these problems should be fully evaluated by the adolescent's doctor.

Heavy or prolonged periods Following their first menstrual periods, after some fairly regular menstrual cycles, some girls experience a longer than usual interval between one period and the next. As the next period begins, it is either heavier or longer, or heavier *and* longer, than any previous one. Both the heavy bleeding and its duration are worrisome to the adolescent, even though this kind of bleeding is usually not accompanied by pain. The problem usually develops when the endometrium (the tissue lining the uterus) is stimulated by estrogen alone for a longer than usual time. In addition, the estrogen level in the bloodstream, though normal, does not trigger the release of large amounts of luteinizing hormone (LH) by the pituitary gland, and ovulation fails to occur. Because ovulation does not occur, progesterone is absent. Eventually the estrogen-stimulated endometrium begins to bleed, but not in a normal fashion. Heavy, prolonged bleeding is the result.

Sometimes this kind of menstrual bleeding, called **dysfunctional uterine bleeding,** ceases without medical intervention. However, clinical evaluation and sometimes treatment are useful. The doctor will review the girl's menstrual history, make sure that the source of the bleeding is the uterus (which it should be), and check that the patient has not lost too much blood. He must also exclude other causes for the bleeding, among them inadequate function of the thyroid gland, iron deficiency, and disorders of the platelets. He may prescribe medication such as estrogen or progesterone, which can help slow and then arrest the bleeding, setting the stage for more normal subsequent menstrual flow. The doctor will also help the adolescent monitor her menstrual function for the next few months to make sure that the heavy, prolonged bleeding does not reappear.

Painful periods　During the first year or so after menarche, ovulation does not occur regularly, and, as a general rule, menstrual periods following non-ovulatory cycles do not produce much discomfort. As ovulation becomes a more frequent occurrence, several changes appear in the menstrual cycle. Compared with cycles during the first year or so after menarche, the interval between the menstrual periods usually becomes more regular, menstrual flow is of shorter duration, and the bleeding is more likely to be accompanied by discomfort. The discomfort consists of crampy lower abdominal and pelvic pain, sometimes in conjunction with other discomforts, such as pain in the thighs or the back, or gastrointestinal problems, particularly nausea or diarrhea. The symptoms, collectively called **dysmenorrhea,** contribute to school absenteeism for many girls. The discomfort begins with the start of the menstrual period and is usually most bothersome during the first two days of the period. A plausible explanation of these symptoms has evolved slowly among medical researchers. Evidence points to a **prostaglandin** as the cause of the symptoms. This is an interesting and complex chemical substance produced in the endometrium (the lining of the uterus) in larger quantities during ovulatory menstrual cycles than during cycles when ovulation does not occur. It has been shown that when the levels of the prostaglandin are reduced, the cramping pains and other symptoms tend to decrease. It is not necessary for a girl to endure these symptoms each month, as several forms of medication either prevent or relieve them.

When taken at the beginning of a menstrual period, aspirin—or other medication, such as naproxen, ibuprofen, and mefenamic acid—decreases the production of prostaglandins and effectively prevents much of the discomfort of dysmenorrhea. Because they prevent ovulation, oral contraceptive pills (see p. 196) also reduce or prevent menstrual pains. Although oral contraceptive pills are not primarily recommended for the treatment of dysmenorrhea, it may be a desirable side effect of their use.

Mittelschmerz, which means "mid-cycle pain," is a common occurrence in girls having ovulatory menstrual cycles. The discomfort, typically a dull ache in the lower abdomen and perhaps noted more often on the right side than the left, develops just before or after the ovary releases an ovum. Therefore it appears at mid-cycle, or more precisely, about fourteen days before the onset of the next menstrual period. A girl who is aware of this mild and short-lived symptom can pinpoint the moment when she ovulates. She requires no treatment, and has no need to worry that the symptom is being caused by an abnormal condition.

Persistent sexual immaturity

Problems in reproductive function that go along with the normal sexual maturation process are fairly common, and tend to occur during the process of sexual maturation. Much less often, adolescents are faced with a complete lack of *any* physical changes indicating sexual maturation. Before becoming concerned about an abnormal lack of sexual maturation, however, consider how old the adolescent is. The age-maturation linkage is never precise. When a child grows normally, but slowly, during childhood, when one or more family members have begun to mature at relatively late ages, and when a child has been chronically ill, he or she often reaches adolescence and moves through the process of sexual maturation somewhat more slowly than other children.

In members of either sex, the first physical sign of the start of sexual maturation can be used as a milestone. Among girls, it is the earliest stage of breast development (see p. 170): a small amount of breast tissue beneath the areolae, which may not develop until girls are 13 to 13 1/2 years old. Among boys, the sign is accelerated growth of the testes, and this may not begin until the age of 13 1/2 to 14 years (see p. 123). Healthy boys and girls who are growing normally and who have no abnormal physical symptoms should not become unduly concerned about a lack of sexual maturation until they reach these ages, which are at the upper end of the normal range. When these ages are passed, and no evidence of sexual maturation appears, it may be useful to consult a doctor for an evaluation. The physical examination may well yield other more subtle evidence of the onset of sexual maturation. Or, if not, it will suggest further diagnostic steps aimed at revealing what might be delaying the process. As suggested by the discussion of sexual maturation earlier (see p. 15), the difficulty might reside in the regulatory centers of the brain or the pituitary gland, or it might represent an inability of the ovaries or testes to respond to stimulation by the gonadotropins. Using a systematic approach, the doctor evaluates the functional ability of each part of the reproductive system and assesses the prospects for further growth. In most cases, the complete evaluation reveals no particular abnormality, and we can safely conclude that the process of sexual maturation is simply (and mysteriously) delayed; in time it will begin and progress normally. In a smaller number of instances, the evaluation identifies a specific problem somewhere in the system. With this information, the doctor can start treatment.

Because sexual maturation is so central to the entire adolescent process, and because its effects are so visible, adolescents who do not mature at the usual time tend to compare themselves unfavorably with their peers and become very depressed. What is worse, adults and other teenagers frequently treat sexually immature adolescents as if they are much younger than they really are, and thus add to their emotional burdens. A clinical evaluation of persistent sexual immaturity and a discussion with a sympathetic doctor give an adolescent the information he or she needs to understand what is happening and what the future holds. This knowledge is generally far preferable to continued worry and ignorance.

Delayed menarche As discussed earlier in this section, some fluctuation in menstrual function is not at all unusual after menstrual periods begin during adolescence, and menarche does not occur in girls who remain sexually immature. Apart from these circumstances, another condition called delayed menarche can sometimes appear. Delayed menarche describes a situation in which sexual maturation begins and progresses to a level at which menstrual function customarily starts, yet does not. It is often due to the same causes that interrupt menstrual function after menarche (see p. 159). Remember that the average age at menarche is just under 13 years, and ranges from 10 to 15. Girls afflicted by delayed menarche might well be approaching the end of their physical growth spurts; and they might have nearly mature breast development and pubic and underarm hair growth. Much less often, menarche is delayed in girls who have quite mature breast development, but who have not developed any appreciable amount of pubic or underarm hair: in these girls, the problem may be hormonal. For others, the actual onset of menstrual function is blocked by an anatomical oddity in the reproductive tract; for example, a small portion of the outflow tract in the vagina may be closed, preventing menstrual flow. Such an obstruction can cause intermittent lower abdominal discomfort and fullness. Whatever the cause, delayed menarche should be fully evaluated by the adolescent's doctor.

Common skeletal disorders

During adolescent growth, the size of the skeleton increases considerably, the weight carried on it nearly doubles, and the muscles attached to it increase in size and strength. It is not surprising, under these circumstances, that several problems can arise that specifically involve the growing skeleton. To a great extent, the problems follow the general skeletal growth pattern, beginning in the extremities, then affecting the hips, and finally the spine. Though there are a few other skeletal problems that occasionally bother adolescents, those particularly linked to the adolescent growth process include Osgood-Schlatter disease, slipped capital femoral epiphysis, and idiopathic scoliosis. Each is presented here with a concise guide to the symptoms that usually signal its presence. Another skeletal problem—bone tumors—is discussed in the section on cancer in adolescence (see p. 227).

Osgood-Schlatter disease

Early in the adolescent growth spurt, when the legs are growing more rapidly than the upper body, an otherwise healthy adolescent may feel sharp pain just below the knee. The pain is located over a small bony prominence, two or three inches below the patella (knee cap). This bony prominence, called the anterior tibial tubercle, is the place where the tendon from the thigh muscles attaches to the tibia, the larger of the lower leg bones. The pain can appear during participation in vigorous sports, such as basketball or track, and not be present at any other time; or it can occur when the adolescent climbs stairs or reaches for something on an overhead shelf. In other adolescents, the discomfort is more or less constant. The area of pain may display a slight swelling, a small increase in local warmth, and perhaps a high degree of tenderness when one presses on the bony prominence. Tensing the thigh muscles and straightening the leg can often reproduce the pain noted in various physical activities that require the same movement. This grouping of symptoms is typical of Osgood-Schlatter disease (named for the two physicians who first described the disorder in 1903). Many adolescents develop it only in one leg, while some have the problem in both legs. Girls seem to develop Osgood-Schlatter less frequently than boys. As might be expected from the fact that girls begin their adolescent growth earlier than boys, girls tend to develop Osgood-Schlatter disease at 10 or 11 years of age, and boys at 12 or 13 years.

The swelling and discomfort that characterize this problem have nothing to do with the knee joint itself. Instead, it appears to result in part from the considerable force that the thigh muscles exert through their tendon on the anterior tibial tubercle. In addition, when Osgood-Schlatter disease appears, the bone in the tubercle has not reached full maturity, and under the constant forces applied by the muscles, small fragments break free from the surface of the bone and irritate the tendon. The swelling and pain of Osgood-Schlatter disease result from this process.

In milder forms, Osgood-Schlatter disease heals readily, and the symptoms disappear. Treatment is usually rest, enough to relieve the discomfort and to allow healing to get underway. Some pain-relieving medication, such as aspirin or acetaminophen, can also help, particularly when the amount of discomfort is severe or is constant. Avoidance of strenuous physical activity is very important during the healing phase. A few adolescents, whose symptoms are very troublesome and do not respond to the customary forms of care, need to have a short cast applied to the leg for several weeks: the complete immobilization of the knee relieves the symptoms and promotes healing. Most cases heal themselves completely, but some affected adolescents may notice that a slight protrusion of the tibial tubercle at the location of the swelling is visible for many years.

Slipped capital femoral epiphysis

A slipped capital femoral epiphysis is an epiphysis, or growth plate (see p. 13), in the hip that slips from its normal position. As the slipping begins, the teenager notices pain in the hip or groin, usually mild. Because pains originating in the hip do not always feel as though they are in the hip, some adolescents feel the pain in the thigh or the region around the knee instead. The pain is usually made worse by movement of the hip, and may cause a limp. Boys develop this problem more frequently than girls. It usually appears somewhat later than Osgood-Schlatter disease. Most adolescents who develop a slipped capital femoral epiphysis are considerably overweight.

From time to time, adolescents strain muscles or get bruised, both of which can produce similar aches in their legs. However, when a leg pain or a limp cannot be readily associated with a recent strain or bruise, or when aches of this kind last more than a few days without improving considerably, it is of the utmost importance to find out whether slipped capital femoral epiphysis may be causing the trouble. Clinical evaluation of the disorder consists of a careful physical examination and X rays of the hips. In general, the sooner a slipped epiphysis is recognized, the less likely it will be for additional injury to the hip to occur. An orthopedic surgeon will treat the slippage by surgical means, pinning the epiphysis to the rest of the bone until adolescent growth is finished and fusion of the epiphysis is completed. Unfortunately, adolescents who have this problem in one hip are also likely to develop it in the other hip, and part of their care consists of carefully watching the growth and position of the other epiphysis.

Idiopathic scoliosis

A normal spine, viewed from the back, looks straight. Scoliosis is a side-to-side curvature of the spine. Potentially serious scoliosis is curvature that is rather rigid or inflexible: it does not "unwind" or straighten out when the adolescent bends to the side of the curve. In addition, the curvature of scoliosis is accompanied by a second deformation that is responsible for many of its most unpleasant effects. This consists of rotation of the vertebral bodies of the spinal column around their common axis, the degree of vertebral rotation being greatest at the center of the curvature. The importance of the combination of spinal curvature and rotation is that as the spine is deformed, so are the structures attached to it, especially the ribs.

168

For example, if a girl has developed scoliosis in the section of her spine to which the ribs are attached, and if the curvature points to the right side of her body, then it is likely that her ribs will be more prominent on the right side of her back than they are on the left side. In addition, scoliosis is frequently accompanied by some unevenness in the heights of the shoulders and the appearance of the shoulder blades, and by a tendency for the pelvis to be thrust more to one side than the other.

The term "idiopathic"—which refers to a disease without an obvious cause—applies to most cases of scoliosis that develop in adolescents. (But children and adolescents who have any one of a variety of diseases involving the nervous system or the muscles can develop scoliosis as part of their illness.) Scoliosis may be discovered by a doctor who notices the curvature while performing a regular physical examination, or perhaps by an adolescent's parent or friend. Scoliosis requiring treatment is quite a bit more common in adolescent girls than in boys of the same age. When one female in a family has it, chances are greater that other female members of the family will have it too, as it is frequently hereditary. Clinical assessment of the problem focuses on the amounts of curvature and rotation, on the degree of flexibility of the scoliosis, and on how much further growth the adolescent can expect. Scoliosis that is already marked benefits from treatment by orthopedic surgeons, as does scoliosis that is progressing rapidly. Milder degrees of scoliosis are managed in ways that prevent the deformity from getting worse. Many therapeutic advances, including exercises, bracing, and surgery, have been made in the management of patients with scoliosis, and a doctor or orthopedic specialist can choose an appropriate treatment.

Breast disorders

It is possible for both boys and girls to experience some breast disorders during the process of sexual maturation. Most people don't realize, in fact, that during adolescence boys are more likely to have breast disorders than girls. Fortunately, many of these problems come and go quickly, appearing and disappearing during the process of sexual maturation; other disorders require special treatment. In general, the problems may be characterized as involving changes in the size or shape of the breasts, masses within the breast, or secretion from the breast. Since adolescence also presents an opportune time for girls to become familiar with an easy and reliable method of examining their own breasts, this section concludes with a description of breast examination technique.

Changes in girls' breast size and shape

As breast development takes place, one breast may begin to mature earlier than the other, and continue to be larger and more advanced in development for some time. Eventually their appearances become similar. Girls may also notice that the shape of one breast is not exactly like the other, a difference that may vanish as the breasts become mature. These irregularities are not necessarily abnormal. To see why, let us briefly review changes that occur during breast growth in girls.

In preadolescence, before the ovaries begin to produce increased amounts of estrogen, the breasts contain none of the firm tissue that is typical of more mature breasts. The tissue beneath the **areola** (the smooth, more darkly colored circular area that eventually becomes the nipple) consists only of the muscle and ribs of the chest wall. In the center of the areola, there is a small nubbin, called the **papilla,** which usually projects slightly. As the immature breast tissue is stimulated by estrogen produced by the maturing ovaries, firm breast tissue appears beneath the areola, and the entire areola begins to project slightly from the chest. Eventually a stage is reached in which the areola projects from the contour of the rest of the breast. When this developmental stage is reached earlier in one breast than in the other, the breasts can appear noticeably dissimilar. As the breast reaches its mature form, the projection of the areola usually disappears, and only the papilla remains elevated above the contour of the entire breast.

After menarche, breasts frequently become slightly more full, or firm, and sometimes slightly tender, several days before the onset of a menstrual period. The fullness and tenderness disappear toward the end of the menstrual period.

Given the variety of normal changes in the appearance and size of the breasts during adolescence, it is plain why it may be wise to wait until development is complete before taking any steps, such as cosmetic surgery, which might permanently influence the form of the breasts.

Changes in boys' breasts

During their sexual maturation, boys also frequently undergo some unexpected breast enlargement. This is called **gynecomastia**. While it seldom reaches the extent normally seen in girls, it is more than enough to catch a boy's attention. Some breast enlargement tends to occur in two-thirds to three-quarters of all adolescent boys. When it occurs, it is usually confined to the region beneath the areola. Much less often, it may spread beyond the border of the areola. A boy may notice changes in the size of one or both breasts, and his attention may be drawn by the fact that the breast has become moderately sensitive to touch. Even a loose-fitting shirt may be uncomfortable. When gynecomastia appears during the growth spurt, it does not usually indicate any serious, underlying problem. Instead, it probably represents a passing imbalance between the amounts of estrogen and androgen in the boy's body. Gynecomastia is likely to go away entirely without treatment. Even in cases where a moderately large amount of breast development has occurred, the problem may resolve itself completely, sometimes in a year to a year and a half, sometimes more quickly. Occasionally cases do require treatment. When the breast size is large, or when it does not return fully to normal size, it makes sense to get a doctor's opinion, and surgical removal of the unnecessary breast tissue may be recommended. The removal of the tissue is accomplished through an incision along the border of the areola. The areola is, of course, left intact and afterwards the chest appears normal again.

Breast masses

A mass within the breast occurs almost exclusively in girls. It may be found by the girl as she dresses, showers, or periodically examines her own breasts. A breast mass should be distinguished from the general increase in fullness or firmness that can precede a menstrual period. The term "mass" refers to a lump in the breast that is firmer than the breast tissue itself. Most of the breast masses that develop in adolescents are benign tumors, and they possess no ability to spread to another area of the body. The most common breast mass is a small, firm, smooth, nontender, rubbery mass that can be easily felt and moved slightly within the breast. Sometimes more than one is present, in the same breast or in both breasts. Masses of this kind that are removed surgically, examined by a pathologist, and found to be benign are usually **fibroadenomas.** Other kinds of benign breast masses do develop during adolescence, but they are much less common than fibroadenomas, and masses that are actually malignant cancers are very infrequent.

Because breast masses make no useful contribution to the adolescent, nor do they get better and disappear by themselves, and because they cannot be identified with certainty unless they are examined by a pathologist, a girl who discovers a mass in her breast should notify her physician and have it evaluated clinically. This usually involves having it removed surgically. Knowing the exact nature of the mass is reassuring when it is benign, and in the uncommon event that it is *not* benign, identification is imperative. Adolescents should note that removal of a breast mass, depending on its size, is a relatively minor matter, and not disfiguring. It has nothing to do with such major surgery as a mastectomy, which can involve the removal of an entire breast.

Secretion from the breast

As the female breast matures during adolescence, it acquires the potential for producing milk to nourish an infant. Secretions from the breasts at times other than the end of pregnancy need to be viewed as separate problems, and should be evaluated by a physician.

Milky secretions coming from the breasts of young women who have not recently given birth to a child (a condition called **galactorrhea**) can occur when a higher than normal amount of the hormone prolactin is circulating in the body. Increased amounts of prolactin can be produced by the pituitary gland acting on its own, or under the influence of various medications in the system, or when the thyroid gland supplies the body with insufficient thyroid hormone. Occasionally secretions of this kind appear *during* pregnancy. Though much less commonly, boys occasionally develop milky secretions from their breasts.

Other secretions from the breasts include those produced by infections and masses in the breast. In the presence of infection, the breast may be increased in size, warmer than usual, perhaps reddened, and tender to touch; the secretion is likely to be yellow. Some breast masses (but not a fibroadenoma) produce a small amount of blood-tinged secretion, which is itself a clue to the presence of the mass.

Breast self-examination

During the adolescent years, girls should begin to examine their own breasts. They will then find it easy to continue the practice into adulthood, when there is a greater possibility of locating an abnormality in the breast. Breast self-examination is aimed at discovering a breast mass—a lump that stands out from the normal texture of the breast tissue. Girls whose breasts become full or tender just before menstrual periods should wait until a period has ended before performing the examination. In this way, the prominence of some of the normal breast structures in the premenstrual phase of the cycle will not be mistaken for masses, nor will the increased fullness of the breast obscure any mass which might be present.

The procedure begins with the girl lying on her back, with a small pillow under her right shoulder. The pillow lifts the side of the chest enough to flatten the right breast, making it easier to examine. Then the girl places the palm of her right hand under her head. With her right arm in this position, she uses her left hand to examine the inner half of the right breast thoroughly. Usually more information is obtained by examining the breasts for masses by pressing down with the flat surfaces of the ends of the fingers than by using the fingertips. Before examining the outer half of her breast, she places her right arm alongside her body. Having completed the examination of the right breast, she shifts the pillow to a similar position beneath the left shoulder, and examines the left breast in the same manner, using the right hand. Self-examination of the breast does not take long, and should be performed each month, usually during the week that follows a menstrual period.

Skin problems

Skin problems are among the most numerous and varied of all the problems of adolescence. Some of the skin problems teenagers encounter are similar to those of children and adults, while others begin and are most noticeable during adolescence. The latter include acne, changes in the growth of hair, and certain kinds of fungal infections involving the skin. Other skin problems that are common in adolescents include atopic dermatitis, psoriasis, allergic contact dermatitis, pityriasis rosea, dry skin, warts, moles, and sunburn (which is discussed in the section on cosmetic problems—see p. 234).

As sexual maturation progresses, changes occur in the functions of several glands located in the skin. On the face, scalp, back, shoulders, and chest, an increase in the production of fatty substances by the **sebaceous glands** makes the skin and hair much more oily than it was during childhood, necessitating more use of shampoo and a general increase in the frequency of washing. Androgens also stimulate the growth of the beard in boys, and after needing to shave only once a week or less at the start, boys find that more shaving is becoming necessary. The development of other skin glands, called **apocrine glands,** most numerous under the arms, leads to the production of substances that can be broken down by bacteria that live on the skin. In turn, this process promotes an increase in body odor that makes attractive the use of more soap and deodorant.

Acne

Probably no other skin disorder is as universally recognized as acne. It appears during adolescence, lasts (when untreated) for several years in most boys and girls, and then usually clears up in early adult life. As with most disorders involving the skin, acne has a rather specific distribution on the body. Several forms of acne lesions develop, each representing different stages of the problem. Acne appears only in those areas of the skin containing structures known as **pilo-sebaceous follicles.** This awesome term describes a test-tube-shaped structure lined by skin, in which a small, barely visible hair grows. Most important, a sebaceous gland—one of those that produces most of the oily material found on the skin—is attached to the follicle. The oily products of the gland are delivered into the follicle, and then make their way to the surface of the skin. The areas of the skin containing appreciable numbers of pilo-sebaceous follicles include the face, neck, chest, shoulders, and back; thus, acne is mostly limited to these areas. Similar follicles exist elsewhere—particularly on the scalp—but the larger hairs they produce may help prevent acne from occurring in them.

Acne develops as a result of a complex interaction in the follicle of the skin cells, the oily material, and bacteria—specifically, *Propionibacterium acnes.* The bacteria are present during childhood, but the production of oily material by the sebaceous glands does not reach full capacity until the sebaceous glands are stimulated by androgens, increased amounts of which appear during adolescence. Boys tend to develop more acne than girls, and some of the difference can be explained by the generally lower levels of androgens, and higher levels of estrogens, in girls during adolescence.

The bacteria, which increase in number at adolescence, do not cause a typical infection. They seem to act on the oily material and skin cells to create an acne lesion in the absence of the usual signs of infection. The skin cells lining the follicle are normally shed regularly into the follicle, where along with the oily material made by the sebaceous gland, they make their way to the surface of the skin. This shedding of old skin cells does not proceed normally in a follicle beginning to develop an acne lesion. Instead, the skin cells unite, forming a plug that gradually fills the follicle and closes it off. When the mass within the follicle acquires enough bulk, it becomes visible in the skin. Depending on its depth in the follicle, it is given one of two names. If it comes to the surface, it is called a "blackhead"; if it occupies a deeper portion of the follicle, it is called a "whitehead." Both blackheads and whiteheads, collectively known as **comedones,** are unattractive. They also encourage the follicles they occupy to develop into more serious acne lesions. These serious lesions occur when the wall of a follicle containing a comedone ruptures, and the material that was confined within the follicle runs out into the surrounding tissues. When this happens, redness and swelling ensue, and the adolescent notices a red bump, or pimple, which can be tender. Apart from the appearance and discomfort of such bumps, they can leave scars when they heal.

Once these basic concepts about the evolution of acne lesions are understood, it is easier to deal with some of the myths about acne that have survived over the years. An old myth links sexual activity with the development of acne; it is a good example of the confusion of cause-and-effect with coincidence. Other myths include insufficient washing of the skin and improper dietary habits. Yet even those adolescents who scrupulously wash their faces several times a day can develop acne, and the elimination of favorite foods such as cola drinks, french fries, and chocolate from your diet may make you feel as though you deserve something special in return, but it seldom does the acne much good.

Some adolescents learn that their acne becomes more troublesome when they are in hot, humid environments, or when they perspire a great deal. Girls sometimes notice a flaring up of their acne just before a menstrual period. In addition, many afflicted teenagers blame stress from a variety of sources (exams, arguments, being tired) for increasing the severity of their acne, although no firm basis for this connection has ever been established.

A tour through the dermatological section of a drugstore quickly reveals that a wide array of acne treatments exists. Many of the same ingredients are found in the different preparations for treating acne, and guidelines can be drawn for choosing something that will be helpful. In addition, it is good to know when to seek professional help for acne.

Mild acne, which consists of blackheads and whiteheads, is helped considerably with the use of **benzoyl peroxide,** now available as an over-the-counter medication. Usually provided in a concentration of 5 percent in a gel or liquid form, benzoyl peroxide is applied to the skin once a day. It works by reducing the action of the bacteria that inhabit the follicle, and also by breaking up some of the comedones that have formed. A convenient and practical method involves washing the skin with mild soap and water, rinsing it well, and allowing it to dry completely before applying a thin film of medication at bedtime. In the morning, the medication is washed off—it might bleach clothing that it touches. The beneficial effect produced by benzoyl peroxide may take several weeks to appear, but after a month or more of its use improvement begins to be quite noticeable. The quantity and the size of the blackheads and whiteheads decrease, and the tendency to develop red bumps also diminishes. If adequate improvement does not occur, the strength of the benzoyl peroxide preparation can be raised to 7 1/2 or 10 percent. As the skin becomes more completely clear, the frequency with which the medication is used can be decreased, perhaps at first to every other day, and then if there is no relapse, even less often.

Other over-the-counter preparations for acne accomplish less impressive results. Many are solvents or astringents that remove oily material from the skin surface, and leave the skin feeling dry and clean: these preparations do not usually have much effect on the acne lesions in the follicles. Similar results are also obtained from sun exposure, short of sunburn, which makes the skin drier, and also produces a tan, hiding some of the redness that accompanies more serious acne lesions.

Physicians who treat adolescents with acne can prescribe other kinds of medication that are also helpful when acne is either stubborn or more severe than the mild form mentioned. Vitamin A acid, also known as **retinoic acid,** can be prescribed by a doctor, and is particularly effective in reversing the development of whiteheads and blackheads. Antibiotics, which impair the activity of the bacteria in the follicles, can also be very helpful. Both tetracycline and erythromycin, as well as a few others that are used less often, are effective when applied to the skin or taken by mouth. In addition to providing some of these medications, a physician can help an adolescent with acne in two other ways. One is to remove blackheads and whiteheads from the skin. An instrument called a comedone extractor is used to exert pressure around the opening of the follicle: this simple maneuver squeezes the comedone out of the follicle, and large numbers of comedones can be dealt with quickly in this way. The other procedure available to a physician is the use of a steroid medication injected directly into the more severe red bumps. This causes them to improve quickly, and perhaps avoids or lessens the possibility of developing acne scars. Often, after a serious acne lesion has improved, an adolescent may notice a dark-colored area of the skin in the immediate vicinity. The color, which is bluish-red or brown, fades slowly. It does not mean that the lesion is still active or that additional treatment is needed.

When acne lesions cause much inflammation in the skin, a scar can form as healing takes place. In many instances, the scars are very small, and they frequently become less noticeable as time passes. When numerous acne scars exist and detract from the adolescent's appearance, a physician may be able to offer advice about their treatment. **Dermabrasion** is one technique that some dermatologists and plastic surgeons employ to remove or reduce the degree of scarring present in the skin, by scraping off the top layer. In general, dermabrasion is not performed until all of the active acne lesions have disappeared and the scars have shrunk as much as they are likely to without treatment.

Changes in the growth of hair

In the description of the growth of sexual and body hair earlier (p. 17), the usual appearance of hair on the face, chest, and abdomen of boys was mentioned. In addition, during the latter part of adolescence, some hair loss also begins. It is often unnoticed, but the hairline at the temples normally recedes slightly.

Alopecia refers to an abnormal condition in which many hair follicles stop producing hair, and when the hairs in the follicles are shed, none replace them. As a result, an adolescent can suffer the complete loss of hair in a small, quarter-sized area of the scalp, eyebrow, or beard, or more extensive loss of hair from the scalp or any other body surface from which it normally grows. In severe alopecia only a few sparse hairs remain on the scalp or the body. Sometimes the only hair that is spared is the sexual hair around the genitalia and under the arms. Alopecia occasionally results from exposure to chemicals. It can also be caused by infections, particularly fungal infections in preadolescents, that interfere with the normal growth of hair. Most of the time, however, the cause of alopecia remains obscure. Alopecia should be evaluated by a physician, usually in consultation with a dermatologist, so that any obvious cause can be identified and treated.

Among girls, the appearance of hair resembling that usually found in boys is called **hirsutism,** and it can be a source of considerable worry. Girls notice the growth of coarse hair along the jaw, in front of the ears, beneath the chin, on the neck, or on the chest. The appearance of hair in these locations in girls may be noted in several female members of a family, or it may be limited to a single person. Clinicians dealing with this problem consider the girl's general state of health, and check to see whether she has an excessive amount of androgen, which is most often responsible for stimulating the growth of the hair. The doctor also studies the source of the androgen, which can be the adrenal glands or the ovaries, or both, and works out a treatment designed to improve the condition.

Fungal infections of the skin

Ringworm of the scalp, caused by a fungal infection, is common in children but is much less likely to occur during and after adolescence. Ringworm of the skin does occur from time to time, and is a round, quarter- or half-dollar-sized, flat lesion that is slightly raised at the edges, and somewhat scaly. It may itch, or may not. Other fungal infections, however, are more typical during the adolescent years. Specifically, *tinea cruris* (familiarly known as "jock itch"), *tinea pedis* ("athlete's foot"), and *tinea versicolor* appear more frequently in adolescents than in younger children.

Tinea cruris   Despite its popular name and greater frequency in boys, tinea cruris also develops in girls. Adolescents who acquire this fungal infection notice one or more patches of reddened skin with a definite border, on the inner surfaces of the thighs, and occasionally on the genitalia and the lower surface of the abdomen. Sometimes, additional small red bumps are located outside the border of the main rash. Both itching and burning are common symptoms in the affected skin. The development of this infection seems to be encouraged by the skin's being slightly moist and protected from exposure to the air. Diagnosis is based on identifying the infecting fungus in the skin, and treatment consists of the use of an effective antifungal medication, such as clotrimazole or tolnaftate.

Tinea pedis Just as ringworm of the scalp is common in young children and uncommon in adolescents, athlete's foot is common in adolescents and almost nonexistent in young children. Athlete's foot usually develops between and below the toes and on the soles of the feet. Cracks in the skin, and softening and peeling of the skin, are characteristic. The infected area itches or burns and may be sensitive to touch. Treatment consists of drying the skin by providing more exposure to the air and use of footwear that does not cause a build-up of moisture, as well as application of antifungal medications such as clotrimazole, miconazole nitrate, or tolnaftate. There is no need to be an athlete to get athlete's foot, and the chances of getting it may be reduced by keeping the skin on the feet fairly dry.

Tinea versicolor In comparison with other fungal infections, tinea versicolor makes a less dramatic appearance, but almost always involves a larger area of the skin, most often on the chest, back, and neck. The fungus that causes this infection lives in the outermost layer of the skin and, as a rule, does not cause redness or itching. Instead, it produces greasy-looking irregularly shaped accumulations of skin cells. During winter months, when the summer's tan has faded from an adolescent with a fair complexion, the infected skin appears slightly darker than the surrounding normal skin. With increased sun exposure during the summer months, particularly in more dark-skinned boys and girls, the infected skin does not tan as well as the normal skin, and thus appears lighter. The variety of the changes in the skin's appearance are reflected in the name given to the infection ("versicolor" means variegated). Following the identification of the infection, treatment consists of the use of medication that removes the infected outer layers of the skin, as well as obliterating any fungus remaining on adjoining skin areas. Though tinea versicolor can be a persistent problem, it usually responds to patient and attentive care.

Other skin problems

Atopic dermatitis   Atopic dermatitis, a moderately common skin problem, often occurs in families where some members have asthma or hay fever. It usually appears during childhood, and its predominant symptom is severe itching that tends to occur in a seasonal pattern. The areas of the body affected in adolescents often include the eyelids, neck, inner surfaces of the elbows, hands, backs of the knees, and the feet. The involved skin is often red, thickened, and dry; at times it may be moist.

Treatment is aimed at relieving the itching—which otherwise leads to scratching and more skin damage—and reducing the inflammation in the skin. Steroid preparations are applied to control itching and inflammation, and measures are taken to rehydrate the dry skin; antihistamines taken orally are also very helpful in controlling the itching.

Psoriasis   Compared to other skin problems discussed in this section, psoriasis is much less frequently a problem of adolescents. However, it does occur, somewhat more often in girls than in boys, and often more than one person in a family has it. The appearance of psoriatic skin is more likely to distress an adolescent than the itching that sometimes accompanies it. Psoriasis consists of rapidly growing red, thickened, dry skin —called **plaques**—which have a thick silvery scale on their surfaces. These patches can appear almost anywhere on the body, but the scalp and hairline, lower back, elbows, knees, and shins are common sites. In addition, fingernails and toenails may be slightly pitted or severely distorted by psoriasis. Often, the psoriatic patches are sizable—one to two inches in diameter—but occasionally very small lesions develop in considerable numbers.

Treatment programs tend to combine, in various proportions, the application of tar-based medications and steroids, and the use of ultraviolet light.

Allergic contact dermatitis Many adolescents are all too familiar with the skin eruption caused by poison ivy, poison sumac, or poison oak: tiny blisters develop in the skin, accompanied by itching and oozing. Similar allergic reactions can occur to other substances: ingredients in cosmetics and medications are among the most common offenders, and the metal nickel is another. At the place where the chemical or metal touches the skin, the reaction develops. Therefore, a necklace containing nickel may cause an allergic contact dermatitis in a necklace pattern, while an ingredient in a deodorant may produce a rash under the arms.

Avoiding the probable offending agent is the first step in treatment, and it is completed by the use of cool wet dressings and steroid medication on the skin, and medicine to relieve the itching. Sometimes, in severe allergic contact dermatitis— usually widespread poison ivy—steroid medication is also given by mouth for a few days.

Pityriasis rosea The first sign of this moderately common disorder consists of the appearance of a single often-itchy oval-shaped patch one to two inches in diameter, having a slightly raised, reddened, and scaly border and a somewhat crinkled center. Called a *herald patch,* this first lesion usually develops somewhere on the trunk of the body, remaining for several days—or even a week or two—before being joined by numerous miniature versions.

Pityriasis rosea may be caused by a virus, and multiple cases among adolescents (or children) in the same family, gang, or class are not unusual. The illness resolves itself completely over a period ranging from a few weeks to several months, and requires treatment only for the relief of itching.

Dry skin is a very common problem in adolescence: the frequent use of soap and hot water, exposure to wind and sun, and natural predisposition all contribute to it. In general, dry skin improves when the moisture normally present in the skin is replaced, and not allowed to evaporate from the skin. One simple, yet effective, way of managing a dry skin problem is to apply a lubricating cream or lotion to the skin after it has been thoroughly moistened. For example, after a shower, even before reaching for a bath towel, the adolescent can apply a small amount of lotion to the skin and spread it out into a thin film. Suitable lotions include Lubriderm, Nutraderm, Nivea, and Keri, to name a few that are widely available. After applying the lotion to areas of dry skin, use the bath towel to remove any excess water. Similarly, the same procedure can be repeated during the day after washing hands and before drying the hands with a towel. As the skin improves, the lotion can be used less often. If this approach does not improve the skin's dryness noticeably after a week or ten days, the adolescent may be able to make more rapid progress by washing and showering less often, using water that is not as hot as usual, and by using a milder soap (such as Basis, Lowila, or Neutrogena). In addition, instead of using a liquid skin lotion, try a cream form.

Warts Most children know about warts because they have some (or perhaps many) on their hands or knees. A wart is the result of a viral infection within the outer layer of the skin. When they occur during childhood, most warts go away after some months or years whether they are treated or not. Adolescents can develop warts on the same locations as younger children, but they also develop warts in locations not common in children. Plantar warts, named for their location on the sole, or plantar surface, of the foot, are quite common in teenagers, and are exceptionally uncomfortable. Warts also can appear on the genitalia, more often in girls than in boys. All of these wart lesions can be treated successfully: clinicians employ various chemical agents that separate the warts from the surrounding normal skin.

Moles, or nevi, deserve to be removed mostly for cosmetic purposes. Moles are accumulations of pigment-producing cells, called melanocytes, and they may appear as small flat, or fleshy, light or dark brown pigmented lesions almost anywhere on the body. After they appear during childhood and early adolescence, most do not change in size, and some only gradually darken as the adolescent grows older. Their removal can be considered necessary mainly when they interfere with a person's appearance or body functions. When the mole is ugly, or when its location causes it to be irritated by clothing or hair-combing, removal can be accomplished fairly easily by a physician. Because of the concentration of pigment-producing cells in moles, they have been associated with transformation to the form of skin cancer called **malignant melanoma.** However, this change is probably no more likely with a pigment cell in a mole than with any pigment cell elsewhere in the skin. Malignant melanoma, which is rare in childhood and adolescence and tends to be found in older adults, usually begins with the appearance of an irregular, somewhat bumpy skin lesion that is multicolored, with red, white, and blue colors being especially characteristic. A lesion of this description on anyone's skin should be evaluated promptly by a physician.

Hives Among adolescents, hives—smooth, raised, itchy skin lesions that tend to wax and wane quickly—frequently occur as a reaction to the use of various medications (particularly penicillin and aspirin), the consumption of certain foods (notably seafoods, nuts, eggs, and fresh berries), and insect bites. Hives can also be produced by sun exposure, pressure on the skin, and contact with ice or very cold water. Some adolescents occasionally develop hives during vigorous physical exercise (this is fortunately a problem that lasts only a few years and then disappears). Each form of hives can be evaluated by a doctor who can help uncover the cause as well as provide appropriate treatment to clear them up and prevent them from recurring.

Problems associated with sexual activity

Several different categories of medical problems are found under this general heading. One category includes infectious diseases that involve the genitalia and reproductive tract. Some of these illnesses are transmitted only during sexual intercourse, and some are acquired both sexually and in other ways. Another category covers the problem of pregnancy during adolescence, and a third involves the use of contraception by adolescents.

Infections of the genitalia and reproductive tract

To make the presentation of this complex subject as clear as possible, we shall discuss most of the infections that adolescent girls acquire separately from those acquired by boys. A few of the infections producing very similar changes in both boys and girls are discussed together in joint entries.

Infections in girls The infections that belong in this group involve the external genitalia, consisting of the labia majora and labia minora, as well as the internal structures of the reproductive tract: the vagina, cervix, uterus, fallopian tubes, and ovaries. The most frequent infections affect the external genitalia, the vagina, and the cervix. Infections of the other parts of the female reproductive tract occur much less often.

Depending on whether they affect the vagina or the cervix, the infections of the lower reproductive tract are generally called **vaginitis** and **cervicitis**. Girls who develop either of these infections usually have one or more of the following symptoms:

Abnormal vaginal discharge   The vaginal secretions during adolescence are normally rather thin and clear, and free of any unpleasant odor. In the presence of an infection, the secretions may increase in quantity, become thicker and cloudy or yellow, and have an undesirable odor.

Itching   The external genitalia may become quite itchy and inflamed (red or slightly swollen).

Discomfort during urination   When the girl urinates, she may feel a burning sensation. She also may feel like urinating more often than usual. When the infection involves only the urethra, the tube that carries urine from the bladder, the discomfort may be confined to that region; however, if the infected vaginal discharge has irritated the outer surfaces of the genitalia, the urine can cause additional burning discomfort as it is passed.

Infection without symptoms   It is important to realize that several different kinds of reproductive tract infections can be carried by girls *without causing any symptoms.* This is most serious in the case of **gonorrhea**. The bacteria that are responsible for this disease may be picked up by a girl during sexual contact, and carried by her unnoticed. This is an important reason why girls who have had sexual contact with a boy with gonorrhea should be examined and treated for it.

Causes of vaginitis and cervicitis   Several microscopic organisms account for most of the vaginal and cervical infections that develop in adolescents. None causes immunity, so any of them can develop more than once. They include three different bacteria. One is called *Haemophilus vaginalis,* and is often (but not always) acquired sexually; another—the cause of gonorrhea—is called *Neisseria gonorrhoeae,* and is almost always sexually transmitted, as is the third, *Chlamydia tra-*

chomatis. In addition, there are two other common causes of vaginal and cervical infection. One is a yeast known as *Candida albicans.* It, of all the infections, is least likely to be spread sexually. The other is a small parasite called *Trichomonas vaginalis,* which is transmitted sexually. Another somewhat infrequent cause of vaginal infection is a foreign substance such as a small piece of toilet tissue, sanitary napkin, or other object, which becomes lodged inadvertently in the vagina. A reaction can develop to its presence there and a profuse discharge with an unpleasant odor results.

In most cases, because the infecting organism can be identified under a microscope in samples of discharge, the right form of treatment can be prescribed during the initial visit to the doctor's office, and brought under control easily and promptly. In other cases, a specimen must be cultured in a laboratory to learn whether any abnormal organisms are present. Treatment consists of the use of proper doses of antibiotics for gonorrhea, Chlamydial and *Haemophilus* infections, intravaginal medication for yeast infections, and medication taken by mouth for *Trichomonas* infections. Particularly when infections are caused by *Trichomonas vaginalis, Chlamydia trachomatis,* or *Neisseria gonorrhoeae,* the girl's sexual partner, who often has no symptoms, should also be examined and receive proper care.

Infections of the upper reproductive tract—the uterus, the fallopian tubes, and the ovaries—are much less common than vaginitis and cervicitis, because most of the infectious agents that cause vaginitis and cervicitis do not affect other parts of the body. Gonorrhea is an exception, and sometimes *Chlamydia* is too. Having been present (often without causing any symptoms at all) in the cervix, the bacteria may travel into, and pass through, the uterus to infect the fallopian tubes and the ovaries. When this happens, the girl begins to have pain in her lower abdomen and pelvis, and fever, and she feels unwell. Though it may happen at any time, the movement of this infection into the upper reproductive tract often takes place at the time of a menstrual period, so the symptoms appear shortly after the period ends. Girls who develop symptoms like these should seek medical attention promptly. The spread of gonorrhea, but not *Chlamydia,* to the skin or the joints occurs occasionally.

Infections in boys Almost all of the genital infections acquired by boys are associated with sexual activity. The symptoms are either a discharge from the penis (**urethritis**), or discomfort during urination, or both. Depending on the cause of the infection, which may be gonorrhea (but doesn't have to be), the interval between the sexual contact during which the infection is acquired and the onset of symptoms can be as little as two to three days, or as long as two weeks. Boys who notice a discharge (which can be thin and clear, or thick and yellow) from the penis and discomfort during urination should see their physicians for tests necessary to identify the cause of the infection. The tests include examination of the discharge under a microscope, as well as cultures of the discharge. Either gonorrhea or an infection caused by *Chlamydia trachomatis* may be found. Boys should realize that they too can carry the bacteria that cause these infections without developing any symptoms: their only clue to the possibility of being infected is that they have had a sexual contact. If his sexual partner is aware of being infected, and tells him, the boy should see a doctor for a checkup. Even when there are no symptoms, the bacteria that cause gonorrhea can be identified in specimens obtained from the urethra. All too often, however, his sexual partner either does not know about the infection, or fails to share knowledge of it, and as a result, the boy carries it and can transmit it to others. Gonorrhea and chlamydial infections can be treated with highly effective antibiotics.

Other infections that result from sexual activity

There are three other infections connected with sexual activity. **Syphilis** is one. It is fortunately much less common than gonorrhea in adolescents. Two others include the infections caused by *Herpes simplex* virus, and **crabs,** the latter being more properly called an **infestation.**

Syphilis is an infectious disease caused by a kind of microscopic organism called a spirochete. The name of the organism is *Treponema pallidum.* As a rule, the first sign of the infection appears at one of the sites of direct contact with a carrier, about three weeks after an infecting sexual contact. The first lesion, called a **chancre** (pronounced "shanker"), is reddened, raised, firm, and moist. It is not painful, often is about half an inch in diameter, and develops on the penis or scrotum of a boy, or on a girl's external genitalia. However, a girl's first lesion may be inside the vagina, or on the cervix, and thus may easily escape notice. When syphilis is not diagnosed and treated during this early stage, the chancre heals, but the infection remains in the body. About six weeks after the appearance of the chancre, a more widespread stage of syphilis begins. In this stage, the victim feels unwell, may lose appetite, and can develop fever, headache, or fatigue. In addition, this stage is accompanied by a most diverse assortment of skin rashes, as well as swelling of the lymph nodes throughout the body. It is possible to diagnose syphilis during these stages by means of clinical examination and laboratory tests, which include examinations of the lesions and the blood. If undiagnosed and untreated, syphilis usually goes on to become a serious, chronic illness. Treatment, usually with penicillin and occasionally with other antibiotics, cures the infection and prevents progression of the illness.

Herpes simplex infections   The most familiar form of *Herpes simplex* virus infection is "cold sores" or "fever blisters," located on or near the lips. A very similar herpetic infection, often transmitted sexually, can involve the genitalia, causing small blisters and, subsequently, shallow ulcers to form on the penis or on the labia. The ulcers are very painful, and they are easily irritated by urine. Unfortunately, no specific treatment cures genital herpetic infections, but they do heal on their own. Treatment is given, however, to relieve the pain and prevent bacteria from invading the already infected parts.

Crabs are not always transmitted directly from one person to another: they may, for example, be spread by contaminated bedding or shared clothing. Crabs is the common name for the infestation caused by the crab louse—a tiny, wingless insect named *Phthirus pubis*—which prefers to live in the seclusion of the genital region of the body, but occasionally accepts lodgings in other places. Crabs announce their arrival by biting their host's skin. As a result of this attack, itching develops, and pinpoint drops of blood may appear on the skin or underwear. By inspecting the troubled area closely, the boy or girl finds the mature crabs, grayish in color and about the size of the head of a pin. Egg cases of incubating crabs can also be seen. They are small, smooth transparent cases attached to the pubic hairs. Crabs are treated effectively with medications such as Kwell, which is available in shampoo and lotion forms. A single treatment with lotion left on for twelve hours should suffice in most cases. Avoid overuse, as this medication can be absorbed through the skin. Sometimes, because the egg cases remain attached to hairs after effective treatment, adolescents worry that they still have the infestation. In fact, the eggs are destroyed quite easily, and even though an egg case remains in place, it is empty and harmless. A fine-tooth comb will sometimes remove them. Discovery of crabs should prompt thorough washing of recently used clothing and bedding. It also makes sense to advise friends with whom one has shared clothing or bedding, or with whom one has been sexually active, that they too may have acquired crabs.

Adolescent pregnancy

As they become fully mature sexually, adolescents who choose to become sexually active need to be aware of the real possibility that their activity can result in pregnancy. The occurrence of pregnancy depends on a number of factors, but the most important obviously is having sexual intercourse without effective contraception at the time in the girl's menstrual cycle when she is susceptible to being impregnated. In general, an ovum is released from one of a girl's ovaries about fourteen days before her next menstrual period begins. Because of the length of time that an ovum or a sperm can remain alive or active, fertilization of the ovum (and thus pregnancy) can occur when sexual intercourse takes place several days *before* or *after* ovulation. Adolescents cannot rely on this general time pattern, however, in making decisions about when it is safe to have intercourse without fear of getting pregnant. The interval between ovulation and the start of the menstrual period is sometimes longer than fourteen days, and frequently it is shorter. In addition, the length of the menstrual cycle can easily vary from one month to the next, and the information from the last cycle can be quite misleading when it is applied to the current cycle.

The hallmarks of pregnancy were discussed in an earlier section, under cessation of menstrual periods (see p. 159). In this section, we take up other aspects of pregnancy during adolescence. Recent data show that adolescents give birth to about one-fifth of the children born in the United States each year; that about one million adolescents between 15 and 19 years of age become pregnant each year; and that of the 10.2 million girls and 10.6 million boys 15 to 19 years of age in the United States, about 4.4 million girls and 6.9 million boys are sexually active. These statistics demonstrate that the problem of adolescent pregnancy must be considered an important issue in the United States.

Problems associated with adolescent pregnancy   When compared with pregnancy in a woman in her twenties, pregnancy in an adolescent is more likely to cause toxemia or iron-deficiency anemia in the mother or result in the delivery of an underweight baby. Fortunately, these problems can be reduced appreciably by very thorough prenatal care for pregnant adolescents, but for several reasons, they seem to plague the adolescent more than they do more mature women. One is the fact that adolescent growth is continuing even as the girl reaches sexual maturity. She must thus meet her own nutritional needs for growth while accommodating the additional nutritional needs of a developing fetus. When pregnancy occurs within two years of a girl's menarche, the chance of having an infant who weighs less than 5 1/2 pounds is almost twice that of an infant born when pregnancy takes place three or more years after menarche.

Other problems associated with adolescent pregnancy are not, strictly speaking, medical ones, but they do have a strong influence on the adolescent's life, as well as that of her infant. Marriage can be considered to be one complication of adolescent pregnancy, particularly when it occurs solely for the purpose of legitimizing the birth of a child. Marriages between adolescents, even under the best of circumstances, are more often than not unsuccessful. In addition, the need to care for a growing infant often combines with other demands to bring an early end to the adolescent's schooling. This limits not only the young mother's education but also her social activity with her peers, and creates a handicap for her when she seeks employment. The adolescent, or her family, must find the resources to feed and clothe a child: the adolescent feels compelled to work, and then may be torn between a job, her wish to attend school, and her sense of responsibility toward taking care of the child at home. Each of these problems, along with the acceptance of an adult role, also forces the adolescent to cut short the amount of time she has for growing up. For many girls that loss represents a major sacrifice the importance of which is sometimes not fully appreciated.

Reasons adolescents become pregnant   In general, sexually active adolescents become pregnant for one of two main reasons. One consistent reason is a lack of effective contraception. When contraceptive use is not planned in advance of the time when it will be needed, the adolescents expose themselves to obvious risks. The other reason is that to some adolescents of both sexes, having a baby may seem very appealing. Becoming pregnant is not necessarily viewed by the adolescent as something either undesirable or better postponed. Having and raising an infant can appear to be a much more satisfying activity than anything else facing the adolescent; and an infant might easily seem welcome as someone who would give, and need, companionship and love. In addition, becoming pregnant and having a baby sometimes looks like a way to break out of a confining family situation, allowing the adolescent to leave home and become more independent.

Questions raised by pregnancy   When an adolescent girl finds that she is pregnant, she has to decide what to do about it. She needs to work through her thoughts about the impact of the pregnancy on her life, on her time for growing up, on friendships, on educational and employment opportunities, and on her family relationships. Perhaps she can do this with the help of her parents, close friends, and physician.

If the girl decides to continue the pregnancy, she must become involved in good prenatal care. Unless she plans to have her baby adopted and raised by someone else, she must also begin to learn about those things she will need to do and know in order to raise a healthy and happy baby. If on reflection she does not wish to continue the pregnancy, it is important to learn what form of abortion is available. Just as postnatal care is important following the delivery of a baby, care after an abortion is also essential. Not only does the adolescent need help in dealing with the impact of the abortion, but she also must understand how she can avoid having another unwanted pregnancy.

Contraception

For sexually active adolescents who do not wish to become pregnant, many forms of contraception are available. For practical purposes, contraceptive methods can be grouped into three main types: "barrier" agents, contraceptives that inhibit ovulation, and the intrauterine device (IUD). They are described below. The "morning-after" pill, a strictly emergency form of contraception, does not belong to any of these types and is discussed separately. Each form has its advantages and limitations, and adolescents can choose a method that best meets their own requirements.

Barrier contraceptives The most frequently used barrier contraceptives include **condoms**—"rubbers"—and **spermicidal preparations**. Both kinds are available in a considerable variety. To insure adequate contraceptive protection, a rubber condom must be slipped securely over the erect penis before intercourse begins, and must remain in place during intercourse and ejaculation. In this way, sperm are prevented from entering the vagina; hence, they cannot reach the ovum and fertilize it. Spermicidal preparations inactivate sperm that are ejaculated within the vagina and therefore the proper quantity of the foam, suppository, or gel must be inserted in the vagina prior to intercourse. A particularly good contraceptive effect is obtained when *both* methods are used together. These barrier contraceptives also afford some protection against transmission of several of the sexually transmitted infections. Barrier contraceptives, both condoms and spermicides, are available in drugstores, and can be obtained without a prescription.

A somewhat similar barrier method is provided by the **diaphragm**, a pliable rubber cap that is placed in the vagina and positioned so that it covers the cervix. Before it is inserted, a special spermicidal preparation is applied to the surface of the diaphragm that covers the cervix; following intercourse, the diaphragm is left in place for about six hours before it is removed. The diaphragm can be prepared for use and inserted in the vagina some time before sexual intercourse begins, thus avoiding any need to interrupt the process once it is underway. Because a diaphragm must fit properly, a pelvic examination by a clinician is necessary before a diaphragm of the correct size can be prescribed. Many girls who use diaphragms find their physician's help useful in learning how to insert the diaphragm and check its proper placement over the cervix.

The "pill" Well-known colloquially as "the pill," the **oral contraceptive** keeps a girl from ovulating, thus offering substantial protection against becoming pregnant. The pill is a combination of two different hormones: an estrogen and a progestin. These components act primarily to prevent the development of an ovum and its release from the ovary. They also make the endometrium (uterine lining) inhospitable to a fertilized ovum, and, by making the cervical mucus thick, make it difficult for sperm to gain access to the upper reproductive tract. These combined actions of the pill are responsible for the nearly 100 percent contraceptive effectiveness of this birth-control method, provided it is used consistently.

Since oral contraceptive pills were introduced a number of years ago, the amount of estrogen in each pill has been reduced substantially. At the present time, the most frequently used pills contain about 30 μg. of estrogen (a μg. is one-millionth of a gram). The reduction in the amount of estrogen in the pill is particularly important since unwanted side effects of the pill have been attributed mainly to its estrogen content. They include increased risks of abnormal blood clotting and gall bladder disease. Despite such increased risks, it is clear that in general the use of the pill is associated with fewer risks for an adolescent than would be posed by pregnancy. The problems arising from use of the pill appear to be more frequent in older women, and some are influenced by other factors such as cigarette smoking. In each instance, the advisability of using the pill must be considered carefully by the adolescent and her doctor. All of the reasons affecting the decision to use the pill should be reviewed, a pelvic examination and "Pap" test performed, and blood tests done before the girl starts using the pill.

Use starts on the fifth day of a new menstrual cycle (the first day of the cycle is the day when the menstrual period *begins*).

A pill containing hormones is taken each day, preferably at the same time of day, for a total of twenty-one days. Then, for the next seven days, the girl takes no hormonal medication, but may take "spacer" tablets that often contain a small amount of medicinal iron. Within two to three days after taking the last hormone pill, a menstrual period starts. This menstrual period may be quite similar to the periods she had when she was not on the pill, or it may be somewhat shorter in duration and lighter in flow. After the seven days during which no hormone pills are taken, a new cycle of medication starts. During the first month or two on the pill, some "break-through" bleeding in the second week of the cycle occurs in many pill users. This is harmless, but when it continues to occur in subsequent cycles, a doctor can take some simple steps to correct the condition.

Contraceptives that inhibit ovulation are prescription medications, available through physicians and family planning clinics such as those sponsored by the Planned Parenthood League, following a clinical examination.

The intrauterine device, or IUD, is similar in some respects to barrier forms of contraception, except that it is placed in the endometrium of the uterus by a doctor, and can remain there for an extended period of time. Though they do not inhibit ovulation, and do not prevent sperm from entering the uterus, various forms of the IUD do prevent the establishment of a pregnancy in the uterus. In adolescents who have never been pregnant the IUD appears to be less effective than it is in adolescents or older women who have had children. Moreover, the presence of an IUD is often associated with heavier and more painful than usual menstrual periods. Unfortunately, some IUDs slip out of place within the uterus, and their protection against pregnancy is lost. (One can check the placement of an IUD by means of a small string attached to it that can be felt as it comes from the cervix.) The IUD also predisposes its user to a greater risk of upper reproductive tract infections.

The "morning-after" pill is an *emergency* form of contraception, used *after* sexual intercourse. Typically, an adolescent who has intercourse without contraception near her time of ovulation realizes that she has taken a risk, and if she consults her doctor within three days of the event, she may be able to take rather large doses of estrogen over a period of five days to prevent pregnancy. After she has a menstrual period, she should make use of one of the standard forms of contraception if she plans to continue to be sexually active.

Infectious mononucleosis

In some respects, infectious mononucleosis presents a quandary for many adolescents. Frequently, adolescents are not exactly sure about the characteristics of the illness, and therefore are not sure if they really have it or not. In addition, they are often unaware that a true case of mononucleosis confers immunity to future infection. Though no preventive immunization in early childhood prevents the development of infectious mononucleosis later on, sometimes natural immunization occurs. Some children become infected with the virus during earlier life, without developing the usual panorama of symptoms found in infected adolescents, and thus they gain immunity from further infection. Consequently, not every adolescent is susceptible to mononucleosis.

The symptoms

Mononucleosis exerts its major effect on the lymphoid system in the body. Therefore, the illness tends to manifest itself in places where lymphoid tissue is abundant. The tonsils, for example, are a large segment of lymphoid tissue in the upper part of the throat, and are customarily among the first organs to become inflamed and enlarged by the infection. Consequently a very sore throat is a principal characteristic of the disease. In addition, the lymph nodes throughout the body become affected, and somewhat tender, enlarged nodes appear in the neck, under the arms, and in the groin. (The spleen and the liver also contain lymphoid tissue, so a considerable enlargement of the spleen, and a lesser degree of liver enlargement, are not unusual during the early stages of mononucleosis.) Other symptoms include low-grade fever, fatigue, and some loss of appetite. These symptoms usually last several weeks, and then begin to diminish: some adolescents have symptoms of shorter duration, and in some they persist longer.

The cause

The cause of infectious mononucleosis, the Epstein-Barr virus, was not conclusively connected with the infection until about 1973, many years after the illness had been well described. The infecting virus is transmitted directly from one person (who usually has no symptoms of infectious mononucleosis at the time, and who may not even have had an apparent infection earlier) to another person who is susceptible to the virus. The person-to-person passage of the virus usually takes place through the transfer of saliva, a mode of transmission that once gave the illness the nickname "kissing disease." The virus infects certain lymphocytes (members of the white blood cell family), and after an incubation period of from four and one half to seven weeks, the symptoms develop. Other lymphocytes respond to the infection, and antibodies to the Epstein-Barr virus begin to appear in the bloodstream. Gradually, the body brings the disease under control.

The diagnosis of mononucleosis is usually based on a combination of things: symptoms in the adolescent who is ill, findings on physical examination, and several laboratory tests that help confirm the presence of the infection. Blood tests reveal atypical lymphocytes and rising antibody levels.

The complications

Fortunately, complications of infectious mononucleosis are not common. The enlarged lymphoid tissues can sometimes partially obstruct the upper throat. In some cases, this change only interferes with swallowing solid foods comfortably; in others, it makes difficult even the swallowing of fluids, and gets in the way of the passage of air to and from the lungs. In such cases, medication reduces the degree of lymphoid swelling and relieves the obstruction. Other complications are much less common, and tend to involve the central nervous system. Doctors treating adolescents with mononucleosis generally advise avoiding contact sports while there is any enlargement of the spleen, and recommend adequate rest to avoid excessive fatigue.

Endocrinological disorders

A substantial group of different kinds of hormones are produced by the endocrine system. Some hormones particularly affect sexual maturation; others affect growth; still others affect metabolic functions, or the maintenance of proper amounts of minerals, glucose, and fluids within the body. The endocrine system includes the pituitary gland and its control centers in the brain, the thyroid and parathyroid glands, the pancreas, the adrenal glands, and the ovaries or testes. In general, the problems that appear in any part of this system tend to reflect either an inability of one gland to supply the needs of the body for the appropriate hormone or hormones, or overproduction by the gland. During the adolescent years, the parts of the endocrine system that most often cause some difficulty include the pituitary and its control centers, the thyroid gland, the pancreas, and the ovaries and testes.

The pituitary gland

Appropriately considered a "master" gland, the pituitary and its control centers within the brain are responsible for monitoring the production of hormones by many of the other endocrine glands. In particular, one part of the pituitary produces hormones that influence the activity of the thyroid gland, the adrenals, and the ovaries and testes. Another segment of the pituitary gland produces a hormone that influences the ability of the kidneys to concentrate the urine. The pituitary also secretes growth hormone, a key factor in the normal growth process, and prolactin. In contrast, the secretion of hormones by the pancreas and the parathyroid glands is not under the direct control of the pituitary gland.

When an adolescent develops an endocrine problem, the first indication of it is usually the onset of various symptoms or physical changes. In the course of a clinical evaluation of these symptoms and changes, it is determined whether the problem originates within the specific endocrine gland, or whether the control of the glands by the pituitary has been altered in some way.

Thyroid function disorders   For most practical purposes, the major problems arising from the functioning of the thyroid gland are caused by the production of either too little thyroid hormone to meet the body's needs (*hypo*thyroidism), or too much (*hyper*thyroidism). The malfunction of the thyroid gland can be traced to several causes, but the effects that they have on the adolescent are quite similar. Girls tend to develop disorders of thyroid function more frequently than boys.

Hypothyroidism   When, at the time of adolescence, the thyroid gland produces too little thyroid hormone, the adolescent begins to develop characteristic symptoms. In particular, he or she notices that the rate of growth in height slows down considerably, while weight gain often continues. This combination often leads to a slight degree of overweight, and to the adolescent's becoming relatively short in comparison with peers of the same age. These changes occur in spite of decreased appetite. The adolescent's ability to tolerate physical activity also diminishes: he or she tires more easily, needs more rest, has little "energy," and may notice that cramps develop in the leg muscles during moderate amounts of exercise. The skin usually becomes drier and cooler than normal, and the hair becomes somewhat dull and brittle. The adolescent notes that bowel movements occur less often than they did in the past. In girls, there may be an increase or decrease in menstrual bleeding.

In addition, hypothyroid adolescents seem to be more sensitive to the cold, and they may have to struggle to keep comfortably warm, particularly during the winter months. In some forms of hypothyroidism, the thyroid gland is quite small, and no enlargement of the neck occurs; in other forms, the thyroid gland attempts to compensate for the deficient production of thyroid hormone and its size enlarges: as a result, a fullness of the neck develops and some discomfort occurs.

Hyperthyroidism In hyperthyroidism, the supply of thyroid hormone is greater than normal, and the symptoms represent the effects of the excess hormone on the body. As is true in hypothyroidism, hyperthyroidism also starts gradually, and neither the adolescent nor members of the family may become aware of the changes until they are fairly advanced.

Hyperthyroidism strains the cardiovascular system. The heart rate increases and its beating is more noticeable. The adolescent may feel uncomfortably warm all the time, and begins to avoid wearing warm clothing and to use fewer covers at night. Because of the increase in the metabolic rate that is caused by hyperthyroidism, the patient's appetite usually increases. Physical growth in height continues to progress normally or at an increased rate, while weight gain slows. The adolescent becomes thinner as the illness continues. The hyperthyroid adolescent can be irritable and apprehensive for reasons that are not at all apparent, and he or she finds it hard to do physical or academic work for the usual length of time. Boys and girls alike take on a staring appearance. This results from a combination of some widening of the space between the open eyelids, actual protrusion of the eyes from their sockets, and infrequent blinking. The skin is usually warm, moist, and oily. Enlargement of the thyroid gland is customary in hyperthyroidism, and this produces a sensation of pressure, as well as some degree of obvious fullness, in the neck.

Adolescents who develop signs and symptoms of either hypo- or hyperthyroidism should be seen by a doctor. Diagnostic studies to determine why and to what degree the thyroid is malfunctioning lead directly to a plan for treatment. This allows either for replacement of the thyroid hormone that is lacking or for medication or other procedures to slow down the activity of the gland to a normal level.

Growth hormone problems Most children who do not produce enough growth hormone to permit a normal rate of growth throughout childhood and adolescence usually get medical attention during childhood. The size of the child is noticeably smaller than others of the same age. The difference in size between the child deficient in growth hormone and others tends to widen as they grow older, however, and if the condition is overlooked in childhood, it will almost certainly be noticed during adolescence, when sexual maturation may also be somewhat delayed. Blood tests that measure the level of growth hormone in the system are used to establish the diagnosis. Treatment with growth hormone will allow normal growth to resume.

Overproduction of growth hormone during childhood and adolescence leads to quite a different problem—excessive physical growth. It is far more rare than underproduction.

Juvenile diabetes mellitus

Of the endocrine disorders encountered during childhood and adolescence, diabetes mellitus is certainly the most common. Unlike the form of diabetes customarily discovered during the adult years, diabetes appearing during childhood and adolescence is most often caused by a lack of **insulin**, and is accompanied by a number of severe symptoms. In addition, the tendency for acquiring juvenile diabetes mellitus seems to be influenced by several hereditary factors, and more than one member of a family may have this illness.

Diabetes does not usually appear suddenly one day without warning. Instead it tends to make a gradual appearance over a period of several days or weeks. When one understands the basic changes in the body that are responsible for the onset of juvenile diabetes, it is easier to appreciate why certain symptoms accompany the early phase of the illness. Cells in the pancreas that normally produce amounts of insulin adequate to meet physical needs begin to supply less and less of this important hormone. In the absence of normal amounts of insulin, the body loses the ability to transfer glucose (sugar) from the bloodstream into cells for use. For this reason, and because glucose is produced in the body, the glucose level in the blood increases, and some of it begins to be excreted in the urine. As sugar is no longer used efficiently by the body, energy is drawn from another source—the body's fat. However, the fat is not used completely, and some of the breakdown products from it—called **ketones**—accumulate in the bloodstream and also appear in the urine.

With these metabolic changes, the adolescent develops symptoms directly reflecting the disturbances going on in the body. There is an increase in appetite, in an attempt to compensate for the inefficiency of the body's metabolic processes and the loss of energy (glucose and ketones) into the urine; an increased amount of urine is produced by the body, because the glucose lost in the urine draws water along with it; and there is increased thirst and a compensatory increase in water consumption. The increased amounts of ketones also make the body more acidic than normal and result in minerals being lost from the body as well. Despite efforts to maintain a state of balance, the adolescent often loses weight and begins to feel ill. At this point in the development of diabetes, the diagnosis can be established readily by tests of the blood and urine that measure the levels of glucose and ketones. But if nothing is done, more severe symptoms, such as marked fatigue, heavy breathing, lethargy, sleepiness, and abdominal pain can appear rapidly as the chemical changes and dehydration become worse. At this stage, diabetes is a considerable threat to the adolescent's life.

The treatment of newly found diabetes consists of replacement of the minerals and water that have been lost from the body, provision of insulin to reestablish metabolic balance, and gradual nutritional replenishment. Just as adolescents with any other endocrine disorder requiring the replacement of a vital hormone need to take an appropriate amount of the hormone each day, adolescents with diabetes need to have insulin each day. Insulin is not at all effective when given by mouth; it is given by injection through a small needle to a site just beneath the skin. From that location, the insulin is absorbed and used by the body. Some insulin preparations are absorbed rapidly, others slowly, and mixtures are frequently used to supply the body's needs for twelve to twenty-four hours. The dose of insulin is adjusted so that no ketones appear in the urine, and so that the blood glucose level stays as near normal as possible throughout the day and night. Diet, exercise, and growth needs are all taken into account in planning the treatment of a diabetes case. As adolescents grow, it is not unusual for their insulin requirements to increase. This change does not mean that the diabetes is becoming worse, but that the body and its demand for insulin are becoming larger. Exercise, on the other hand, tends to reduce the body's demand for insulin.

One curious phenomenon in diabetes appears quite often within a few months of diagnosis and the start of treatment. The requirement for injected insulin decreases—sometimes disappearing completely—for several weeks or months, as the pancreas resumes insulin production. The reasons why this happens are not understood well at all. Unfortunately, this turn of events is seldom permanent, and gradually the need for administered insulin reasserts itself.

Ovarian and testicular disorders

Apart from endocrine disorders that may cause a delay in sexual maturation (see p. 163), only a few disorders of the ovaries and testes are at all likely to occur during the adolescent years.

Ovarian and testicular masses Masses that increase the size of either the testes or the ovaries can develop during adolescence. Among boys, an increase in the size of one testis is easily recognized by the boy, who may also notice discomfort or pain. A change of this kind should be evaluated immediately by a physician so that the cause of the enlargement can be determined. Sometimes, fluid accumulates around or above one testis causing a harmless condition called a **hydrocele.** In addition, the veins supplying the testis—particularly the left one—may become somewhat dilated, forming another harmless swelling known as a **varicocele.** In some girls, ovarian masses may produce symptoms of lower abdominal pain or fullness. In others, hormones that are produced by the mass in the ovary stimulate the growth of additional hair on the face, neck, and body, and may also interrupt regular menstrual function. These symptoms should also be evaluated by a physician.

Torsion of the testes develops rather suddenly. A healthy adolescent boy may notice pain and swelling in the region of one testis, often without any obvious reason such as being hit there. The symptoms are caused by the twisting of the testis on its supporting structures within the scrotum. These symptoms are an indication for urgent medical attention so that the torsion can be identified and relieved before the testis is permanently damaged.

Disorders of the respiratory tract

Numerous respiratory tract disorders can affect adolescents. Some are well known—the "common cold," hay fever, sore throat, nosebleeds, and sinusitis, as well as bronchitis, pneumonia, and asthma. These are problems that affect only the respiratory tract. There are some disorders that have a major impact on the respiratory tract but disturb the body in other ways as well. A good example in this category would be cystic fibrosis. In addition, respiratory symptoms can be produced by ailments or practices not directly connected to the respiratory tract. The hyperventilation syndrome is an example of this.

Upper respiratory tract problems

The upper portion of the respiratory tract consists of the nose, the sinuses, and the throat.

The **common cold** produces swelling of the inner surfaces of the nose, making it more difficult for air to pass through freely; the inflamed nasal membranes produce moderate or large amounts of watery secretions that make the nose "run," and there is frequently some sneezing and coughing. A sore throat often accompanies the nasal symptoms, and fever, when present at all, is usually mild and short-lasting. The vast majority of this kind of upper respiratory tract infections are caused by viruses that cannot be controlled by antibiotics. Despite claims that various diets, or dosages of vitamin C, can prevent colds or shorten them, no effective preventive methods are uniformly successful, and colds tend to run their course. During the infection, decongestants taken by mouth or used in the form of nasal spray or nose drops for several days may offer some relief from the nasal symptoms, while aspirin or acetaminophen relieves some of the discomfort in the throat and reduces the fever, if any.

Hay fever (also known as rose fever or allergic rhinitis) is occasionally mistaken for a common cold. There are several characteristic differences. Hay fever, an allergic reaction of the nasal membranes to substances in the environment, tends to have a seasonal pattern, appearing when the offending substances—called allergens—are most plentiful, and disappearing at other times. Hay fever also tends to last longer than the common cold, and is marked by itching of the nose and profuse clear watery nasal discharge. It is not accompanied by either sore throat or fever. Adolescents who are sensitive to such substances as pollens, molds, house dust, and animal dander (minute particles of animal hair and skin), which are almost constantly in the air, can develop nearly continuous nasal symptoms, and seldom be comfortable breathing through their noses. Readily available antihistaminic and decongestant medications may relieve these symptoms. But it also makes sense to have a doctor diagnose the allergy and offer suggestions both for reducing exposure to the offending substances and for selecting the best medication. Desensitization is a procedure in which gradually increasing amounts of allergens are injected over an extended period to change the body's response to them and reduce the symptoms of hay fever. It is occasionally considered for adolescents who have symptoms that do not improve with other care.

Sore throat has many causes during adolescence. One cause, infectious mononucleosis, has already been discussed (see p. 198). Sore throat can be caused by a number of viruses, but the single most important cause of sore throat is not a virus at all but the **beta-hemolytic streptococcus** (Group A). Infections—called "strep" throat—caused by this bacteria are often found in adolescents who have painful sore throats, fever, and swelling and tenderness of the lymph nodes in the neck. They feel quite ill. Swallowing food and beverages can be very uncomfortable for them because of the inflammation. Some adolescents with strep throat also develop either abdominal pain or a reddish-brown, sandpapery skin rash (scarlet fever), or both. A doctor can make a probable diagnosis on the basis of the adolescent's symptoms and physical examination, but it is best confirmed by taking a throat culture. While antibiotics do no good for viral throat infections, they will cure streptococcal infections. Such infections should be identified promptly and treated with penicillin or a suitable alternate antibiotic both to clear up the infection and to prevent complications. The most important complication of beta-hemolytic streptococcal infections is acute rheumatic fever, discussed in the section on cardiovascular problems (see p. 215).

Nosebleeds are, for the most part, unfortunate consequences of the way the nose protrudes from the face, and of its normal function as an air passage. When the nose is bumped, or when air that passes through the nose contains little moisture or abundant quantities of substances that easily irritate the nasal membranes, a nosebleed is apt to follow. The most common forms of nosebleed occur from the front of the nose, starting in a small area on the nasal septum, the partition separating the total nasal space in half.

Other causes of nosebleed include stifling a sneeze and strenuous coughing, both of which raise the pressure within the small nasal blood vessels to the point where they may break; blood disorders that cause abnormal bleeding; and disorders of small blood vessels in which the vessels are prone to break easily. A tumor in the nasal space may be responsible for recurrent or severe nosebleeds, but this is rare.

Because the nasal membrane does not heal immediately, another nosebleed may follow in a short time if the small scab that forms at the site of the nosebleed is jarred loose. This usually happens when the person unthinkingly blows or rubs the nose.

When a nosebleed starts, the best thing to do is to sit down comfortably, and squeeze the nose very firmly between the thumb and the index finger for at least five minutes. This maneuver stops most nosebleeds. Later on, a thin film of Vaseline can be applied to the nasal membrane with a cotton swab; renewing this film once or twice a day for several days allows the membrane to heal before another nosebleed occurs. When nosebleeds seem more serious, either in frequency, duration, or amount of blood, or when a blow to the nose results in pain, a doctor should assess the nosebleed and discover its source, and identify any additional injury, such as a nasal fracture.

Sinusitis can cause inflammation in any of the sinus chambers in the head. The most common symptoms include nasal congestion and discharge, pain, and fever. Because adolescents who develop sinusitis sometimes have had previous difficulty with allergic rhinitis (hay fever), they may not be as aware that the nasal congestion is a different symptom as those who have had no difficulty before. However, the nature of the nasal discharge in sinusitis is usually distinctive: it is thick and yellowish. Though the discharge can flow to the front of the nose, sometimes it travels to the back of the nose, becoming an annoying postnasal drip and the cause of an irritant cough. Pain emanating from the inflamed sinuses is felt in the cheeks, behind the eyes, or in the middle of the forehead; it also may be noticed at the top of the head or be experienced as a toothache. For many adolescents, sinusitis pain is an unremitting feeling of pressure inside part of the head. Fever is not always present in sinus infection, but can be.

Since each sinus empties into the nose, clinical examination of the nose provides useful information about the presence, location, and cause of sinus infections. In addition, the sinuses in the cheeks can be examined with lights, and all of them can be seen with the assistance of X ray studies. The treatment of sinusitis is aimed at relieving any sinus obstruction, and eradicating the infection using antibiotics. In addition, efforts are made to deal with any condition in the respiratory tract that might encourage sinusitis to start.

Lower respiratory tract problems

Infections involving the respiratory tract below the level of the throat are termed lower respiratory tract infections. Among adolescents, these infections include such ailments as tracheobronchitis and pneumonia, as well as generalized infections as influenza, which also affect other parts of the body. Infections of the passages between the larynx (voice box) and the most distant portions of the lungs affect the trachea (the windpipe) and the bronchi (the tubes which carry air from the trachea to the lung chambers where oxygen and carbon dioxide are exchanged) to an equal degree. Many of these infections are caused by viruses, and are characterized by coughing that sometimes produces quantities of sputum. Pneumonia is an infection of the lungs themselves, caused by viruses, bacteria, and other organisms, as well as by chemical agents. Pneumonia usually causes fever, discomfort or pain in the chest, cough, and some distress in breathing. Depending on the cause of the infection and its distribution in the lungs, the adolescent can seem only slightly ill or very sick. Each of these problems should be evaluated by a physician.

Asthma is a disorder in which narrowing of the bronchi occurs intermittently and interferes with the free passage of air into and from the lungs. The most common symptoms include difficulty in breathing, and wheezing. Not only do the bronchi narrow, but also the bronchial passageway becomes further obstructed by the swelling of its lining and by the presence of sticky mucus. In the early stages of an asthmatic attack, the difficulty in breathing is most noticeable when breathing out, whereas as the attack progresses, extra effort is also needed to get air into the lungs. When the bronchial air passages narrow, wheezing develops: wheezes are rather high-pitched musical sounds that can often be heard by someone who is several feet away from an adolescent having an asthmatic attack. Sometimes there is so marked a narrowing of the bronchi that little air is able to pass through them, and the adolescent is virtually strangling. At such times, wheezing may disappear.

Several different factors play a role in the occurrence of asthma. Asthma and other allergic disorders, such as hay fever and atopic dermatitis, tend to develop among members of a family, and are believed to be at least partly hereditary. Asthma may be triggered as the body responds to a variety of substances in the environment, to infections in the respiratory tract, to exercise, and sometimes to emotional changes.

During childhood and adolescence, asthma is often caused by the reaction of the cells in the lungs to substances in the environment. Sensitizing agents include such things as house dust, animal dander, pollens from trees, flowers and grasses, and molds. Particular foods, though possible offenders, are less commonly responsible than other substances. After taking into account the season and the type of weather that appear to be associated with the onset of asthma, it is sometimes possible to determine that one substance is more important than another. Asthma is often more troublesome during the night when the adolescent lies down and sleeps than it is during the daytime.

Asthma is related to infection in the lungs, but to a lesser extent in children and adolescents than in older people. Exercise does sometimes induce asthmatic attacks in adolescents, and may become noticeable during the exercise, or not until shortly after the exercise ends.

Symptoms suggestive of asthma are a good reason to see a physician. Sometimes allergy to one or several substances in the environment can be confirmed by skin tests employing tiny amounts of the various substances. Adolescents who have asthma should receive proper medication, which can prevent the narrowing of the bronchi despite continued exposure to allergens or exercise. This step permits the teenage asthma sufferer to live a fairly normal life. It is sometimes possible to get relief from asthma by avoiding contact with allergens, or by going through a series of desensitizing shots (see p. 207).

Cystic fibrosis

Cystic fibrosis, a complex disorder with widespread effects in the body, usually makes its appearance during infancy or early childhood. The disease affects many glands in the body, especially those which produce mucus and sweat. It is acquired in hereditary fashion: the parents, without symptoms themselves, each carry a recessive gene for the disease. The child who is affected with cystic fibrosis receives the gene from both parents. Since the gene for cystic fibrosis is carried by about 5 percent of the population, screening tests for this disease are being developed. Some screening tests currently in use can identify those people who have genes for the disease—but they are as yet unable to distinguish accurately between those with one gene, who are just carriers, and those with two, who actually have the disease.

Two major characteristics of cystic fibrosis usually appear in early life. One results from the inadequate production of digestive enzymes by the pancreas. These enzymes promote the normal use of food in the intestinal tract, and in their absence protein and fat are poorly digested and absorbed. The child fails to grow well, and produces bowel movements that are bulky and malodorous. The other important characteristic results from the production of abnormal secretions by mucus glands in the bronchi. It consists of coughing, difficulty with breathing, and recurrent pulmonary infections. Of these two major manifestations, the pulmonary disease is relentless, moderately resistant to treatment, and the most important cause of disability in children with cystic fibrosis.

Apart from pulmonary and pancreatic involvement, cystic fibrosis also affects the function of the liver, the sinuses, the salivary glands, and the reproductive system. The sweat glands produce sweat containing a much higher than normal concentration of both sodium and chloride, and this is used to establish the diagnosis of cystic fibrosis. Sometimes the involvement of the lungs or pancreas is not very striking during the early years of life, but the symptoms become more noticeable in late childhood and early adolescence. Once in a while an adolescent not known to have cystic fibrosis comes to a physician because of pulmonary symptoms, poor growth, or recurrent abdominal pain. Once the diagnosis of cystic fibrosis is confirmed, treatment is aimed at improving digestion and absorption of food from the intestinal tract by supplementing the diet with digestive enzymes; at controlling the recurrent pulmonary infections; and at removing as much of the mucus from the lower respiratory tract as possible.

The hyperventilation syndrome

The term "hyperventilation" or overbreathing simply describes a process in which the volume of air circulated through the lungs in a given length of time is excessive. During exercise the volume of air passing in and out of the lungs is increased, when compared with that during rest, but the amount is considered normal because it meets the immediate demands of the body for more oxygen and a quicker removal of carbon dioxide. In cases of hyperventilation the excess volume of air is not required. Teenagers who overbreathe may not even be aware of what they are doing. As a result, however, they have an adequate level of oxygen in their bodies, but an abnormally low level of carbon dioxide.

Adolescents who hyperventilate usually complain of several things. One problem is a feeling of being unable to get enough air, and discomfort, or tightness, in the chest is another. Usually these symptoms become increasingly bothersome as an attack progresses, and are accompanied by numbness of the lips and tongue, and either numbness or "pins and needles" in the fingers. A sensation of being light-headed is common, and an adolescent may feel as though he or she is about to faint, though that doesn't often happen.

In some adolescents, the amount of hyperventilation necessary to produce the symptoms is not very great, while others have to overbreathe markedly for the symptoms to appear. Often, the adolescents are in an uncomfortable, restless, or anxious situation or frame of mind, and the hyperventilation begins insidiously as a response to those conditions. As the effects of the hyperventilation begin to appear, the adolescent feels even less comfortable, and unless the overbreathing is brought under control promptly, the situation progresses from uncomfortable to unbearable.

Once they understand the underlying process, adolescents can avoid the tendency to overbreathe, or can deliberately slow the rate of breathing and take smaller breaths until they become more comfortable. Rebreathing air from a small paper bag is also helpful, as it restores the carbon dioxide level to normal. However, it is important to determine what triggers the attacks in the first place. (An aspect of hyperventilation is the occasionally used ritual of repeated deep breathing before an underwater swim. Though this is done in hopes of increasing the length of time the swimmer can hold his or her breath, the process entails the dangerous risk of losing consciousness under water. The possible gain from such over-breathing before diving or swimming underwater is vastly outweighed by its potential dangers.)

Cardiovascular problems

Few health problems receive as much attention and generate as much concern as those that involve the heart and circulatory system. They can make themselves known at the time of birth or in early childhood, or not develop until adolescence or adult life. Some are minor, but others can be dangerous, especially if they are permitted to go undiagnosed and untreated.

Murmurs

Murmurs are but one of several different sounds that can be produced by the heart as it beats. Just as most of the other sounds signify very normal cardiac function, murmurs are also frequently "innocent," and thus not indicative of any abnormality. When doctors listen to the heart with a stethoscope, murmurs heard at certain locations in the chest, and having particular acoustic qualities, are classified as belonging to the innocent variety. Sometimes, an innocent murmur is heard during one physical examination, but not at all during the next one. A trained person can usually distinguish a murmur that represents the flow of blood through a normal heart from a murmur caused by some abnormality. Sometimes murmurs are present for reasons having nothing to do with the heart. For example, a murmur may be heard in anemic adolescents, in cases of hyperthyroidism, and in the presence of fever or excitement. When any doubt exists about the cause of a murmur, additional tests such as an electrocardiogram and chest X rays can provide more specific information about the heart's size and function. An innocent murmur can remain for many years, or vanish completely. However, because no heart disease is responsible for an innocent murmur, whether it remains or goes away is really unimportant.

Blood pressure

As the heart pumps a volume of blood through the body, the blood vessels offer some resistance to the flow, and the combination of these factors is called blood pressure. Because both output from the heart and vessel resistance influence its level, blood pressure changes one way or another whenever either of these forces is altered.

An instrument called a sphygmomanometer, plus a stethoscope, is used to measure blood pressure. A sphygmomanometer has three parts: a cuff, containing an inner tube, which is wrapped snugly around the upper arm; a small pump, which inflates the inner tube with air; and a meter, which measures the air pressure in the inner tube. With the patient either sitting or lying down, the doctor puts on the cuff and pumps up the inner tube. He then releases the air slowly from the inner tube while he listens with a stethoscope on the inner surface of the elbow for the sound of the heartbeat. The pressure at which the sound of the heartbeat is first heard determines the **systolic** blood pressure. As the air pressure in the cuff is reduced further, the sounds of the heartbeat either become muffled or disappear, marking the **diastolic** blood pressure. Blood pressure measurements, expressed in millimeters of mercury, are recorded as systolic/diastolic, for example, 122/72. The normal range of blood pressure moves up with increasing age and tends to be a little higher in adolescent boys than in girls of the same age. Most adolescents have blood pressures of between 120/70 and 140/80, but both lower and higher readings can be normal.

When a blood pressure reading is higher than expected for the adolescent's age, it becomes important to measure the blood pressure again at frequent intervals to see if it remains high. It is not unusual for an adolescent to have a slightly elevated pressure occasionally, and a normal level at other times. Persistent elevated blood pressure indicates a need for further clinical evaluation to determine possible causes for it. Such causes include obesity, kidney disease, and several metabolic and endocrine disorders. In some cases, when no underlying problem is found, the elevated blood pressure is called **primary hypertension.** To treat high blood pressure, the doctor deals with any evident causative factor, and prescribes medication to lower the blood pressure level.

Cholesterol and triglycerides

Among the most rapidly advancing and important topics in preventive medicine is the study of the relationship between the levels of cholesterol and triglycerides in the bloodstream during early life, and the development of **atherosclerosis** in later life. Atherosclerosis is a complex, slowly developing condition in which fatty materials are deposited within the walls of arteries—the blood vessels that carry blood from the heart to other parts of the body. This reduces the flexibility of the vessels and makes it more likely that they will be blocked off entirely, as in a heart attack or, sometimes, a stroke. In addition to higher than normal levels of cholesterol and triglycerides in the blood stream (a condition called hyperlipidemia), smoking, overweight, hypertension, and diabetes mellitus increase the chances of atherosclerotic changes in blood vessels. When elevated levels of either cholesterol or triglycerides, or both, are found in the bloodstream, they may indicate the presence of one of several known forms of **hyperlipidemia,** a condition usually influenced by hereditary factors. The most common forms of hyperlipidemia cause various effects. Fatty masses called xanthomas may appear on the eyelids, elbows, or Achilles tendons, and coronary artery disease begins during the early adult years, rather than in much later life.

It is important for adolescents who are members of families in which young adults have xanthomas or coronary artery disease to have their blood levels of cholesterol and triglycerides checked. All adolescents should probably have their blood levels of these substances tested at some point, in order to make sure that they are in the normal range. It is possible to lower the levels if necessary, mainly through managing the diet, thus probably reducing the danger of atherosclerotic complications in later life.

Fainting and chest pain

Adolescents occasionally faint, but more often they simply feel as though they are about to. Fainting results when the brain temporarily receives less than an adequate supply of blood. Although several different conditions provoke fainting, it probably most often represents a response either to some unpleasant stimulation or to staying in one position—kneeling, for instance—for an extended time. Think how often fainting occurs after a shock—a door slams on your finger, or you twist an ankle—or a guard faints after standing at attention for a long time on a hot day. Some fainting seems to be a sympathetic response; on seeing someone else in pain or distress, the observer faints as if the discomfort were personal. Fainting also follows the loss of blood—in an injury, after having blood drawn for a test, or after donating blood to a blood drive. Adolescents who are very anemic (see p. 230) are more likely to faint than those who have normal blood counts. Because shifts in blood volume and pressure occur when changing position, some adolescents notice that for a brief moment they feel slightly faint and either see "spots" before their eyes or have a brief darkening of their vision as they stand up quickly after lying down, kneeling, or sitting. When the flow of blood from the heart is not increased sufficiently to meet the increased demands of the body for oxygen, as in strenuous exercise, fainting can also occur. With the latter cause of fainting, there may be some associated heart problems. They tend to involve a failure of the heart rate to increase enough, or an obstruction to blood flow as, for example, with a small or narrowed heart valve.

When an adolescent feels faint, actual loss of consciousness is often avoided if the head is lowered to the level of the rest of the body. One way to do this is to sit down and lower your head to, or slightly below, your knees; another is simply to lie down. When fainting does occur, the loss of consciousness is usually brief, and a person who has fainted should be allowed to lie flat with the head turned to one side until fully recovered. There is no need to use smelling salts nor is there any point in throwing cold water on someone who has fainted.

Chest pain, known to be a symptom of serious heart disease in adults, is very infrequently produced by heart trouble in young people. When there is no other symptom suggesting heart trouble—shortness of breath, stomach upset, or weakness—and when the pain is short-lived and confined to the chest, rather than being felt in the shoulder or arm, it is in adolescents much more likely to be caused by something to do with the rib cage and its muscles, or the lungs. A commonly noted kind of chest pain is a quick, jabbing pain that appears and vanishes in moments. Though uncomfortable, it does not have any effect on one's health.

Heart problems

So far, this chapter has focused on the issues of normal heart function, on problems that can be recognized and managed so as to reduce the danger of future complications, and on symptoms that may make adolescents worried about their hearts. Now, attention can be drawn to the forms of heart disease found in adolescents.

Congenital heart disease While there are many different kinds of congenital heart disease, most are present at birth and consist of either a subtle or striking malformation of the heart. Many forms of congenital heart disease are so overwhelmingly important to the health—even life—of the small infant or child that surgical correction must be done as soon after birth as possible. Other problems, however, benefit from waiting until the child is larger, or may not need treatment until their effects begin to interfere with health or normal activity. Therefore, some children with congenital heart disease do not require treatment until they are in their adolescent years.

Heart problems acquired during adolescence The heart, alone or in combination with other organs in the body, can be affected during the adolescent years by a number of different diseases. Some are quite rare, and do not warrant discussion here. One, however, is more common. Acute rheumatic fever is an important form of heart disease, and it is preventable.

Acute rheumatic fever is a generalized illness that may appear several weeks to a month after an adolescent has had an *untreated* infection caused by beta-hemolytic streptococci (Group A) (see p. 208). The streptococcal infection is usually a sore throat, and is not always serious enough to make the adolescent feel particularly ill or seek the care of a physician. Acute rheumatic fever represents a reaction to the strep infection, and can include several different symptoms. Quite frequently there is pain, swelling and tenderness in various joints; in addition, these symptoms migrate from one joint to another, so that an elbow might hurt or be somewhat swollen in the morning, while in the afternoon, the elbow might be fine, but the wrist or another joint will be similarly affected. Fever frequently accompanies the onset of this illness. In addition to the fever and joint symptoms, a fine skin rash may develop on the chest or the back, and some nodules—hard bumps—can appear beneath the skin near the elbows and knees, on the scalp, or along the spine. In some adolescents one exceptional sign of the illness is an inability to control the position and motion of their bodies. These adolescents appear to be clumsy, and their faces, heads, and arms often move abruptly and involuntarily. This condition, called **chorea,** interferes with normal speech and with the ability to write legibly. The most dangerous aspect of rheumatic fever, however, is its effect on the heart. **Rheumatic carditis** (inflammation of the heart) causes symptoms such as fatigue, chest pain, shortness of breath, and an inability to sleep comfortably without using several pillows.

The possibility of developing rheumatic fever after a streptococcal throat infection is largely prevented by adequate treatment of the infection once it has been identified. As mentioned earlier, the diagnosis of streptococcal infections is made certain by taking a throat culture. Once identified, it can be cured relatively easily with antibiotics. Rheumatic fever itself can be treated to relieve the symptoms it causes; however, damage to the heart can still occur. Young people who suffer one attack of rheumatic fever run an increased risk of having another attack. For this reason, they may be given penicillin or another antibiotic every day to minimize the chance of acquiring another beta-hemolytic streptococcal infection.

Gastrointestinal diseases

When the length—some nine yards—and the variety of functions of the mature gastrointestinal system are considered, it is surprising that more doesn't go wrong with it. Of the symptoms accompanying gastrointestinal disorders, many are combined in one of the most commonly experienced ailments: acute gastroenteritis. They include nausea, loss of appetite, vomiting, diarrhea, and pain in the abdomen. These symptoms, and three others—fever, jaundice, and change in the color of bowel movements—are found in varying combinations in most disorders affecting the gastrointestinal system. In addition, some gastrointestinal diseases are associated with an adolescent's failing to grow normally or losing weight.

Gastroenteritis

The term gastroenteritis is often used to describe an unpleasant, but limited, illness involving nausea, vomiting, abdominal discomfort, and diarrhea. Other symptoms are minimal. In some adolescents, however, the illness tends to affect one portion of the gastrointestinal tract more than the other; thus, one might have "gastritis" or "enteritis." Infections with viral and bacterial agents can cause these ailments, as can toxic agents. Examples of the latter include the toxins that cause food poisoning.

Gastritis can also be caused occasionally by alcohol or aspirin. This form of gastritis, resulting from irritation of the lining of the stomach, often appears as vomiting and abdominal pain. At times, the material vomited from the stomach contains blood that may be bright red or (because of the action of stomach acid on the blood) black and dispersed in flecks (looking like coffee grounds).

Enteritis predominates when the infection involves the lower portions of the intestinal tract, and crampy abdominal pain and diarrhea develop. At times, the bowel movements contain blood.

When an adolescent has a sudden attack of gastroenteritis, but does not have much fever or abdominal pain, and has no evidence of bleeding from the upper or lower parts of the intestinal tract, it is wise to manage the problem by taking a little time off from usual activities to rest, and by making minor changes in dietary practices for a few days. When vomiting occurs, it is very helpful to avoid any intake of food and fluids for about six hours, and then begin to take small amounts of only clear fluids—such as two to four ounces of apple juice, flat soda, or Jell-O made with twice as much water as usual— every thirty minutes. The amounts can be increased gradually, and the interval between drinks can be extended as the adolescent feels better and is able to keep down larger amounts. When vomiting is not a problem and diarrhea is, clear fluids can be taken from the start, and while they will not overload the intestinal tract, they will help to prevent the adolescent from becoming too dehydrated. As either condition improves with time and the use of clear fluids, solid foods can be reintroduced into the diet, starting with bread and crackers, then foods with little fat or milk (because of its lactose content), and finally a full diet.

When an episode of gastroenteritis is accompanied by more severe symptoms, or does not clear up promptly, or when bleeding is evident, a teenager should consult a doctor about the problem.

Ulcers   One is apt to think of the typical ulcer patient as the stereotypical harried businessman; however, ulcers do occur in children, and seem to become fairly common during adolescence. Ulcers are produced by a combination of factors that cause the lining of the stomach or duodenum to be worn away at one or several points. The symptoms in ulcer disease may be slight or marked. In the latter case they can include upper abdominal pain (sometimes relieved after eating, and sometimes appearing in the middle of the night), vomiting of blood or "coffee-ground" material (see gastroenteritis, p. 221), and change in the color of bowel movements from normal to blackish. The latter indicates presence of blood from a source in the upper part of the gastrointestinal tract. Medical care is important in the diagnosis and management of ulcer disease. It is frequently possible to find the ulcer or ulcers during an X ray examination of the upper gastrointestinal tract, or by directly inspecting the lining of the stomach and duodenum with an instrument called an endoscope. Treatment, aimed at allowing the ulcers to heal, includes the use of antacid preparations and other medicines, and avoidance of any foods that cause an increase in discomfort.

Hepatitis   The liver serves a vital function in the digestive process, as well as in the removal of waste substances from the bloodstream. Liver disease symptoms depend upon which of these functions is more affected. Hepatitis is the most commonly acquired disease of the liver during late childhood and in adolescence. While hepatitis can be caused by a wide variety of infections and chemical agents, most hepatitis is caused by one of two viruses. One hepatitis virus, called virus A, is associated with typical infectious hepatitis, an illness that is caused by swallowing the virus in contaminated foodstuffs. Usually two to seven weeks elapse between exposure to the virus and the onset of the illness. The other cause, virus B, causes "serum" hepatitis, named for the usual transmission of the virus via a blood transfusion or contaminated needle; however, this virus is also transmitted orally. Hepatitis caused by virus B usually begins six weeks to six months after the exposure.

In many respects, the illnesses caused by these viruses are similar. Nausea and vomiting, upper abdominal discomfort or pain, loss of appetite, and fever are common. The urine darkens, the stools may become lighter in color, and jaundice (yellowing of the skin) appears. In addition, some adolescents who have infections caused by virus B also develop pains in the joints and skin rashes. Once hepatitis has been diagnosed and proper care provided, each infection runs its course in four to six weeks.

Adolescents who are exposed to virus A infections by family members or close friends with the illness benefit from preventive treatment with a form of gamma globulin called immune serum globulin. This form of passive immunization supplies antibodies capable of preventing or reducing the effects of virus A. Another form of immune serum globulin is available for the prevention of accidental infections with virus B.

Gallbladder disease Though not particularly common in adolescents, gallbladder disease does occur. Most of the symptoms that herald problems in this part of the digestive tract are preceded by the formation of **gallstones.** Gallstones act to produce inflammation and obstruction in the biliary tract— the system that collects bile from the liver, stores it in the gallbladder, and transports it to the upper intestinal tract. The patient notices their presence because of pain in the right upper portion of the abdomen, jaundice, and fever. Although pregnancy, the use of oral contraceptive pills, and the increased turnover of red blood cells in certain forms of anemia all are associated with an increased risk of gallbladder disease, the reason for gallstone formation is in fact not always clearly understood. Some gallstones can be seen on a regular X ray of the abdomen; others are invisible in such X rays, but show up on X rays taken after a special diagnostic chemical is absorbed from the gastrointestinal tract and deposited in the gallbladder. While major advances have been made in the medical treatment of gallbladder disease, the most common and effective treatment still consists of surgical removal of the gallbladder.

Crohn's disease, also known as regional enteritis, is a chronic gastrointestinal disorder in which inflammatory changes affect and change the normal structure of the wall of the bowel, usually in the small intestine, but also in the large bowel (colon), and to a lesser extent in the stomach. Sometimes only a small section of the bowel is affected; sometimes the disease is more widespread. Unlike most other forms of gastrointestinal disease, Crohn's disease appears over several months or more with a constellation of symptoms, not all of which appear in the gastrointestinal tract. Among the general symptoms are fever, slowing of growth, weight loss, and pains in the joints. Gastrointestinal symptoms include abdominal pain, diarrhea, and sometimes rectal bleeding. Adolescents who notice these persistent symptoms should see a doctor. Once the extent of the disease is known, treatment can be planned to relieve the symptoms and reduce the underlying inflammation.

Appendicitis is a sudden inflammation of the appendix, a narrow tubelike intestinal structure, three to four inches in length, closed at its free end and attached at the other end to the first part of the large intestine. Invariably an attack of appendicitis begins with pain above or around the navel. Vomiting, either short-lived or persistent, usually begins a little later, and is frequently accompanied by nausea or a loss of appetite. Then, in most cases, the pain shifts to the right side of the lower part of the abdomen and becomes more severe. Subsequently, when the adolescent presses on the abdomen below and to the right of the navel, the discomfort is increased; and walking or jumping may also accentuate the pain. By the time appendicitis has reached this stage, a low-grade fever (up to 101° F.) may also have developed.

Pain, vomiting, fever, and tenderness—in that order—so typically point to a diagnosis of appendicitis that the boy or girl who has them should see a doctor without delay. Prompt diagnosis of appendicitis leads to equally prompt surgical removal of the inflamed appendix—before it perforates (breaks open), sending bacteria and irritating substances into the abdominal cavity to cause other mischief. The diagnosis is based on the sequence of symptoms, a physical examination, a white blood cell count and differential white cell count, and often a regular X ray of the abdomen.

Constipation

While the small intestine takes on the important function of digesting food and absorbing nutrients, the large intestine absorbs minerals and water from the intestinal contents that reach it, and transforms the remaining waste into a form that can be easily excreted. Some adolescents normally have bowel movements less often than once a day, and yet have no difficulty emptying their bowels. Constipation refers to a condition in which there is pain during or following bowel movements, which may be accompanied by small amounts of bleeding and incomplete emptying of the bowel leading to a gradual accumulation of feces in the colon. If the colon eventually becomes overstuffed with waste material, the victim of constipation may experience intermittent abdominal discomfort, and soiling of the underwear between bowel movements may begin.

While temporary constipation can often be relieved by the use of extra fluids and fiber in the diet, more persistent forms ought to be evaluated by a doctor.

Ulcerative colitis

Unlike Crohn's disease, which tends to be widely distributed in the gastrointestinal tract, ulcerative colitis affects only the colon. It gradually produces symptoms of diarrhea, often with bleeding and weight loss. Abdominal pain, fever, pallor, and fatigue also develop frequently. Ulcerative colitis is somewhat less likely to interfere with growth than Crohn's disease. Clinical evaluation and medical treatment of this serious condition should be obtained without delay.

Cancer

Previous sections have mentioned tumors that can appear in several different body systems. Among these are malignant tumors of the pigment cells of the skin, of the ovary or testis, and of the breast. All are quite rare during adolescence. Before considering, in this section, other forms of cancer which *do* appear with relative frequency during adolescence, it is worthwhile to note that cancer is far from being the most common cause of death in adolescence. In the United States, three other causes of adolescent death consistently outrun cancer: accidental deaths, deaths caused by homicide, and suicide. Deaths from cardiovascular diseases rank fifth, after cancer.

Some of the forms of cancer that do affect adolescents in some numbers are those of the blood-forming tissues, mainly the leukemias; the cancers of the lymphatic system; cancers of bone; and cancers involving the central nervous system.

Leukemia

Leukemia is the name given to a group of conditions in which the normal cells of the bone marrow are replaced by immature white blood cells, which also begin to inhabit other parts of the body. Any, or all, of the three different kinds of blood cells (red cells, white cells, and platelets) normally produced in the bone marrow can be affected by the disease. When the population of the red blood cells is reduced, the adolescent develops anemia (see p. 230); when the normal white cell population is reduced, infections become more frequent and more severe; and reduction in the number of platelets, which control the rate of blood clotting, increases the possibility of abnormal bruising and bleeding. The afflicted adolescent may become pale, tired, develop fever, have nosebleeds, and perhaps increased menstrual bleeding.

As the leukemic cells spread throughout the body, the lymph glands, liver, and spleen enlarge, while involvement of the central nervous system causes headaches. There may be pain in the bones or joints.

A diagnosis of leukemia depends on blood count findings and the results of an examination of cells from the bone marrow. Treatment of leukemia has advanced tremendously in the past decade. In fact, it has become so successful in making the disease disappear and in preventing its reemergence that many patients now appear to be cured of their disease.

Cancer of the lymphatic system

Hodgkin's disease is the best-known disease in this category, while **lymphosarcoma** is another, less well known. Hodgkin's disease is a disorder in which one or more lymph nodes, either in a single region of the body, or in several regions, enlarge painlessly over a period of months. Though the adolescent may be able to continue with schoolwork and other activities, fatigue increases, and there is often a loss of weight. Fever commonly develops, and some patients experience night sweats. There may also be considerable and widespread itching of the skin.

Lymphosarcoma is also marked by the increasing size of one or more lymph nodes. However, as lymphosarcoma evolves, it frequently turns into an illness indistinguishable from leukemia.

Bone cancer

During adolescence, it is far more common to discover a benign bone tumor than a malignant one. Noncancerous **bone** cysts—fluid-filled spaces within bones—may account for pain in the bone that harbors them. An abnormal growth of bone called an **osteoid osteoma,** a benign bone tumor, causes pain that is rather characteristically greater during the night than in the daytime and, unlike the pain produced by most other bone lesions, responds quite well to the use of aspirin. Malignant bone tumors are sometimes found during adolescence, and they tend to be associated with bone pain, and often with swelling of the tissues near the site of the pain. Adolescents who notice pain in a bone that cannot be linked to a recent bruise or bump, and that does not vanish entirely within a short time, as well as those who notice an unexplained swelling in the vicinity of a bone, should tell a doctor about it promptly.

Central nervous system tumors

Certain types of brain tumors are more common in adults than in young children. In adults, tumors tend to appear in the upper portion of the brain, while they affect the lower regions of the brain more often in children. Brain tumors occurring during adolescence resemble those found in adults more closely than those found in younger children, although some overlap exists. The symptoms that develop from the presence of a brain tumor depend on the location of the tumor within the brain: rarely does a tumor cause headache alone. Symptoms more suggestive of brain tumors consist of changes in vision, especially double vision or blurring of vision; seizures; weakness in the face or an arm or leg; difficulty with coordination or with maintaining balance; difficulty with speech; a change in personality; and vomiting, especially in the absence of any other signs of gastrointestinal problems. An adolescent who develops one or more of these symptoms should have them investigated by his or her doctor.

Anemia

Anemia is a general term describing a state in which the number of red blood cells or the amount of hemoglobin in the bloodstream is below normal, or in which the overall quantity of blood in the body is decreased. These definitions reflect the fact that anemia can result from three different things: from insufficient production of red blood cells or hemoglobin (the oxygen-carrying protein in the red cell) by the bone marrow, from abnormally rapid destruction of red blood cells in the bloodstream, or from loss of blood through bleeding.

Insufficient red cell or hemoglobin production New red blood cells are produced in the bone marrow and released to circulate in the blood. In general, two problems may cause abnormal production of red cells or hemoglobin. In one, an important building block of the cells (such as iron) is missing or present in only small quantity. In the other, the building blocks are present in normal amounts, but some other process interferes with the manufacturing process. For example, if the center of the bone is occupied by other tissue—some sort of abnormal growth, for example—the normal marrow is crowded and cannot do its work. Also, in the presence of infection and other systemic illnesses, the production of red cells by the bone marrow may be partially shut down for a time.

Abnormal red cell destruction After they enter the bloodstream, red cells normally circulate for 120 days before they become too old to do their job and are removed. Anything that noticeably shortens the lifetime of the red cell can result in anemia if the production of new red cells by the bone marrow is not able to keep pace with the rate of destruction. Sometimes, the structure of the red cell itself leads to a shortened life; at other times, substances in the bloodstream affect the stability of the red cell and lead to its early demise. An example of the latter state of affairs is found in some adolescents, usually of African, Mediterranean, or Oriental ancestry, who become anemic when they consume such things as sulfa drugs, aspirin, antimalarial medications, or fava beans. Adolescents who respond to these substances by developing anemia often have a red blood cell deficiency of an enzyme called glucose-6-phosphate dehydrogenase.

Loss of blood Bleeding, particularly when it occurs suddenly and leads to the loss of a considerable volume of blood, results in anemia. Such bleeding is obvious, but bleeding that progresses at a slower rate can occur without the adolescent noticing it at all. Most bleeding copious enough to lead to anemia occurs in the gastrointestinal tract (as from a bleeding ulcer), but heavy nosebleeds and profuse menstrual bleeding can cause anemia.

Symptoms of anemia

Most symptoms of anemia result from a decrease in the oxygen-carrying capacity of the blood, because of a smaller number of red cells or a decrease in the hemoglobin level. Adolescents who are anemic may have rather imprecise symptoms such as tiring easily and low energy, but non-anemic adolescents often feel the same way. Light-headedness and getting "winded" after moderate activity are often suggestive of anemia, however. When anemia develops suddenly, as it can when blood cells are destroyed rapidly or when bleeding occurs, the symptoms are apt to be much more bothersome than when anemia develops gradually over a longer period of time. Changes in the appearance of bowel movements can point to gastrointestinal bleeding: obvious red blood when bleeding is massive or when the bleeding comes from the lower part of the bowel; and a change in the color of normal bowel movements to a blackish color when small or moderate amounts of blood escape into the upper part of the intestinal tract. As anemia develops, adolescents may be able to see that they are becoming noticeably paler, and they may even sense that their hearts beat more rapidly in an attempt to compensate for the anemia.

Iron-deficiency anemia

During periods of rapid growth, which occur during the early childhood years and again at adolescence, anemia caused by iron deficiency is most likely to appear. It does so at such times because the growing child or adolescent is not getting enough iron from the diet to meet the needs of an increasing blood volume. Just as the premature baby—who has less iron in its body at birth than a full-term baby—is more likely to become iron-deficient during early life, the preteenager who has marginal iron stores is more likely to become iron-deficient during adolescence. In each instance the enormous demands for iron during the growth phases simply may not be met by the daily nutritional intake. In addition to the foods mentioned on page 29 as being natural sources of iron, many other foods are fortified with iron—breads and cereals especially.

Several forms of anemia, both of nutritional origin like iron-deficiency anemia and from other causes, can be identified by proper diagnostic tests and then treated. Because iron deficiency occurs so often among adolescents, checking an adolescent's blood count once or twice during the years of rapid growth makes good sense.

Cosmetic problems

Two cosmetic problems have already been discussed in other contexts: the possible use of surgery to correct irregularities in breast formation, and the availability of dermabrasion to reduce the scars of acne. In this section, several other cosmetic problems of concern to teenagers are covered. They include rhinoplasty, treatment available for tattoos, care of the skin to prevent sunburn and accelerated aging of the skin, and keloids.

Rhinoplasty

Rhinoplasty (in slang a "nose job") may be indicated for medical reasons, cosmetic reasons, or both. Particularly after the nose has been broken and heals unsatisfactorily, the distortion may interfere with the passage of air and with drainage from the sinuses, and may lead to nose infections. Or the shape of the nose may be unattractive to the adolescent, and rhinoplasty is an effective way of making some desirable adjustments.

Rhinoplasty is a procedure carried out by both otolaryngologists and plastic surgeons. It involves the rearrangement or removal of enough nasal bone to reshape the nose and to create an adequate passageway on each side of the nose for air. The procedure is performed under anesthesia and results in quite a bit of soft tissue swelling, as well as bruising around the nose and eyes. The latter is caused by the seepage of small amounts of blood under the skin, and goes away in a week or so. The swelling that accompanies the surgery disappears more quickly. Most adolescents who choose to have rhinoplasties usually prefer to have the surgery performed during the early part of a school vacation, or during the summer, when their friends do not see them regularly and when their responsibilities are minimal.

Tattoos

Tattoos, and the methods by which they are applied to the skin, have been associated with a number of medical complications. Hepatitis (see p. 223) and other infections have been transmitted through the use of tattooing equipment that does not meet standards of good hygiene. Also, some of the chemical agents used in tattooing are capable of producing quite undesirable reactions in the skin, sometimes right away but often not until many years later. Occasionally for these reasons, but usually because he or she simply wants to get rid of an unwanted adornment, an adolescent wishes to have a tattoo removed. Contrary to widely held belief, the situation is not hopeless, and surgery is not necessary for the removal of unwanted tattoos. Instead, a simple and effective method consists of the use of **salabrasion,** literally "abrasion using salt," to disperse and remove the pigmentation responsible for the tattoo.

Sunburn and aging of the skin

Adolescents spend a lot of time in the sun. Whether on a mountain in winter, at the beach in the summer, or on a construction job, the skin is bombarded with sunlight. This light contains rays that have the ability to burn and to accelerate the aging of the skin while producing its more valued effect, a suntan.

A sunburn is one form of damage, produced by certain light rays, that may appear after exposure to the sun. Anyone who has suffered from a sunburn knows the way the skin becomes tender, swollen, and red, and how blistering and weeping of the skin follow. In many respects, a sunburn resembles a burn produced by other injuries such as hot water. Sunlight can also affect the components of the skin that are responsible for its softness and elasticity. If these components are damaged by too much exposure, the skin becomes drier, more wrinkled, and sometimes thicker. Each of these effects tends to be more striking in light-skinned people than in those whose skin and hair color are darker.

Tanning of the skin is, generally speaking, fashionable. Having a "decent" tan is, in many quarters, almost as essential as having the right clothing and the correct length of hair. Many people who prize suntans also believe that they feel better when they are tanned. From a practical medical point of view, the important thing is to reduce the untoward effects of sunlight as much as possible while permitting attractive tanning to occur. This goal is best achieved through the regular use of screening agents—creams and lotions—that filter the sunlight before it reaches the skin.

It is possible to modify the effect of sunlight on the skin completely or partially. When an agent totally excludes light from reaching the skin, it is called a "blocking" agent. Zinc oxide and titanium dioxide are examples of these. Other agents filter out the particular light rays that can burn and damage the skin: these are called sunscreens. The prime example of an effective sunscreen is para-aminobenzoic acid, often called "PABA." Other sunscreens include such agents as benzophenones and cinnamates. PABA and several of its chemical cousins are ingredients in many of the sun lotions and creams on the market, and adolescents should examine package labels carefully to make sure that the preparation they are purchasing contains an effective sunscreen. PABA is particularly effective when applied in a concentration of 5 percent. With few exceptions, the preparations require repeated application in the course of a day outdoors: swimming and perspiration wash them off. Even though a "good" tan does provide some built-in protection against sunburn, it is advisable to continue to use sunscreen to prevent overexposure of the skin to sunlight and the development of skin problems in later life. These problems include wrinkling, dryness, and other cosmetic problems, as well as skin cancers.

Keloids

Sometimes when the skin is injured, instead of healing neatly it produces a keloid—a bulky, smooth, unattractive scar. Keloids can form when the skin is simply cut. They are sometimes a consequence of acne or a smallpox vaccination, or they can appear on pierced earlobes. Black adolescents develop keloids more often than those of other racial backgrounds. Keloids can be treated in several ways: some can be reduced appreciably by the application of a form of cortisone to the skin; others by injection of the keloid with similar medicine; and a few benefit from combined medical and surgical treatment.

Other common physical problems

No discussion of the health concerns of adolescence would be complete without mention of two problems that do not belong to any of the categories covered in the foregoing sections. One problem is urinary tract infections. The other is migraine.

Urinary tract infections

The urinary tract encompasses the kidneys, the ureters (tubes that carry urine from the kidneys to the bladder), the bladder, and the urethra (which transports urine from the bladder to outside the body). Urinary tract infections, which appear more often in girls than in boys, can affect any of the structures in the urinary tract, but the kidneys are less often involved.

An adolescent who develops an infection in the urinary tract usually notices one or more symptoms. One of the most common is a burning discomfort in the lower abdomen or in the region of the urethra, during or after urination (see also p. 187). Another symptom may be an increased frequency of urination, or of an urgent feeling of a need to urinate: the adolescent may worry about getting to a toilet in time to avoid an accident. Sometimes, after urinating, he or she will feel as though the bladder has not been fully emptied. These symptoms are especially common in infections of the bladder (cystitis) and urethra; they may also arise in cases of infection in the upper part of the urinary tract (the ureters and kidneys). When the kidneys become infected, symptoms are more likely to be abdominal pain, nausea, back pain, and fever; and the adolescent will probably feel very ill.

A urinary tract infection is usually diagnosed by identification of abnormal amounts of bacteria in the urine (though there is also strong reason for suspicion when many white blood cells are found in the urine.) A fresh urine specimen is examined for bacteria and cultured. Special tests are also done to learn what antibiotic would be most effective against the particular bacteria involved.

When an adolescent has had urinary tract infections in earlier life, the urine should be checked periodically to make sure that bacteria is not present, even without other symptoms. When an adolescent develops a urinary tract infection for the first time, the anatomy of the urinary tract is checked by X ray after the infection has been treated. In this way, any structural abnormality of the urinary tract that might contribute to the development of infections can be identified. A doctor will probably also have suggestions to make about hygiene aimed at avoiding or controlling chronic infections.

Migraine

Headache is a common complaint of adolescents who are subject to many of the same stresses and strains that produce headaches in adults. Hunger, fatigue, pressure from multiple demands that compete for the adolescent's time and energy, and brief emotional upsets can all be associated with development of a headache. Headaches that appear under any of these circumstances often increase gradually over several hours and are more noticeable over the muscles at the back of the head and upper neck, or at the temples or forehead. Removal of the underlying tension, some relaxation, and use of aspirin or acetaminophen and an ice pack are usually very helpful in relieving such headaches. An adolescent who has a persistent headache often benefits from having it evaluated by a doctor: a sinus infection, depression, or some other cause of headache may well be behind it.

A migraine headache is a special kind of headache whose causes and symptoms are distinctly different from most other forms of headache. A migraine headache typically affects one side of the head but not the other, and is marked with certain symptoms that appear in advance of the headache itself, and by others that accompany it.

The adolescent who begins to have a migraine attack may

realize that an attack is imminent before any headache develops. The most noticeable of the warning signals is an unmistakable alteration in vision. Instead of being able to see clearly, a portion of the view is blocked by a large "blind spot." The blind spot seems to be present in both eyes, and looks much like a bright light that has bright, zigzag lines flowing through it. Soon after the blind spot appears, the adolescent may notice a "pins and needles" feeling in the face or hands, and generalized weakness. After these symptoms develop, a headache appears, a remarkably unpleasant headache. It often feels vise-like and may be accompanied by nausea and vomiting, and sometimes by a chill.

It is harder to identify a migraine when the early signs are not so pronounced, or when they consist mainly of feeling very confused. Migraine attacks do tend to occur in more than one member of a family, and it is difficult to ascertain their cause. Because effective treatment is available for most adolescents who suffer from migraine, clinical evaluation and treatment are certainly recommended.

Psychological Problems

Anxiety

Anxiety is a feeling experienced by everyone at one time or another. It is a kind of mental pain, a generalized apprehension unconnected to any particular source or type of danger. The physical and mental manifestations are those of fear, although with fear the person knows what the cause is and knows that the danger is worthy of the discomfort.

Some psychologists theorize that anxiety is the modern expression of ancient adaptive mechanisms. When our caveman and cavewoman ancestors spotted or were spotted by a saber-toothed tiger, for example, they had two choices, flight or fight. In either case it was to their advantage for the pupils of their eyes to dilate, their lungs and hearts to work at full capacity, and for more blood to be shunted to the muscles of their arms and legs. Those whose bodies worked best in this manner were most likely to survive and have many offspring like themselves. In the twentieth century, when we feel fearful, the same physical reactions are repeated, but fleeing or fighting are now seldom the best solutions to a problem. The consequence of this is that the modern individual who is about to enter an exam unprepared or to call a possibly unreceptive girl for a date may be inappropriately struck with pallor, dry mouth, excessive perspiration, trembling, and increased heart and respiration rates.

Such feelings are uncomfortable enough when you know what causes them, but when they appear for no apparent reason, they may be even worse. The latter is true anxiety. Since, however, the signs of anxiety and fear are the same, and the two states are sometimes difficult to differentiate, they will be discussed together.

"Normal" anxiety

Anxiety is not an all-or-none phenomenon. At one end of the spectrum there can be terror and panic for no conscious reason, and this is unquestionably a sign of emotional disorder. The complete absence of anxiety, however, is also abnormal. Even though we would rather do without the full-blown physical symptoms, fear and anxiety are the body's early warning system for danger. Without having to think about it consciously, the uneasy feeling you get when swimming far from shore or foolishly signing up for advanced calculus or telling a member of the Hell's Angels that he doesn't know what he is talking about warns you that you should be aware of what is going on and should decide whether or not you really want to do what you are doing. Without the signal of anxiety we would get into a lot more trouble than we do.

A good example of the usefulness of normal anxiety is the excitement felt before taking a test in school or participating in some important competition. If you did not have any anxiety, there would be little motive to study and you would do poorly on the exam. On the other hand, if you have an abnormally high amount of anxiety, your ability to study and do well on the exam is hampered by distractibility and short attention span. Coaches of athletic teams are very aware of the importance of normal anxiety. They know they want their players

240

"up" for a big game, but not so high that they will be nervous and make a lot of mistakes. The latter is more apt to occur in students who are not accustomed to taking important exams or in teams that are not used to championship play-off pressure.

Abnormal anxiety

As has already been pointed out, a certain amount of anxiety is necessary in order to function well in life. Speaking strictly, true anxiety differs from ordinary fear in that the person does not know why he or she feels afraid. It is a feeling of a danger without any danger being apparent. Everyone has such feelings from time to time, but they are usually infrequent and relatively mild. Some adolescents, however, feel waves of panic and do not know why. It is difficult to convey in words how uncomfortable this feeling is, but in essence there is the foreboding that a calamity is about to strike, without knowing what or when. The body goes through its pointless physical preparedness routine, and to increase vigilance the stimulus barrier that we all use to protect us from registering every little event in the environment is lowered. This means that the anxious person is overaware of noises and nuances that he or she might otherwise ignore. Everything is startling. Unfortunately, since the victim does not know the source of the danger (and there might not even be one), no amount of attentiveness or activity can bring more than partial or temporary relief, and most often such tactics are counterproductive. A body always tense and on the alert soon becomes weary; as the old saying has it, nervous sweat is more tiring than work sweat. In addition, a body that is nervously alert has trouble falling asleep to recoup the extra energy expended during the day.

When your body is tense and tired all the time, other physical symptoms are likely to result. Usually the first clue a physician has that a patient is suffering from anxiety attacks is a request for a checkup for a sleep disorder, eating disorder, generalized weakness, or other physical complaint. Another manifestation of anxiety is overbreathing, also called hyperventilation syndrome (see p. 213).

Why should people have anxiety? It certainly seems like an unnecessary bother that evolution would have done well to have eliminated. As already noted, however, it can be a useful signal that keeps us alert to danger. What is bad about it comes when the signal is too strong or its meaning cannot be under-stood. Such anxiety means that the mind has picked up some-thing within us that is considered dangerous, but that still lies in our **unconscious.**

The concept of the unconscious is a difficult one for some people to grasp, although for others it is obvious from what they see in their own and other people's lives. Although there are a number of everyday examples of the fact of the uncon-scious, **amnesia** and **hypnotism** are probably most graphic and obvious. Although some people lose their memories following a blow on the head, amnesia more commonly follows an emo-tional shock. Hearing bad news or seeing a loved one killed are examples of experiences that may blank out one's memory for varying periods of time. This is the brain's protection against a massive onslaught of anxiety. It is common in large city hospital emergency rooms. Through hypnosis one's memory can be tampered with in all sorts of ways, including forgetting you were hypnotized, not knowing members of your own family, carrying out silly suggestions without knowing why, and so on. The brain at all times has the capacity to keep things that might be stressful hidden from us. This is one way of understanding anxiety attacks. They come in response to fears that we are not consciously aware of, yet at an unconscious level they are perceived and responded to by the body with all of the physical preparations used in the face of danger. The mind does not always distinguish between fears touched off outside the body and those originating within oneself.

Typical types of adolescent anxiety

Problems caused by anxiety can occur before adolescence and certainly occur afterwards, but there are aspects of the adoles-cent experience that tend to encourage certain types of anxiety. One is involved with breaking free of parents; the other arises from sexual pressures.

Separating emotionally from parents is difficult for even the most independent adolescent. Since a crucial part of being independent is not being (or seeming) afraid of independence, the enormity of the feeling of loss is often unconscious. Therefore, anxiety attacks sometimes occur around seemingly trivial experiences. For some adolescents this may involve going to school. School avoidance is most common around the beginning of grade school and again during adolescence. This type of avoidance is not the same as truancy, but it is associated with the adolescent's fear that something bad will happen if he or she does not remain at home. Stage fright can occur at any age but is often most common during adolescence. The idea of going out and doing something alone can be terrifying. Success anxiety is another variation of separation fear that may be exaggerated during adolescence. It seems paradoxical that a teenager should become anxious following a highly acclaimed success, but some adolescents associate succeeding with no longer needing to be looked after. Fearing the success will preclude still being able to be taken care of, and believing they still need such care, these adolescents find discomfort rather than joy in their honored accomplishments. Finally, death anxiety occurs fairly commonly during adolescence. Around the age of 4 or 5 many children worry about their parents dying, but the child of that age has little grasp of the concept of death. During adolescence the inevitability and the permanence of death are better realized. Although for many people the certainty of death does not form until middle age, some adolescents become preoccupied with death. Suicide attempts (but not successful suicides) are more common during late adolescence than during other periods of life, and death is not an unusual theme for the work of especially creative adolescents. William Cullen Bryant, for example, wrote "Thanatopsis," one of the best-known poems about death, when he was only 18. In psychotherapy, adolescents' preoccupation with death is often related to their breaking away from the parents who gave them life.

A second major source of adolescent anxiety stems from sexual pressures. As noted before, there is an unfortunate discrepancy between the time teenagers are capable of having sex physically and the time that either they are ready emotionally to handle the consequences or society is ready to offer its approval. The result is considerable frustration for many adolescents, since sexual urges at this age can be very strong. If conscious, these urges lead either to action or frustration. When because of fear of detection the urges are unconscious, their very presence can lead to anxiety. Sometimes this anxiety is expressed chiefly through concern about bodily fitness and leads to symptoms without physical cause. For others, anxiety reveals itself through hyperactivity and tenseness. Sports and other physical releases help some adolescents feel better. For still others, sexual anxiety is characterized more by weariness than hyperactivity. Especially in the last century it was quite common for adolescent girls to faint or swoon when exposed to too much sexual attention. Although such behavior is less frequent now, some adolescents today do become excessively moralistic or even ascetic in order to help ward off unacceptable sexual urges and thereby prevent anxiety attacks.

Psychological maneuvers used to cope with anxiety

Anxiety is distinguished from other common psychological reactions by the fact that its symptoms fall into no particular pattern. The constant tension and need for vigilance caused by pathological anxiety are so disagreeable that in most cases there is an attempt by the mind to construct some alternative to fear of what one doesn't know. Four of the most common alternatives are phobias, conversion reactions, obsessive-compulsive reactions, and reactions in which one part of the personality is dissociated from the others.

In a **phobia,** the adolescent decides he or she "knows" what is causing the anxiety, even though it may not make any sense either to the adolescent or to others. For example, leaving the house, going to school, being in enclosed spaces, or being high up may terrorize the teenager, even though he or she cannot explain why. Phobias are irrational fears, and they can occur at any age. They have one advantage over free-floating anxiety: that is, if a person believes something in the environment frightens him, he can avoid it. This may cause some limitations on one's life, but makes the anxiety potentially manageable.

Especially during adolescence, there are also opposite variations of phobias called **counterphobic reactions**. These are expressions of persons meeting their anxieties head on. At a younger age this is done through play as children actively participate in the reenactment of a situation that frightened them as passive participants. A child, for example, may act out over and over again a visit to the doctor, an accident, or a fight. In the play, the child is active, willing, and in control of the situation, instead of being acted upon, unwilling, and helpless. During adolescence, one sometimes sees teenagers deliberately rush in where they really fear to tread. The hope remains the same: that by attempting actively to control the situation, the fear can be overcome. This response can be dangerous; "playing chicken" or daring one another is common during adolescence. Especially in regard to driving risks and to abusing drugs and alcohol, the results can be fatal. Intellectual types of counterphobic behavior can, however, be very useful. Studying law out of the fear of conflict, studying medicine out of the fear of death, or becoming an expert swimmer because of a fear of water are such examples. Examples of other adaptive counterphobic maneuvers include becoming proficient at something earlier failed, returning to a situation associated with an accident, and overcoming a physical disability through painful or difficult exercise.

A second approach the mind can use to give structure to incomprehensible anxiety is to convert it to a bodily complaint. These are called **conversion reactions** and the symptom often has a symbolic meaning in regard to the unconscious conflict. The three most common conversion reactions are paralysis of a limb, blindness, and pain. The symptoms have no anatomical or physiological basis, but are frequently very effective in relieving anxiety. In fact, it is often surprising how little concern the person has about the disability. As with a phobia, in a conversion reaction, organization is provided by giving reasonableness, or at least meaning, to any concern the adolescent feels. The difference is that the purported problem in a phobia is directed toward an external object, while a conversion reaction involves part of the person's own body.

A third psychic maneuver the mind uses in order to avoid anxiety is the development of **obsessive-compulsive reactions.** A certain amount of tenacity is very useful in mastering any pursuit, and such determination is sometimes erroneously labeled "compulsive." What is being described here, however, is more problematic and indicates repetitive thoughts and/or actions that don't really have any constructive purpose but that must be carried out as a sort of magic ritual to avoid feelings of danger or anxiety. These thoughts and actions may seem ridiculous to the person as well as to others, but no matter how intrusive and disruptive they become, they must be continued for the sake of peace of mind. Accompanying the symptoms are often guilt feelings as well as preoccupation with opposites such as orderliness and disorder, right and wrong, cleanliness and dirt. The adolescent usually tries to compromise by maintaining the ritual while trying to make it as inconspicuous as possible. This may not be easy, and peers may ridicule the boy or girl who has to touch certain objects, walk in certain patterns, or say things in a certain way. Like Linus with his blanket, however, people whose obsessions or compulsions are not too severe draw great comfort from them. There is the story of the man who was driving with a friend down Fifth Avenue in New York City. As they rode, he tore up small bits of paper and dropped them out of the window. When his friend asked him why, the man replied, "It keeps the tigers away."

"Why," scoffed his friend, "there are no tigers in New York."

"Yes," the man replied. "Effective, isn't it?"

The most radical maneuver of the mind in dealing with

anxiety is the **dissociation of one part of the personality from the other.** In amnesia (which is relatively common during adolescence), when the anxiety level is too high, the person "forgets" everything or at least as much as is necessary. A much more rare occurrence is for the personality to become "split." When anxiety becomes extreme, rather than blanking out all memory, a different personality comes to the fore. The book *Sybil* and the movie *The Three Faces of Eve* are popular descriptions of this sort of defense.

Treatment

What must first be stressed and repeated is the fact that everyone experiences some anxiety and that feelings of uneasiness are not only *not* abnormal, but can be useful signals of danger or spurs to accomplishment. What separates "abnormal" anxiety from "normal" anxiety is its intensity and frequency. When an adolescent's anxiety is so strong as to disrupt school and social activities or it occurs frequently without any understandable basis, help is called for.

The adolescent usually first tries self-help. This may include trying to think positive thoughts or at least not think such "bad" ones, becoming more religious, taking up a structured plan of physical exercise, becoming reclusive, beginning or stopping to smoke tobacco or marijuana, experimenting with street drugs, or going on a diet or an eating binge.

If attempts at self-help don't work or cause still more problems, or if parents and others become concerned about the adolescent's discomfort or behavior, there are several ways to handle the situation. Since this book is written by physicians, we will begin with the medical approaches, although many adolescents and their families will want to begin elsewhere. A decision on treatment should be based on what is available and from whom the adolescent can most easily accept help. The family physician, pediatrician, internist, and medical clinic represent one set of choices. All physicians have some training and much experience in dealing with people with anxiety. Physicians' tolerance for such patients varies, however, and either a version of the statement "You're physically fine so don't worry" or the hasty prescription of a tranquilizer should be the tip-off to look elsewhere for relief. Within the medical profession, this means psychiatry. Since mental illness bothers people even more than medical illness does, psychiatry has long been the butt of jokes. Jokes, however, are a way of contending with anything in society that makes us uneasy. It is also true that psychiatry has occasionally come up with some rather strange theories, and some rather strange people have occasionally become psychiatrists. Actually, psychiatry is a very broad field, and psychiatrists are not at all the same in terms of therapeutic approach, personality, or area of interest. It is certainly not true that only crazy people go to psychiatrists. By far the majority of people who see psychiatrists are not then nor ever will be considered crazy. They are people who are troubled about their lives or worried about what is happening to them, and seek relief. Many adolescents fall into this category, and when their difficulties are acute enough, talking with a psychiatrist is an obvious, realistic, and sensible answer. For most adolescents, personality compatibility is very important, so it may be a good idea to have initial interviews with several psychiatrists before settling on one. The psychiatrist should want to find out in some detail what the symptoms are, what the background has been, and what the adolescent believes might be the problem. The parents may or may not be involved, depending on the style of the therapist. Some psychiatrists will emphasize the conflicts in the mind that are the root of the anxiety, some will concentrate on interpersonal factors, some will use relaxation and other behavior modification techniques, and still others will combine medication with one or more of the above. An interested nonpsychiatrist physician may also use some or all of the above approaches.

Cities of even moderate size now have clinical psychologists and psychiatric social workers who work either in clinics or private practice and can, except for the prescribing of drugs, provide counseling of a wide variety of types. Some states license psychotherapists, so adolescents and parents can be assured that at least minimum standards have been met.

The clergy have long been turned to in times of emotional need and especially when religious guilt is prominent in causing the adolescent's anxiety. Counsel with a rabbi, priest, or minister may be useful either in itself or in preparing the way for a mental health referral.

Some adolescents prefer to consult with practitioners of transcendental meditation and other forms of spiritual relaxation. As with the other approaches, this technique works best when the adolescent has confidence in the helping person.

Finally, a note of caution: whenever one person seeks help from another, there is the potential for the latter to take psychological or sexual advantage of the former. Adolescents are especially vulnerable because of their wish to be taken care of, their impressionability, and their youthful sexuality. Besides knowing the reputation of the therapist, a good rule of thumb in this regard is that the person who has the most to lose is going to be the least tempted to lose it. While one can report a priest or sue a physician, there is usually very little redress one can obtain from an unlicensed "counselor." These issues are discussed more thoroughly in the section on psychotherapy (see p. 293).

Depression

As with anxiety, many adolescents are sad at one time or another, but it is usually short-lived. In general, adolescents speak of sadness and depression as being synonymous. From a medical point of view, however, depression may be defined as sadness plus pessimism. In other words, it is one thing to feel sad or "blue," but depressed persons believe the sadness will be with them always.

It should be kept in mind that it is the *domination* of the individual by the depressive feelings rather than the occurrence of the feelings that is pathological in depression. Mood swings are expected and usual in adolescence.

For a long time it was believed that depression did not occur prior to adolescence. It is true that younger children usually do not appear depressed in the same way that adolescents and adults do, but it is now generally agreed that depression can take place prior to adolescence. In such young patients, however, depression is often "masked" by hyperactivity or school learning problems. In adolescence, the symptoms of depression are similar to those seen in adults and commonly include social withdrawal, crying, sleep and eating problems, feelings of guilt, dejection, helplessness, hopelessness, and/or worthlessness. Bodily complaints and lack of sexual interest or concern are also frequently present. Depression may be masked in adolescence by delinquency or promiscuity. The latter is the result not of a desire for sexual excitement so much as for a feeling that someone cares. Both the delinquency and promiscuity are often compulsive and give little enjoyment. More often than not these forms of behavior cause shame and guilt that deepen the depression.

Depression is not a single disorder but represents a group of symptoms that vary in emphasis in different depressed adolescents. The cause of the onset of a depression is also variable. As is true for many emotional disorders, there seems to be an interaction between a person's biological susceptibility and all the other circumstances, conditions, and events that affect his or her psychological state. Since the latter are much easier to pinpoint than the former, more investigation over the years has gone into the psychological determinants of depression. During the past decade, however, an enormous amount of research has focused on changes in the balance of chemicals in the brain that seem to influence the progress of depression, as well as recovery from it. How much and how often the adolescent's experiences affect the brain chemistry and how much and how often disturbed brain chemistry brings on depression are still unknown.

Psychological factors

With their prolonged state of dependency, humans are highly vulnerable to the effects of separation and subsequent feelings of helplessness. The symptoms of depression have long been noted to be similar to those of mourning, and investigations have shown that frequently (although not universally) a loss of some sort occurs shortly before an adolescent becomes depressed. Adolescence, of course, is a time of a great many losses. There are the losses of childhood dependency, of sexual innocence, of a relative freedom from responsibility.

There may also be feelings of loss of self-esteem, and this is a very personal loss. Although it is not always clear why one adolescent feels humiliated by a thought or action that will cause no such self-devaluation in most others, at least in part the basis of self-esteem is determined by how the adolescent was treated and valued as a child. It is difficult to value oneself when one has not been valued. This pertains especially to past and present parental values and expectations. While many adolescent depressions are not due to parental actions, some are. Most parents encourage their children through positive reinforcement of good behavior, but others use mainly shame and punishment. When a child has been led to feel worthless, he or she may feel less able to be worthwhile. In short, negative parental expectations may become self-fulfilling prophecies.

Studies have shown that anger is a very important emotion in depression. This is usually either unexpressed anger at others or anger at oneself. For adolescents who had previously obeyed their parents chiefly out of fear and awe, past anger may come to the surface now that they have grown older and larger. Depressions in adolescents treated badly by their parents may be compounded by hostility toward the parents that has been building up in the teenagers. Adolescents may, however, harbor anger at even the best of parents. It is during adolescence that the normal childhood idealization of parents first decreases, and the resulting disillusionment and disappointment may trigger feelings of anger. Another type of anger at parents that sometimes makes depression worse is anger directed by adolescents toward those parts of their own personality that they associate with their parents. The realization by an adolescent that he or she is acting "just like my mother" or "just like my father" can sometimes be very depressing.

Some parents want to keep their adolescents dependent, and this can lead to depression. Even when these adolescents agree with their parents, a conflict cannot be avoided, because societal pressures to grow up and out of the family are ubiquitous. Since these teenagers are usually *overvalued* by their parents and during their whole lives have been spared comparison with their peers, exposure to job or college competition can be eye-opening in a demoralizing way that reinforces their wish to stay at home and be dependent. It might be said that the great futures of these adolescents lie behind them.

Depression routinely leads to a number of behavioral problems that can usually be recognized by parents. Body concerns are common, since if the adolescent feels worthless, he or she may also assume that the body is worthless. Eating may be increased or decreased, and sleep patterns are often disrupted. Depressed persons may be slowed down and unable to be active either mentally or physically. Withdrawal is frequent, since social interactions seem too demanding. Friends may therefore be dropped, with the adolescent becoming increasingly a loner.

How other people interact with the depressed adolescent is very important. First, with depression there is usually a desire to be taken care of. By stressing how bad they are and feel, depressed adolescents can often conjure up contrary opinions from persons around them. They may, for example, be told that everything is going to be all right or (more importantly) that *they* are all right. Such reassurance may suffice to lift a depressed adolescent's spirits and terminate a depressive episode. Most people, however, have a definite tolerance limit beyond which they can no longer respond sympathetically to complaining. When this limit is reached, parents, friends, teachers, and others will either avoid the depressed person or begin agreeing with the adolescent's self-condemnations. While in the movies a slap in the face or the admonition to "stop acting like a baby and pull yourself together" almost always does the trick, such shock treatment seldom works in real life and usually causes the depression to deepen.

A second common psychological interaction between the depressed adolescent and those around him or her involves attributing the expressions of self-condemnation to others. Through this psychological trick the adolescent may put off on others his or her own self-contempt. Then "I am no good; I hate myself" can be changed to "I hate them because they hold me in contempt." Such mental gymnastics can at times provide sufficient righteous indignation to relieve the depression. The danger, of course, is that others will be driven away or that the depressed adolescent will slide into increased resignation rather than rising in anger. In either case the depression is usually deepened.

A third psychological reaction to depression that is seen in some adolescents is a kind of grandiosity. Under the thin guise of humility are notions such as "Nobody is as bad as I am" or "Nobody has ever had worse parents than I have." As with the other approaches, if this one is pushed too far, it has the unfortunate tendency to exasperate and drive off potential comforters.

Physiological factors

It should be stressed again that although for convenience the psychological and physiological factors contributing to depression are discussed separately, clinical experience has shown clearly that such a split proves oversimplified when applied in life. This is true for all of the common psychiatric illnesses. There may be hereditary or physical factors that predispose an adolescent to depression, but very often there is also an environmental "trigger." With a strong biological predisposition, the environmental trigger may need to be small indeed.

Certain illnesses, such as hepatitis, infectious mononucleosis, and some strains of influenza, typically increase the likelihood that the patient will feel depressed. The use of some medications, such as barbiturates, can cause an increased incidence of depression, while depression is a common occurrence upon withdrawal of other drugs, such as amphetamines. Alcohol use is frequently associated with depression, and the drinking and depression may make each other worse.

Depression also has a tendency to run in families. Although in part this may be due to a learned behavior pattern, it also seems likely that a tendency toward depression can be inherited.

There has recently been a great deal of research on changes in brain chemistry that occur during depression. How much the changes are secondary to the depression is still quite controversial. The most favored physiological theory at this time suggests that depressed persons' brains have a deficit of certain neurotransmitter chemicals (substances that carry nerve impulses). Medications that increase the amounts of these particular neurotransmitters tend to brighten the mood of depressed people, while drugs that deplete the supply of neurotransmitters may slow people down and cause depression. This theory is strengthened by the fact that often persons who exhibit manic behavior (see next section) have higher than normal levels of these same brain neurotransmitters, and these levels are returned to normal by medication that corrects manic behavior.

Although much is still to be learned about the physical causes of depression, what is already known has been very useful in developing a wide variety of drugs that are effective in depression and are described in the section on treatment (p. 259).

Manic-depression

Manic-depressive illness is a malady that is to some extent inherited. This disorder occasionally begins in adolescence and consists of episodes of both mania and depression. These episodes may alternate or be chiefly of one type or the other. Episodes may be short-lived or may last for months, and episodes may follow each other closely or be separated by many years.

In terms of behavior, mania is close to being the opposite of depression. The adolescent in a manic episode is elated, self-assured, and full of energy. Speech comes rapidly; so do ideas. The upbeat excitement is at first infectious. Brief contact with a manic person is stimulating, but longer contact becomes wearing, and closer scrutiny of the person reveals a short attention span, easy distractibility, and an impatience with those who do not agree with the schemes or laugh at the jokes. As with other emotional disorders, mania exists in many degrees. For some, the symptoms are very mild and difficult to distinguish, except for their episodic nature, from the regular behavior of a healthy adolescent with an exuberant personality. At the other end of the spectrum, mania can be severe enough to exhaust the person completely.

The depressive aspect of manic-depressive illness is no different from the description of depression just given above. But with this malady it occurs in combination with episodes of manic behavior.

It has recently been found that a compound called **lithium carbonate** is quite effective in the treatment of manic-depressive disorders. Antidepressant medication, which will be described in more detail below (p. 262), and various types of psychotherapy are also often used, but nowadays usually in conjunction with lithium.

Suicide

Although not every adolescent who attempts suicide is depressed, the two often go together. Suicide attempts are rare prior to adolescence and become more common as the teen years progress. For example, there are ten times as many suicide attempts in adolescents in the 15- to 19-year-old age range as there are among those 10 to 14 years old. It may be that for various reasons younger adolescents run away when faced with the types of pressures that cause older adolescents to hurt themselves. Runaways seem to feel that they can find a better life if they can get away from home. Suicidal older teenagers, perhaps because the option of leaving home is more available or because their greater maturity suggests that you can seldom really run away from unhappiness, are more prone to believe that death is the only way out of their problems. Surveys show that many, if not most, adolescents in their late teens have already contemplated suicide at least briefly at one time or another. Such brief thoughts are not in themselves evidence of emotional illness. What is pathological is the persistence of such thoughts or the adolescent's belief that the urges cannot be resisted.

The suicide rate has risen sharply during recent decades. For example, the suicide rate for young people increased by 70 percent from 1960 to 1970, while the suicide rate for the general population decreased. Three times as many girls as boys *attempt* suicide in adolescence, while three times as many boys as girls succeed. There is evidence, however, that teenage girls' attempts are becoming more successful. It must be noted that it is always difficult to gather accurate statistics on suicide, because it is such a taboo topic. There are states that still have laws against attempting suicide, although almost no one is ever prosecuted, and it is difficult to imagine the punishment if the act has been successful.

The usual expression—that a person "threatened" suicide—is well chosen. Most of us consider the maintenance and preservation of meaningful life to be a primary goal of people both individually and collectively as a society. To be told by someone that we have failed so badly that he or she would rather be dead is a tremendous insult and rebuff. Guilt and a sense of failure are inevitable if the person is a relative or friend. When one's own child makes such a statement, it is often taken as an attack on oneself, no matter how sincere the communication or dangerous the situation. It is difficult to imagine a feeling of greater parental failure than being told by one's adolescent that he or she has been so poorly raised and is so unprepared to carry on that the only answer is to cancel out the life you have given. Following the initial shock, anger is a common reaction. Unfortunately, parental anger is often the reaction most likely to promote the adolescent's wish to commit suicide.

In adolescence, suicidal behavior is usually impulsive and not based on a true wish to die. The biggest discrepancy between the number of suicide attempts and the number of successes occurs during adolescence. In other words, more people at this age than at any other try suicide but fail. Since adolescence is a time of impulsiveness, this statistic should not be surprising. Suicide may be attempted out of spite, to punish the self, to turn aggression on the self, to search for peace, or to achieve reunification with a loved one. Very often suicide is a response to feeling uncared for. A suicide *threat* is also a cry for help. Suicidal behavior in adolescence frequently follows a quarrel with a parent or loved peer, and the teenager wants the person to reconsider. It is sometimes said that a person who talks about suicide will not carry it out. This is simply not true. Although suicidal behavior is a call for help, a suicide may well take place if the help is not forthcoming.

Unfortunately, many adolescents commit suicide by mistake. A surprisingly large number of teenagers do not fully comprehend the finality of death and mistakenly believe they will somehow be able both to commit suicide and to be around to see how repentant and sad are those they hold responsible for their death. In our own experience we have repeatedly encountered suicidal teenagers who are surprised to be reminded that if their suicides are successful, they will not be around to gloat over the guilt thus laid on the mourning boyfriend, girlfriend, or parent who wronged them. When death occurs under such a delusion, it can rightfully be described as a mistake. A second cause of mistaken deaths by suicide is miscalculation. Although most adolescents who exhibit suicidal behavior do not want to die, sometimes they are not knowledgeable and sophisticated enough to make the gesture believable enough to be taken seriously but not serious enough to succeed. Stepping over the line here is literally fatal. This is especially likely when the attempt is impulsive. As has been noted elsewhere in this book, adolescents often have a faulty sense of the future and a strong sense of omnipotence. Not always knowing which actions can prove fatal, some adolescents die by either underestimating the lethality of their action or overestimating their own powers of immortality.

Some experts in adolescent behavior believe that two recent changes in the American culture have contributed to the rapid rise in adolescent suicides. One is the increase in drug abuse. Most drugs that are abused can interfere with clear thinking as well as enhance depression either during use or withdrawal. Many adolescent suicides, for example, take place in teenagers who abuse alcohol. Other drugs, especially those introduced directly into the bloodstream, can be used by overdose as a means of committing suicide. Since alcoholic and drug-addicted adolescents are especially vulnerable to suicide, the recent increase in these problems may well have swelled the numbers of teenage suicides. The second cultural change that may be associated with the increase in suicides is the rise in the divorce rate. Most studies show that one-half to two-thirds of adolescent suicides come from homes where parents are divorced or separated. The impact of this increase in family breakdown and parental loss can be modified if the couple strives to give the adolescent the opportunity to have enjoyable contact with both parents.

It is important to know what signs to look for in adolescents who are in the high-risk category for suicide. The signs already listed for depression (see p. 249) are important danger signals here too. Although many adolescent suicide actions are impulsive and follow a quarrel or disappointment, the more serious attempts occur in teenagers who are depressed. In fact, the outlook is most grim when no obvious circumstantial reason for the attempt can be found. Some adolescents give warning by asking about, talking about, or becoming preoccupied with the subject of suicide. Such interest may be accompanied by withdrawal, a loss of interest in events generally, or a drop in school performance. A sudden involvement in drugs or alcohol has already been mentioned. An especially worrisome sign is when adolescents give away prized possessions or talk of joining those who have died or of being dead where it is quiet and peaceful. Although a suicide note may be left, it is generally unusual for adolescents to do so.

If a parent suspects that a teenager may be contemplating suicide, it is important to confront the possibility directly. As already noted, it is common for adolescents to have such thoughts, at least fleetingly, so there is little danger that you will be suggesting something that hasn't already come up. Although the question should be direct, it should not be done angrily or in a confrontational style. Recognition of the fact that the adolescent has seemed worried or unhappy and expression of the parent's concern are good first steps. Sometimes the adolescent will respond spontaneously that he or she has thought of suicide. If not, the parent may wish to ask directly whether the adolescent has wondered whether or not life is worth living.

Suicidal adolescents are usually ambivalent. Only very rarely are teenagers 100 percent sure that what they really want to do is die. When there is any real suspicion that an adolescent may be suicidal, it is important to obtain professional assistance. If in doubt, it is essential to err on the safe side. A family physician, a pediatrician, a local mental health clinic, or a hospital emergency room can provide a thorough evaluation. Occasionally an adolescent will refuse such an evaluation, but all states have laws that allow compulsory evaluation if an individual is a threat to himself or others. Reluctant adolescents usually want to be stopped, but are testing parents or other adults to see how much they are cared for. As with the younger runaways, suicidal adolescents often believe, correctly or not, that their parents do not want them and that they should get out of the parents' lives. In most cases, if it is made clear to the reluctant adolescent that, if she or he does not obtain an evaluation voluntarily, the police will be called to provide escort service to the hospital, the adolescent will concede. Although parents are sometimes reluctant to force a possibly suicidal teenager to obtain an evaluation for fear that the force will be resented, it is much more likely that the adolescent will resent it more if the parents avoid any action. The adolescent is relieved to know that parents and others care enough to take a stand in favor of their child's life. This is most true when the "force" is expressed with a helpful rather than a punitive attitude.

Since adolescents' suicidal behavior is more frequently a wish to communicate feelings of unhappiness or hopelessness than a wish to die, establishment or reestablishment of meaningful adolescent-parent communication is often the most important goal of treatment. If this is going to work, it requires effort from both parties. The use of the threat of murdering oneself to win an argument is never successful in the long term, and the illusion that it is tends to encourage the adolescent to turn again to such behavior in the future.

Treatment of depression

A number of psychotherapies (discussed in more detail on p. 293) have been helpful in the treatment of depression. The choice of which one to use depends on the life situation of the adolescent and the special skills of the therapist being seen. If the adolescent and/or parents have a preference as to type of treatment, they should seek out a therapist who offers this approach.

Individual psychotherapy usually emphasizes the unconscious conflicts experienced by the adolescent and how these interact with outside influences. The therapist may see the parents occasionally with the adolescent, or the parents may be counseled separately by the same or another therapist. A major premise in individual psychotherapy is that since a major task of the adolescent is to become a separate, independent adult, the adolescents are helped most by learning to make decisions for themselves.

A second popular type of psychotherapy for depression is **family therapy.** Although members of the family may occasionally be seen individually, the main concern of the therapy is that the offspring's problems are a reflection of the way the family works—or fails to work—and the most thorough treatment for these problems is to correct family interactions. Since the adolescent is still living in the family milieu, family therapists believe that the adolescent's individual change will not survive unless it is accompanied by change in other family members.

The third major approach to psychotherapy for depressed adolescents is **group therapy.** In this method a number of adolescents are seen together with a professional leader. All the patients may be depressed or the group may include members having a variety of problems. A major premise of this approach is that the adolescent does not live in a vacuum and is increasingly moving beyond the world of his or her family. The idea is that feedback from peers in a controlled setting presents depressed adolescents with an opportunity to see that their pessimistic views of themselves are in fact not shared by others. The group process is used not only for insights but also for support and the opportunity to test thoughts and feelings for validations by others.

Good and bad results can be obtained by these various approaches to psychotherapy. Most important in making a decision are the reputation of the particular therapist or clinic and which therapeutic approach seems most comfortable to the adolescent.

In addition to psychotherapy, medication may be used in treating adolescent depressions. During the past two decades, a number of drugs have been found to be helpful in some types of adolescent depression. These drugs are, however, very potent, and side effects and danger from overdosage are great. The two types of drugs most commonly prescribed for depression can be lethal when taken in excess. This, of course, is a real problem when treating a disorder that may be manifested by feelings of hopelessness and a desire to commit suicide. There is the additional need with some **antidepressant drugs** to monitor the adolescent's diet and other medications or drugs carefully, since the mix of the antidepressant and these other compounds can lead to toxic and sometimes lethal side reactions.

Since it often takes three to four weeks of administration of the group of drugs that are the most useful before they begin working fully, it is important that the adolescent be either hospitalized or closely followed during this relatively long lag period. Drug treatment alone, however, should never be considered the best treatment for a person suffering from an emotional disorder. Emotional support, environmental change, and/or counseling should be routinely offered along with the drugs.

Electric convulsive therapy (E.C.T.)—colloquially called shock therapy—is sometimes used in the treatment of depressions that respond to nothing else. Little is known about why applying electricity to a depressed person's brain and causing a convulsion should be so effective in treating depression, but it is. Although the procedure does not hurt, because it seems so barbaric and because no one really knows why it works make it a last-resort procedure. At this point, the misuse of E.C.T. dramatized in the film *One Flew Over the Cuckoo's Nest* notwithstanding, the patient will suffer much, much less from a series of E.C.T. than from the excruciating pain of intractable depression. Fortunately, E.C.T. is rarely needed by adolescents with depression.

The drug lithium carbonate has already been mentioned in conjunction with the treatment of adolescents who suffer from episodes of mania, which may or may not be associated with periods of depression. In these cases, lithium along with other supportive treatment is often helpful. Lithium is occasionally used to treat adolescents who do not have periods of mania but only depressive symptoms, although in these so-called "unipolar" depressions, antidepressant medications are much more likely to be effective.

Finally, it is always wise not to put chemicals in one's body if one can avoid it. To repeat an important point made earlier, it is the *domination* of the adolescent by the depressive feeling rather than the *occurrence* of the feeling that constitutes illness. Mood swings are usual in adolescence. Most periods of sadness pass with time, many others can be helped through psychotherapy, and only a minority of adolescents will suffer depressions severe enough to require prescribed medication.

Psychosis

Psychosis is a medical term referring to the most serious group of mental illnesses. It is difficult to define the term exactly, but what is generally meant is that the person affected has lost contact with reality. In other words, psychotic individuals cannot accurately separate perceptions originating in their own minds from perceptions originating in the outside world. We all, of course, process through our minds what we see, hear, touch, taste, and smell. Even for the same individual the ability to test reality fluctuates with stress, fatigue, or strong emotions. We have all noted, for example, that love may at times be "blind" or that a mother's kiss can, as if by magic, assuage the pain of a child's bruise or cut.

For the person who is psychotic, internal needs and perceptions to a large extent replace what is experienced as reality by other people. Although no single symptom can be taken as absolutely confirming the diagnosis of psychosis, the increased quantity and the bizarre quality of the person's misperceptions are usually the key.

It is in the area of relationships that another important symptomatic change occurs. Characteristically in psychosis, there is a progressive decline in the quality of relationships, and there are fewer and fewer contacts with other people. Although many adolescents like to spend time alone in their rooms, a psychotic adolescent may refuse to come out at all, or to leave the house. Friendships and even casual relationships may be allowed to lapse.

Another common aspect of psychosis that interferes with relationships is that the adolescent's communication may be difficult to understand or be entirely elusive. While it is not unusual for adults to have difficulty at times in following the average adolescent's speech, the psychotic's speech is incomprehensible for peer and adult alike. Because the psychotic's version of reality is to such a large degree determined internally and idiosyncratically, he or she may participate in a conversation or a situation in an extremely personal and peculiar way. For example, although a psychotic's language is symbolic of internal pressures or insights, this symbolism is often impossible for anyone other than the psychotic person to comprehend. It is this bizarreness that signals to a stranger or even a rather young child that the psychotic adolescent is "strange" or "weird." In short, the psychotic adolescent is on a different wavelength from everyone else. Normal people may also exhibit peculiar behavior occasionally (most people in fact do), but because they maintain the knowledge of what is expected by society and convention, nonpsychotic persons tend to keep their strangeness pretty much to themselves.

Nonverbal communication of psychotic thinking may occur in the forms of strange movements, sounds, facial grimaces, or extremes in activity or inactivity.

Delusions are another common symptom of psychosis. Delusions are false ideas that cannot be corrected by reasoning and that are not generally held in the culture. Common delusions are of imagined enemies or of exaggerated self-importance. It sometimes is not entirely clear what is a delusion and what is not. Social acceptance plays a role. For example, if you can get enough people to believe in your belief, odd as it may be, it is no longer considered delusional and may even help you begin a political movement or become the leader of a religious sect. The psychiatric principle seems to be if you are going to talk about a strange belief, make sure you are not alone in holding it.

Still another common symptom in psychosis is **hallucinations**. A hallucination is a sensory experience or perception that is not the result of a stimulus outside oneself. Hallucinations may be of smell, touch, or taste, but much more commonly are of sight or sound. Visual hallucinations, or visions, are quite common, especially when the psychosis results from temporary or permanent brain damage. The most frequent type of hallucination, however, is auditory. The person hears voices that are not in fact there. The voice may be of God, the devil, or less grand personages. Often the voices are heard talking about the adolescent in the third person, and the things said are often unflattering or may be in the form of commands.

Although psychosis may be the result of temporary or permanent brain damage arising from injury, drugs, alcohol, syphilis, metabolic imbalance, and a myriad of other agents and conditions, its most common and baffling form is the group of disorders known as schizophrenia. A psychosis of the former type is best treated by correcting—or attempting to correct—the brain damage. Schizophrenia, because it has no obvious cause, is far more difficult to deal with.

What is schizophrenia?

As has already been noted, psychosis is diagnosed on the basis of disorders of thinking and behavior. By more or less worldwide mutual agreement, when the symptoms described in the preceding section occur without anything having caused demonstrable damage to the brain, the person is diagnosed as having schizophrenia. Written records of such individuals date back to 1400 B.C. Although some writers insist that mental illness is a myth or that schizophrenia is only a label pinned by a culture on those deviant from its particular norms, this does not really seem to be the case. Studies made of a variety of industrial and primitive societies indicate that all have a small subpopulation believed to be "crazy"; each has a special term used to refer to them. People who exhibit delusions, hallucinations, or irrational fears or suspicions fall into this group and are separated by the culture from those who act crazy in a controlled way (such as witch doctors) and from those who are purely troublemakers trying through deviousness or violence to get what they do not deserve.

Historically in western culture, what we now call schizophrenia was often associated with religion. Countless adolescent schizophrenics were judged to be witches or possessed by the devil. They were usually dealt with in cruel ways. Insanity has also long been considered a punishment for wrongdoing or wrong-thinking. Until recently, for example, it was common to warn adolescents that masturbation led to insanity.

Not until the end of the last century were the various common symptoms of insanity or "lunacy" put together as a single entity, called *dementia praecox,* a Latin term meaning literally a mental deterioration occurring in youth. The term schizophrenia, meaning "split mind," replaced dementia praecox early in the present century. This new term was an outgrowth of the discovery that the disorder did not necessarily lead to mental deterioration and did not begin only in adolescence. It is still true today, however, that schizophrenia is most often first diagnosed in persons between the ages of 15 and 24, at least in the case of males.

Background   Studies have shown that the percentage of persons who can be diagnosed as schizophrenic is quite constant throughout various cultures around the world. In the United States about one person out of one hundred will sometime in his or her lifetime be hospitalized for schizophrenia. Nonwhites and poorer people are more likely in this country to be diagnosed as schizophrenic than are whites and those better off financially. This does not necessarily mean that nonwhites are really more susceptible, but may reflect a tendency to diagnose nonwhites as schizophrenic more readily than whites. So far as economic standing is concerned, there is some evidence that parents of schizophrenics are distributed across the social spectrum, but that because of their disorder, offspring who are diagnosed as schizophrenic "drift" to a lower financial state.

Although most researchers agree that there is no single "cause" of schizophrenia, there is strong evidence that at least the tendency to become schizophrenic is inherited. Compared, for example, to the one percent occurrence in the general population, the statistical expectation is 12 percent for the children of one schizophrenic parent and 35 to 44 percent for the children of both schizophrenic parents. Geneticists believe that about 40 percent of all cases of schizophrenia are clearly attributable to genetic factors. Since even in identical twins schizophrenia may be present in one and not the other, it seems most accurate to think of the *vulnerability* for schizophrenia as being what is inherited. For those inheriting a great vulnerability, even less than average environmental stress can cause the disorder. For those with little or no genetic vulnerability, much greater than average environmental pressures are required to produce the condition. A way to illustrate this concept is to use the example of sensory deprivation or the abuse of hallucinogenic drugs. Every adolescent, or adult for that matter, can be made psychotic if kept long enough under certain sensory deprivation conditions or if given enough LSD. Although everyone will eventually succumb to these techniques, the amount required to cause a psychosis will vary greatly. Some will "go crazy" at just the thought of the experiment, and others will first withstand long periods of deprivation or large doses of the drug.

Many researchers have tried to determine whether certain types of children or certain styles of parenting are more likely than others to be associated with schizophrenia during adolescence or later life. Although there are many theories, all of which have advocates, it seems truthful to say that no specific conclusions can be drawn. In the childhoods of some schizophrenics it has been found that family communication was confusing or misleading, or that the child was abused, or that the child was belittled or ridiculed. While some children with healthy constitutions may be able to survive such unfortunate childhoods relatively intact, a child vulnerable to schizophrenia will be devastated.

A further confusion in attempting to sort out a link between parenting and schizophrenia is the fact that schizophrenic offspring are frequently very difficult to deal with. In such cases it is often impossible to tell whether the parents' childrearing approach is the cause of the condition or only a frustrated response to it.

Researchers studying the brain chemistry of schizophrenic adolescents have discovered that many seem to be overinfluenced by a neurotransmitter chemical called **dopamine.** Other drugs, amphetamines or "speed," for example, cause dopamine hyperfunction and at high dosages can cause an emotional state that is very much like schizophrenia. Another finding that suggests that dopamine may be an important factor in schizophrenia is that the drugs used successfully to treat the disorder block the action of dopamine. Much research is still necessary to pinpoint a neurochemical "cause" of schizophrenia, but it is truly humbling to realize that such a profound change in behavior and thinking can occur with such a bafflingly small change in measurable brain function.

Outlook Schizophrenia is a serious disorder. The younger the adolescent is when he or she becomes sick the less likely it is that there will be complete recovery. There are, however, a number of other factors that, if they are present, indicate a better outlook. A sudden onset suggests a more favorable course than a more gradual beginning. A past history of good social adjustment at home and school is a hopeful sign for relatively good recovery. If there is a precipitating event, such as an emotional shock or an illness, the outlook is better than if the disorder seems to develop for no reason. In general, schizophrenic adolescents whose symptoms include a depressive and/or elated element do better than patients without. Finally, beyond any genetic factor, the family plays an extremely important role in the outlook for the adolescent. If the family is supportive and willing to follow good professional advice, to look after the patient as much as possible, and to help make sure that he or she takes prescribed medication, the prospects are improved. This last point—medication—is especially important; in recent years, conscientiousness in following prescribed drug maintenance therapy has become an increasingly important part of the treatment of schizophrenia.

A schizophrenic patient's chances of being "cured" or substantially helped are at least four times better today than they were at the beginning of the century. Although hospitalization may be required for full evaluation and initial treatment, this is not always necessary. Medication and outpatient psychotherapy may prove sufficient to modify the patient's symptoms successfully. Even though this disorder has the most grave outlook of all the psychiatric problems of adolescence, lifelong hospitalization, which was once common, is now rare. Good follow-up care, outpatient treatment, and well-controlled maintenance drug therapy reduce relapse rates to about one-quarter of what they are when the adolescent refuses or forgets to follow his or her treatment plan. Although relapses may occur even with close follow-up, such relapses tend to be less frequent and less severe.

The abuse of drugs by those vulnerable to schizophrenia is particularly dangerous. The so-called mind-expanding or hallucinogenic drugs may trigger a schizophrenic reaction in an adolescent who never had the disorder; they are likely to cause a relapse in those who have. Stimulants such as "speed" or depressants such as alcohol are also capable of bringing on a relapse. Although there is much debate about the possibility that marijuana is less dangerous than these other drugs, some careful research has shown that a schizophrenic patient who takes to regular marijuana use *does* increase the risk of relapse or of worsening an otherwise well-controlled illness. It is important that an adolescent with a history of this disorder use *no* drug without the approval of a physician who knows his or her psychiatric history.

Treatment Most adolescents who are diagnosed as having schizophrenia realize that something dreadfully strange is happening to their minds or their bodies, perhaps both. This realization is often coupled with shame or fear. One obvious response is to withdraw. While withdrawal may temporarily save the adolescent from having to recognize his or her "strangeness" so often, the tactic may also prevent early detection and treatment of the sickness.

The withdrawal that commonly accompanies the development of schizophrenia causes a dilemma for parents. When a family member acts obviously bizarre or "crazy," there is seldom any doubt about the fact that some action must be taken. When, however, the adolescent causes no special trouble, but merely withdraws from schoolwork, social contacts, or perhaps from communication in general, it is much more difficult for parents to know what to do. There is a great temptation to put off doing anything. Is the problem "only adolescence"? Will the adolescent "snap out of it"? Will questioning him or her only make matters worse? In addition, there is still unwarranted shame connected to emotional illness in the United States, and this fact keeps some parents from acknowledging and acting upon a situation they know is there, but cannot face.

When parents suspect that their adolescent might be having emotional problems, it is better to find out sooner than later. If the adolescent seems open to questions, that is the best first approach. Questions should be directed toward finding out whether there have been changes in the adolescent's thoughts and attitudes, what they have been, and whether any unexplainable phenomena have occurred. If the adolescent ignores or rebuffs questions, it can be useful to find out whether others have noticed a change in his or her behavior and, if so, whether these changes are similar to those you have observed.

If after inquiries a parent believes it is possible or likely that the adolescent is emotionally ill, a reasonable next step is to speak to the pediatrician or family doctor. A physician can not only help diagnose the problem but also can give advice about what community resources are available for evaluation and treatment. It may also make sense for the physician to see and talk with the adolescent. Parents sometimes prefer to deal with their own doctor before consulting a psychiatrist or mental health facility. In addition, the pediatrician or family doctor has the advantage of having known the adolescent over a period of time and may therefore be better able than a stranger to judge whether behavioral changes have taken place, and what they consist of. The physician may also be helpful in influencing a reluctant adolescent to seek psychological care or in aiding parents to obtain ambulance or police support if the adolescent requires attention but refuses to cooperate. The latter is not common, but occasionally does occur.

The treatment of schizophrenia usually consists of a combination of drugs, of counseling the adolescent and his family, and of aid in educational or vocational planning. It used to be thought that schizophrenia lowered a patient's intellectual ability, but this is now known to be untrue. Although while ill an adolescent may not be able to make as much practical use of his or her intellect, there is no evidence to support the idea of permanent impairment after recovery or when the schizophrenia is in remission.

Drug therapy is usually very helpful. Although side effects may prove bothersome, these can often be kept to a minimum. As noted for other emotional disturbances, drug therapy is not as effective alone as when it is combined with psychotherapy or case work. The latter usually includes parents and other family members.

Mental retardation

Intelligence is as intelligence does. Although most people think of mental retardation in terms of low I.Q., mental retardation is more accurately defined by whether or not there is failure to adapt to the environment because of a low level of intellectual functioning.

By this practical definition of mental retardation, many people stop being mentally retarded during their adolescence because less is demanded of them in purely intellectual terms. Thus, while it is estimated that 3 percent of the United States population have I.Q.s below seventy and are considered mentally retarded, the highest incidence of retardation is found in school-aged children. In late adolescence, when a person is beyond school age, about two-thirds of those who were earlier diagnosed as retarded find work, support themselves, and cease being called retarded.

Causes

Birth injuries, metabolic disorders, neurological disease, and brain injury are responsible for a relatively small proportion of mental retardation, but victims of these conditions are often the most severely limited both mentally and physically. There is no medical cause for the overwhelming majority of the mentally retarded. The diagnosis of mild mental retardation occurs more often for adolescents and children from the lower socioeconomic groups than it does for more privileged children. It is the former who, perhaps because their families and teachers lack interest or faith in their academic success, are called retarded while in school but who adjust adequately thereafter.

A question raised in regard to adolescents and retardation is whether retarded persons should have children. In terms of numbers, there are very few causes of retardation that can be inherited and in these rare cases the retarded persons and their parents should have the genetic risks explained to them. A physician can do it. Since the great majority of retarded persons of all levels of severity are born to parents who are not themselves classed as retarded, there would be little reduction in the frequency of retardation in this country even if all known retardates refrained from having children. Problems in the family's social and economic environment are the cause of the great bulk of mental retardation. There is, however, an increased likelihood of retardation in babies born to mothers both younger and older than the usual childbearing age, especially among those who fail to get adequate medical care during pregnancy.

Outcome

The majority of retarded adolescents can develop social and communication skills that in adulthood are not distinguishable from those of the rest of the population. The 87 percent of the mentally retarded who are in the borderline or mild categories can usually master academic skills at least at the sixth-grade level and can learn vocational skills adequate to support themselves, at least minimally.

The family's acceptance and support are crucial in regard to adjustment. When parents are willing and the retardation is not too severe, most families can absorb the retarded child without upsetting the equilibrium of the home or jeopardizing the well-being of other family members. Interestingly, studies show that this kind of positive family acceptance is more common in poorer families.

There are some severely retarded children who can be managed at home when they are relatively small but whose parents worry about what will happen after their pubertal spurt in growth and sexuality. Although the retarded are of normal size, a decrease in sexual drive usually accompanies the more severe degrees of retardation. While severely retarded adolescent girls are sometimes taken advantage of sexually and therefore require protection in this regard, severely retarded adolescent boys are *not* likely to be sexually active. Since institutionalization tends to make the retarded function at an even lower level, it is better for adolescents to be kept at home, if at all possible. Federal legislation now makes it mandatory for communities to provide educational and/or vocational services to the retarded; thus, the time spent at home need be only from evening to morning. Information regarding the services and facilities available for the mentally retarded in your area may be obtained from the national or local chapter of the National Association for the Help of Retarded Children or The American Association of Mental Deficiency. Halfway houses for the moderately retarded adolescent have been used extensively and successfully in Western Europe and are becoming more common in this country. When institutionalization is necessary, important contact between the adolescent and his or her family can be maintained by means of frequent visits and, when feasible, regular trips home.

Care and treatment

Often in the past there has been too great an emphasis placed on learning academic skills. With the retarded, this approach usually leads to discouragement. Hard work and great effort simply don't pay off. While academics should not be ignored, vocational and prevocational training are often both more possible and practical. The sooner and the more the retarded adolescent can be integrated into the community the better the long-range adjustment will be. It is particularly important to understand exactly in what areas the retarded adolescent can function normally, and to make a careful judgment of his or her assets. Employers, for example, should be aware that these young workers are often more careful, patient, and diligent with simple, repetitive tasks than are their more impulsive peers with higher intelligence.

Physical rehabilitation is necessary for some of the more

severely retarded. This group has an exceptionally high frequency of accompanying physical handicaps, but physical therapy can often do much to remove these added roadblocks.

Finally, a substantial number of retarded adolescents also have emotional difficulties. These stem not only from their basic disorder but from the increased stresses involved in trying to adjust to society's expectations and prejudices. The types of psychopathology found in retarded adolescents are no different from those found in nonretarded adolescents. Psychiatric techniques, including psychotherapy, behavior modification, and medication, can be helpful, and mental and emotional disorders should not be ignored or treatment refused because the adolescent is mentally retarded.

Smoking

Early adolescence is the time when a person who will become a smoker has that first cigarette. Although smoking gives adolescents something to do with their hands and thus reduces a feeling of awkwardness, the wish to act adult is probably the chief reason why adolescents take up the habit. In early adolescence the choice by far is cigarette smoking; cigar and pipe smoking are more likely to begin in late adolescence or early adulthood. Everyone is familiar with advertisements aimed at glorifying the image of what smokers are like: usually young, healthy, attractive, popular people who are always having great fun. For the adolescent who is trying to find out how to be that kind of an adult, smoking seems to offer an instant identity. Also, what starts out as curiosity may be encouraged by a wish to imitate peers. Smoking may appear to be "daring," with only the childish or cowardly unwilling to take the same chances as their friends, especially when the health hazard seems remote. Many teenagers also view adults' disapproval as inspired mainly by a selfish wish to keep the new generation uninitiated in adult delights. In this case cigarette smoking becomes a parent-child issue of rebellion rather than simply one of health.

In this country between 1965 and 1975, cigarette smoking in adults declined by almost 20 percent, while teenage smoking rose by almost 43 percent. This rise in adolescent smoking mostly represents girls beginning to smoke, and almost as many adolescent girls as boys now smoke. The slogan "You've Come a Long Way, Baby" seems to work. (It reminds us of Will Rogers's remark in the 1930s that "The time ain't far off when a woman won't know any more than a man.")

It must be stated as strongly as possible that the habit of inhaling smoke offers nothing but trouble. Smoking is the greatest public health hazard in this country, and is the nation's most preventable cause of death. More than 300 years ago King James I of England wrote that smoking is "a custome lothsome to the eye, hateful to the Nose, harmefull to the braine, dangerous to the Lungs, and the blacke stinking fume thereof, neerest resembling the horrible Stigian smoke of the pit that is bottomlesse." That is a good description for starters, but the true health danger of smoking did not become known until the 1950s. While both inhalers and noninhalers may offend those around them, inhalers jeopardize their own health more significantly. Smokers who do not inhale absorb 25 to 50 percent of the nicotine in the smoke, while with inhaling, 90 percent is absorbed. The most dangerous part of a cigarette is the last inch, since the toxic residues pile up behind the early portion as it burns.

Statisticians estimate that life is shortened by fourteen minutes for every cigarette smoked and inhaled. Cancer of the lung favors smokers eleven to one, and under the age of 65, smokers are two to three times as likely to die of heart disease as nonsmokers. A third common problem is "smokers' respiratory syndrome," an unattractive group of symptoms consisting of a cough, wheezing, and the spitting up of thick, yellow phlegm. The latter is most bothersome after awakening in the morning. Babies of pregnant adolescents who smoke tend to have lower birth weights, and the rate of miscarriages for smokers is almost double that of nonsmokers. Respiratory infections are also much more frequent during the first year for babies of smoking mothers.

Smoking not only damages health directly, but also increases the potential damage of other harmful agents in the environment. For example, people who live or work around radiation are not more likely to get lung cancer than those who don't as long as they do not smoke. Those who smoke *and* are exposed to radiation, however, are much more likely to die of lung cancer than smokers not exposed. The same additive effect is seen with heart disease. Smokers not only get heart disease more frequently than nonsmokers, but their disease is also likely to be more severe than that of those relatively few nonsmokers who develop heart disease.

Starting and stopping

Through smoking, **nicotine** is usually the first drug used regularly by adolescents. Nicotine is both a stimulant and a depressant, and since its actions are unpredictable and often contradictory, it has no practical use as a medical drug. Its only medical significance is its high toxicity. Nicotine, in short, is poisonous. Smoking causes both habituation and physical dependence. "Habituation" refers to a psychological need. The person needs to smoke because he or she is used to doing it. "Physical dependence" refers to the fact that the body becomes used to nicotine, and when the supply of nicotine stops, the body experiences a painful period of getting used to being without it. The combination of psychological and physical withdrawal symptoms makes smoking so difficult to give up.

By far the easiest way to stop smoking is never to start. The earlier in life one starts smoking the more damage is done to the body. In the mid 1970s the World Health Organization did an extensive survey of cigarette smoking by young people in Western Europe. The survey showed that after the age of 19 or 20 the proportion of smokers in a country does not increase.

In other words, if someone is going to start smoking at any time in life, that time is almost sure to be before age 20. In a similar survey in this country, 84 percent of the adolescents who smoked cigarettes realized that it was harmful to their health and almost half said they were going to stop in some unspecified time in the next five years. Unfortunately, most adolescents have a faulty concept of time, especially in terms of the future, and use this in the service of self-deception. Added to the all-too-human belief that "statistics don't mean me" is the adolescents' rationalization that smoking only harms health later in life and that there is plenty of time to quit. The facts, however, are that health damage begins immediately and that only one out of three persons who seriously tries to stop smoking is able to do so. Most people are like Mark Twain, who inhaled cigars, and who boasted that giving up smoking must be easy because he had done it so often. Indeed, the World Health Organization concluded after its survey that once an adolescent has become dependent on cigarettes, all subsequent antismoking efforts, facts, and propaganda are likely to fail.

Although cigarette ads have been removed from television and there are health warnings on cigarette packages, to date this country has been less vigorous than some others in publicizing the bodily dangers of smoking. To a certain degree it is because the United States is a large tobacco-growing country. This fact does not necessarily mean that tobacco interests are in favor of "hooking" teenagers and sending many of them to their deaths, but it can be said safely that the business people involved demonstrate little concern over the fact that kids continue to begin smoking and die prematurely as a result. Let the buyer beware! Presumably, like bombardiers in high-flying planes, advertising executives who do not see their victims maimed or killed can feel comfortable in the excuse that they are only doing their job.

There is no doubt that the most important influences on smoking arise before or during early adolescence. The strongest influences come from the home. Although most adolescents try cigarettes under the pressure of peer experimentation, the more powerful models are parents, brothers, and sisters. One out of four teenagers living in families that contain at least one other smoker will become a regular smoker, while fewer than one out of twenty teenagers from nonsmoking households will acquire the habit. Clearly, parents have an obligation not only to look after their own lives by not smoking cigarettes, but also to do so as a way to help preserve the health of their offspring.

Drinking

Except for tobacco, alcohol is society's most tolerated drug. It is without question the drug that causes the most misery, debilitation, and financial loss. Parents who would be shocked to learn that their teenager smokes marijuana often are relatively unconcerned about drinking. This common finding is probably due mostly to the fact that the parents use alcohol themselves and remember using it when they were adolescents.

In the United States, two-thirds of all adults use alcohol at least occasionally, and about 12 percent of those who drink can be classified as heavy users. In the mid 1970s, $30 billion, or 3 percent of the nation's total disposable income, was spent yearly on five billion gallons of alcoholic beverages. Over nine million people in this country are dependent on alcohol, and alcoholism is the fourth most common cause of death in the 35- to 55-year-old age range. It is estimated that the combined medical and social costs arising from alcohol use in this country exceed $15 billion annually. With inflation these amounts, of course, rise every year and do not include the huge amount and great variety of personal pain and anguish.

Teenagers and alcohol   Alcohol is usually the second drug, following smoking, which is used by adolescents. It is the most popular drug, however. More than twice as many teenagers drink than smoke cigarettes. Surveys show that about half of high school students go to drinking parties at least once a month, and over 60 percent of these students get drunk at least once a month. Alcohol is definitely more popular than marijuana, although multiple drug use is the rule rather than the exception with adolescents. Probably because they are so widely used by adults, most adolescents incorrectly believe that tobacco and alcohol are not "drugs." Indeed, alcohol, although the biggest offender, is sometimes omitted from drug education programs.

As with smoking cigarettes, family and peer influences are important in initiating drinking patterns. While many adults use alcohol as a tranquilizer, more often it is used as a social lubricant. This is also true with teenagers. Especially if one's parents drink, drinking represents adult behavior. Alcohol allows an adolescent to seem bravely unafraid, to be more socially open, and to have an excuse if social endeavors go wrong. It is probably impossible to overestimate for those who are unsure of themselves the value of having an excuse, other than themselves, to offer when things go wrong. Alcohol is the most universally available "outside-of-the-self" excuse that this society has to offer. Unfortunately, the use of alcohol rapidly progresses from "excuse for" to "cause of" life problems.

Alcohol causes problems for adolescents in two other areas, sex and aggression. There is no question that human beings are more sexually receptive when they are tipsy. Men, especially, have through the years taken advantage of this finding. Yet Shakespeare was correct in *Macbeth* when he wrote, "Alcohol provokes the desire but takes away the performance." Alcohol is the major cause of first-time impotence, and the tragedy is that alcohol-induced impotence can lead young men to worry so much about their virility that *chronic* impotence may follow.

The results are often worse when adolescent aggressive impulses are mixed with alcohol. Alcohol releases combativeness, and suicide attempts are much more likely to be successful when coupled with drunkenness. Accidents, the largest cause of death in adolescence, are greatly encouraged by alcohol. For example, automobile crashes are the most common cause of accidental teenage death, and in this country half of all those killed in alcohol-related automobile accidents are adolescents.

Prevention The factors here are the same for all types of drug abuse, and there is the danger that the reader will dismiss their importance because of the redundancy. It might be helpful to remember that one definition of a cliché is a truth that has become boring. Advice emphasizing the importance of prevention over treatment and the importance of parental modeling must be stressed repeatedly, if only because these two factors represent some of the few knowns in an area saturated with exaggerated and faulty claims.

Parents who are chronic drinkers or who rush for the bottle whenever they are under stress provide a pattern that is learned naturally by the children in the house. While some adolescents avoid alcohol because of the memory of overdrinking by a parent, identification is much more the rule.

It is also important for parents to discuss the use and abuse of alcohol with their children, even before the latter become adolescents. Parents who drink socially and moderately should not try to keep this fact a secret, but explain honestly why they drink, what safeguards they take not to drink too much, and what dangers are present. When children become 13, 14, or 15, it is wise to discuss the alcohol content in various beverages, such as beer, wine, whiskeys, and mixed drinks. Pamphlets that outline legal blood level definitions for drunken driving are available from the federal government and in many police stations. Almost all states use the National Safety Council and the American Medical Association recommendations. These define a blood alcohol determination of 100 milligrams (mg. percent) percent or more as constituting intoxication, while a level between 50 and 100 mg.

percent must be supported by other positive evidence in order to determine legal intoxication. Repeated studies have shown that the average drinker with a blood alcohol level above 100 mg. percent is six to seven times more likely to have an accident than the driver with no alcohol in the blood. Alcohol is responsible not only for driver-caused accidents but also for pedestrian-caused accidents. One study of 2,500 pedestrians killed on the highway showed that 30 percent of these people were under the influence of alcohol. Death from alcohol poisoning occurs in the blood level range of 250 to 500 mg. percent.

Although some facts about the potency of alcoholic beverages are indisputable, such as the fact that it is more intoxicating to drink rapidly and on an empty stomach than slowly and along with food, it is unfortunately less easy to say what quantity of alcohol can be safely drunk. The reason for this difficulty is that the individual person's weight, psychological state, usual level of consumption, rate of metabolism, and other factors all influence the degree of intoxication produced from the same amount of alcohol. Knowledge that one-half of a beverage's proof is equal to the percentage of alcohol it contains (for example, one-hundred proof whiskey contains 50 percent alcohol by volume) can be a help in determining what quantities of various beverages can be drunk to give similar degrees of intoxication. For example, for an average person on an empty stomach, four ounces (two drinks of a little over a jigger apiece) of whiskey, three martinis, or two and a half quarts of beer are all likely to give a blood level that is close to the 100 mg. percent mark that defines legal intoxication. Most adolescents metabolize alcohol at the rate of about an ounce of whiskey in an hour; thus, a rough calculation can be made to know when a person will probably become sober. A hangover, however, may linger longer.

While public educational programs for teenagers about alcohol are of some use, there are some other specific steps a community can take. One is the formation of Alateen, an offshoot of the Alcoholics Anonymous movement for the children of alcoholics. This organization can be very helpful in educating teenagers about the emotional and social pressures that go along with alcohol usage.

A second approach that has merit is to raise to 19 the age for the legal purchase of any alcohol. This step would be most useful in regard to decreasing traffic accidents. The rationale is that, compared to 18-year-olds, 19-year-olds are more likely to be out of high school and therefore not as available to buy alcohol for younger classmates who drive.

Treatment An adolescent should receive treatment when his or her drinking either cannot be controlled or when it has led to physical or psychological symptoms. While many treatment approaches exist, none is especially encouraging. Medications, including behavior modification techniques based on a drug that causes the adolescent to vomit when alcohol is consumed, are seldom appropriate. Traditional types of individual psychotherapy and family therapy have not been found to be especially useful either. Group therapy, perhaps combined with other approaches, seems to offer the greatest promise. Alcoholics Anonymous is an organization worth considering, especially if the local group is aware of— and prepared to deal with—the special problems of the adolescent and young adult. An important contribution of AA is that the emphasis is not solely on stopping drinking but also on the general issue of accepting responsibility for whatever one does in life.

At times it may be clear to parents that their teenager needs help to stop drinking, but the adolescent may refuse to seek it. Although sometimes nothing can be done, at other times influential peers, the family physician, priest, rabbi, or minister can be helpful. Occasionally, the police can order treatment, following a legal offense. However, without at least moderate cooperation from the adolescent, treatment attempts almost always fail. Since heavy drinking that starts during adolescence usually continues into adult life and causes physical and mental deterioration, without help the adolescent alcoholic faces a most grim future.

Drug abuse

Marijuana

Marijuana is known by a great many names, including grass, pot, tea, reefer, weed, and Mary Jane. Although it has been used commonly in this country only during the past two decades, marijuana usage is described in written records that date back nearly 4,000 years.

Marijuana comes from hemp (cannabis) plants, which are easily grown in many parts of the world. Although the highest concentration of psychoactive material is obtained from the flowering tops of the female plant, in this country the term marijuana can refer to any part (flower, stalk, or leaf) of the plant. All are cut, dried, chopped, and made into cigarettes. As with all street drugs, various less expensive and sometimes dangerous fillers are mixed with the marijuana in order to swell profits. With drug usage, "Know Thy Dealer" is the first rule.

The active ingredient of marijuana, tetrahydrocannabinol or THC, can be synthesized and is sometimes sold in this more pure and powerful form. It too, however, may be mixed with other ingredients.

No drug has a single, predictable effect. The effect is profoundly influenced by personality, setting, and expectation. The user of pot routinely has reddening of the eyes, acceleration of the heart rate, and, with greater doses, impairment of short-term memory. Adolescents occasionally experience nausea, vomiting, and dizziness, but this is unlikely with regular use. Subjectively, users believe time is passing more slowly than it really is, and the senses seem to be enhanced. Reports of wasting of the brain and decrease in levels of male sex hormone have been made following studies of *heavy, chronic* marijuana users, but confirmatory studies have yet to appear. High doses of the drug, either from hashish, the resinous exudate from only the tops of plants grown in the Middle East and North Africa, or relatively pure THC, can cause psychosis, usually of short duration.

A number of studies have shown personality differences between heavy marijuana users and nonusers. Heavy users show relatively little interest in achievement or attainment of goals. At present there is no evidence that this so-called amotivational syndrome comes from any brain damage resulting from smoking pot. Most likely the results are explained by the selection factor—that is, by the natural nonmotivated disposition of the kind of adolescents who become heavy users. Even so, the possibility that frequent or chronic marijuana use can affect the developing personality adversely cannot be ruled out.

Whether minimal, moderate, or frequent use of marijuana is more or less dangerous than the similar use of alcohol is unknown; however, since the moderate to frequent use of either is unhealthy, the best advice to adolescents is to avoid both of them, or use them only in small doses.

Hallucinogens

Drugs that will cause hallucinations and behavior that mimics psychosis or actually touches off a psychotic state are not as popular now as they were in the 1960s. They remain, however, convenient agents for adolescents who need to avoid reality and responsibility. A number of drugs can be used for this purpose. Glue sniffing, mescaline, tetrahydrocannabinol (THC), atropine, psilocybin, and large doses of amphetamine or cocaine are but a few. The most popular of the hallucinogens is lysergic acid diethylamide (LSD), but phencyclidine (PCP, angel dust) will probably soon take its place.

All of these agents interfere with the normal action of the brain and, for varying lengths of time, produce a behavioral reaction similar to that described in the section on psychosis (see p. 263). Perception is always altered, but consciousness may remain either clear or become clouded. The senses are usually hyperacute, although distorted, and fear and suspicion often accompany the reaction. The length of the response depends on many things: the type of drug, the dose, the expectation, the environmental tone, and the individual's physiological and psychological peculiarities. Another crucial variable is the purity of the drug and, if it isn't pure, what the properties of the impurities are.

PCP has become an increasing drug abuse problem for two reasons. First, it is easily made and can be taken as a powder, tablet, crystal, or solution. Second, it is totally unpredictable in action. Violent and self-destructive behavior seems more common than with other hallucinogens, and overdosage can cause death. It is a very dangerous drug.

As for treatment, the first approach for a "bad trip" on any hallucinatory drug is to take advantage of the user's greatly increased suggestibility and "talk him (or her) down." This is done best by a calm, friendly person, preferably one who is known and who in a quiet environment keeps the adolescent's attention focused on nonfrightening subjects until the drug effects wear off. Various medications can be useful in combating the effects of a hallucinogen, but two potential problems are present. First, since the combination of drugs increases the unpredictability of the body's response, when one chemical is already in the blood, it is best to avoid giving other chemicals. Second, since the identity of the street drug may be unknown, or its purity suspect, there is the danger that the wrong antidote might be used and the situation made worse rather than better.

There is no known treatment for a chronic hallucinogen habit, although increasing age seems to limit usage. Since these agents are not addicting, the adolescent can theoretically stop whenever he or she wishes. But in fact until the person feels capable of facing the world as it is without drugs, hallucinogens will remain a temptation. Although suicide, accidents, and the triggering of schizophrenia are increased with the use of hallucinogens, these facts seldom deter adolescent users. When a chronic adolescent-user stops, it is usually due either to a switch to opiates (see below) or is secondary to some social, philosophical, or religious upheaval.

Opiates

These are the hardest of the "hard" drugs and include the natural and synthetic drugs that act like morphine. Morphine is a particular portion, an alkaloid, of opium. Opium itself is seldom found in this country. **Morphine** is used extensively in medicine to control pain, while **heroin** (H, smack, junk, horse, etc.) is the most common form of street opiate. Heroin's pharmacological action is no different from that of morphine, but since on a weight basis it is about 2 1/2 times more potent, its smaller bulk may be what gives it its popularity for criminal traffic. During the past couple of decades, **methadone,** a synthetic opiate used for treating addiction, has also been increasingly abused. Less frequently abused opiates among adolescents include merperidine (Demerol) and codeine.

Opium and its derivatives come from the milky juice of the poppy. Its attributes seem to have been discovered long ago, since it is known that in about 4000 B.C. the Sumerian symbols for the poppy meant "joy plants." These substances cause analgesia (lessening of pain), drowsiness, changes in mood, mental clouding, constricted pupils, nausea, and a depression of breathing and bowel functions. Although the initial experiences with opiates may be very unpleasant, the abuser seeks a feeling of euphoria and a reduction of pain and of the sexual and aggressive drives.

There are two main problems with opiates. First, tolerance develops; in other words, it takes increasing amounts to give the same response as before. Second, they are addicting. Addiction means that if the drug is discontinued the body will miss the drug, and will suffer various symptoms until the affected systems readjust to the loss. Generally, these symptoms are the opposite of the reactions produced by the drug. Withdrawal of opiates, for example, commonly causes running of the nose, yawning, sweating, dilated pupils, irritability, pain in muscles and bones, abdominal cramps, diarrhea, and muscle spasms. (The latter often causes a lashing out of the legs which may be the origin of the expression "kicking the habit.") When withdrawal occurs without any treatment, the symptoms usually run their course in seven to ten days. An additional skin phenomenon common during withdrawal is waves of gooseflesh. The skin resembles that of a plucked turkey; hence the expression "going cold turkey."

Almost invariably adolescents who become narcotics addicts have already had experiences with alcohol and other drugs first. These earlier substances seem important in making the adolescent aware that chemicals can relieve, at least for a time, feelings of inadequacy, loneliness, and anxiety. Except in melodrama, drug pushers usually do not seek out adolescents to make them addicts, but wait for adolescents to find them. Because narcotics are illegal in this country, they are dangerous and expensive to get. It is the need for money to pay for the habit, rather than any action of the drug, that leads addicts so often to theft and prostitution. Indeed, because of the pacifying effect of opiates, crimes of violence by addicts are uncommon. In Great Britain, for example, where addicts may register and obtain narcotics legally, criminal activity by addicts is unusual.

A number of the social, legal, and medical problems associated with narcotic addiction have already been mentioned. The feeling of satisfaction created by a significant dose of opiates tends to weaken motivation, and the skills of even very talented adolescents usually wither with disuse. Additional medical hazards include blood infections because of dirty hypodermic needle technique and deaths due to overdosage or to impure "stuff," substituted out of malice or for profit. The most poignant account of the ravages of hard drug addiction that we know is Claude Brown's *Manchild in the Promised Land*, in which he describes how the influx of heroin pretty much destroyed his generation of adolescents in Harlem.

Treatment of opiate addiction has been frustrating. The use of one narcotic to wean a person off another is controversial. Methadone is such an agent. It has the same pharmacological action as the commonly abused opiates, but does not produce a "high" and can be given orally and once a day. Addicts who wish to may enter programs to receive methadone legally. Although a helpful service, methadone can also be abused, and most users simply become methadone addicts.

Psychotherapy has not proved very successful with addicts, but group programs run by ex-addicts to rehabilitate present addicts have shown promise. These programs put great emphasis on personal responsibility, and since the leaders have themselves made the difficult transition, they cannot be conned or cajoled as easily as a "straight" therapist can. Since drugs can give the illusion that the taker instantly possesses the power, satisfaction, and peace that others must work years for, unique skills are necessary to break through this fantasy and force the addict to admit that the illusion is not true. Variations of this rehabilitative approach are available from such groups as Daytop and Phoenix House. Information about drug rehabilitation programs in your area can be obtained from the local mental health center or medical society.

Downers, uppers, and tranquilizers

These drugs are generally more popular with adolescents' parents than with adolescents, but amphetamines, barbiturates, certain sleeping pills (such as Quaalude), and certain tranquilizers (such as Valium and Librium) are sometimes abused by teenagers.

Of these substances, **barbiturates** are probably the most dangerous. These include drugs such as phenobarbital and Seconal. They make people sleepy, but dependency and tolerance occur. More and more of the drug is needed to obtain the same response, and if it is suddenly stopped, irritability and insomnia are usual. If large doses of barbiturates are taken and withdrawal takes place, convulsions and even death can occur. An overdose of barbiturates can also cause death and is a commonly chosen agent for suicide.

Amphetamines or "speed" (Dexedrine, Ritalin, etc.) can be either taken by mouth or injected into a vein. Fatigue lifts temporarily, mood becomes lighter, and appetite declines. Unfortunately, the effects of amphetamines are brief, and this is why they have no medical usefulness as either an antidepressant or weight-reduction aid. The body very quickly readjusts its functioning, and the drug no longer works. Understandably, the usual response by the user is to use more and more drug while getting less and less of a reaction. The injection of amphetamine can give a "rush" but also presents all of the dangers inherent in putting a street drug (quite possibly impure) directly into the bloodstream via a probably unsterile needle. High doses of amphetamines often cause a toxic psychosis that is manifested by visual hallucinations, profound fear, and the paranoid belief that the world is conspiring against you. Withdrawal of the "speed" brings on a craving for the drug, prolonged sleep, depression, and a feeling of fatigue. Cocaine abuse, usually through inhaling or "snorting," gives a clinical response similar to that of amphetamine abuse, but cocaine is too expensive for the average adolescent to use.

Tranquilizers are a way of getting through life for many adults. They are the most widely prescribed group of drugs in the country, and family medicine cabinets are often the source for those adolescents who use them. Because tranquilizers are associated with adult use and because they do not give a "high," they are not as popular with adolescents as stimulants and sedatives are. Barbiturates and other "downers" lessen anxiety only through sedation, while tranquilizers have a specific anxiety-reducing action. Since tranquilizers are not addicting and are not as likely to cause heavy sedation, they are generally safer than other abused drugs, but they can cause habituation and withdrawal symptoms.

Delinquency

Delinquency is not a psychiatric or medical diagnosis, but rather a legal term without a fixed meaning. It varies in definition from place to place and from time to time. What constitutes delinquency in one city may not in another, and what is illegal one year may not be the next. In short, the only way to define delinquent behavior is to say that it is what is against the law in a particular location for an adolescent of a particular age at a particular time.

Types of delinquents and delinquency

Since rebellion is a common aspect of adolescence, whenever the population contains a relatively large proportion of adolescents the delinquency rate increases. This was true between 1955 and 1975, when arrests of adolescents rose 1600 percent. As the percentage of adolescents in the United States declines (and it is now declining), we can expect to hear less about delinquency and to regard it as less of a problem.

Some adolescents are delinquent for neurotic reasons. These are adolescents who steal because they are depressed or who set themselves up to be caught as a way of assuaging neurotic guilt.

A much larger group of delinquents is the so-called dyssocial type. They come from environments in which criminality is either encouraged or at least taken for granted as a way of life. For these individuals crime seems normal, and there is usually a ready-made apprentice system for those who are interested. These people are in crime for profit, not individual rebellion, and may feel great loyalty to those in their group. Adolescents with skills move up within the hierarchy, and the criminal factions referred to as "organized crime" are made up largely of dyssocial adults and youths.

A third group of delinquents is made up of so-called "antisocial" adolescents. These individuals are not organized and tend to be loners. They do not fit in well with any network, including a criminal one. They do not want to take orders and tend not to have the relatively strong loyalties that characterize the disciplined gangs of dyssocial delinquents. Because of these defects of personality, members of this group of teenagers are seldom very successful at anything they undertake. Since they tend not to profit from experience or punishment and have no close friends or organization behind them, antisocial delinquents often suffer arrest after arrest without benefit to society or to themselves.

Adolescents account for much of the crime in this country. FBI crime statistics for 1974 showed that arrests of youths between the ages of 10 and 17 accounted for almost one-half of all arrests for serious crime. This figure soars much higher when "status offender" arrests are included. Status offenses are those such as running away and truancy, which would not be against the law if the minor was an adult. In recent years there has been an increasing tendency to be less vigorous in prosecuting and jailing teenagers for status offense crimes.

While jailing serves to protect society from the dangerous adolescent, it usually doesn't help prevent future crime. Reformatories are less likely to reform adolescents than they are to teach them better ways to steal. Most serious crimes are committed by a relatively small core of juvenile offenders who prove to be repeaters regardless of punishment or counseling. Society needs protection from these youths, but it is counterproductive to house them as teachers with first-time and status offenders.

Prevention and treatment

We are much better at predicting delinquency than we are at preventing it or treating it. As noted above, delinquency is more a sociological than psychiatric problem. Patterns of behavior that are often present by first or second grade allow researchers or even teachers to be quite accurate in predicting which child will be significantly delinquent ten years later. An important factor here is family cohesiveness. Delinquency is relatively rare in intact families where parents spend time enjoying their children, as well as effort in disciplining them. Overly strict and cold discipline can exacerbate rebellion once the child is old enough to rebel, and parents who get vicarious pleasure out of their child's misdeeds or wish the child to be caught and punished may in fact encourage delinquency, consciously or unconsciously. It is fairly common, for example, for runaway adolescents to have been encouraged overtly or covertly by parents to leave.

Since "bad" companions may help foster criminal behavior, parents should try to help find alternative companionship if an adolescent son or daughter is in a group of delinquent peers. Medications have so far not been useful in decreasing delinquent actions. Group and individual psychotherapy are sometimes helpful in persuading adolescents that they will get more gratification by going along with society's rules than by flouting them. Family therapy is useful in some cases, especially in exploring how the delinquent may be expressing family problems and in working out consistent and realistic limits for the adolescent's behavior. Occasionally, the adolescent must be separated from the family and worked with in a residential treatment center. Whatever type of intervention is used, it works best early, before there are multiple arrests or jailings.

Psychotherapy

It is safe to say that there is no limit on the varieties of psychotherapy available. This is due to the fact that there is no universally recognized definition for psychotherapy, nor is there a broadly accepted system of regulation for psychotherapists.

To start, as good a definition of psychotherapy as any is this: treatment for emotional problems that is based primarily upon verbal or nonverbal communication as distinguished from the use of drugs or physical treatments. Before one seeks out a therapist, someone, perhaps the adolescent or a parent, the school, or the court, must discern a need. Except for psychosis, which responds best to medication *plus* psychotherapy, there is much difference of opinion about who needs or should receive psychotherapy. If a person's psychological distress is serious enough to disrupt his or her ability to function in society, in school, or in the family, psychotherapy should be considered. It should also be considered if emotional problems are expressed through bodily symptoms that are bad enough to be bothersome. If parents are unsure whether or not psychotherapy is warranted, they and the adolescent may wish to have a discussion with their family physician or pediatrician. If treatment is indicated, the family physician's knowledge of the adolescent and the community can often be helpful in suggesting possible clinics, hospitals, or therapists.

Most psychotherapists belong to a particular school of psychological theory and technique, although some consider themselves eclectic. Eclectic means either that the therapist has a good grasp of many types of therapeutic approaches and chooses the most appropriate parts of each for a specific patient, or it means the therapist has no theoretical grasp and does whatever comes to mind, helter-skelter. As a way of describing a therapeutic approach, eclecticism has little meaning.

There are a number of ways of classifying types of psychotherapy. One way is by the major schools of thought. The **psychoanalytic** or psychodynamic approach stresses the uncovering of unconscious conflicts and defenses. Psychoanalysts believe that by gaining insight into the reasons for self-defeating behavior, a patient gets the opportunity to choose more appropriate and effective defenses and ways of behaving. Although psychoanalysis itself requires four or five meetings a week for a number of years, insight therapy can be done in sessions once or twice a week or in group therapy or transactional analysis, for example.

Behavioral therapy is a second general approach to psychotherapy. While insight therapy stresses links between past experiences and present behavior, behavioral therapy concentrates on changing present behavior. Basically, specific thoughts or actions are used in a consistent manner either to reinforce wanted behavior or to discourage or punish the target symptom. (The use of bells or buzzers to awaken—and thus train—a bed-wetter is an example of such therapy.) The more specific the behavior to be modified, such as a phobia, the better the treatment usually works. Operant conditioning, aversive conditioning, systematic desensitization, and assertiveness training are some of the many types of behavioral therapy.

A third school of thought is the **humanistic.** Practitioners of this approach stress that all people possess more potential than they use. The techniques used to release this potential vary greatly, but include "growth" groups, encounter groups, self-actualization groups, and so on. The humanistic approach is usually less popular with adolescents than with adults.

The fourth important school of thought in the U.S. today is **transpersonal therapy.** In contrast to the humanists who believe we all should and can expand our individual potential, practitioners of transpersonal therapy attempt to expand the person's oneness with the universe. Eastern religions and thought often express this purpose, and transcendental meditation (TM) has become increasingly popular with adolescents during the past decade. A secret mantra or catch phrase having special meaning to the individual is meditated on twice or more a day and is used to bring on a state of relaxation.

Other types of therapy have less to do with a school of thought than with how treatment is delivered. Group therapy, family therapy, and psychodrama represent such techniques.

In practical terms, humanistic and transpersonal approaches are seldom used for serious maladjustment or psychiatric illness. They border more on the philosophical or religious. Insight therapy has long been used for general problems of living, for neuroses, and, in modified forms, as supportive therapy when medication or physical treatments are used for psychotic and psychosomatic disorders. Behavior modification is most useful for very specific phobias, sexual symptoms, and compulsions.

Group therapy may be the right choice when an adolescent is shy, or fearful that he or she is the only one with problems. Family therapy is a type of group therapy. Although it is becoming increasingly popular, teenagers sometimes balk at a family approach, since a major developmental step for adolescents is to separate from the family.

In picking a type of psychotherapy, it is important that it be compatible with the person's own value system and that it offers some reason to believe that it will be helpful. For example, if the adolescent believes it is important to "understand" things, behavior modification will not seem a very attractive approach. On the other hand, if the person would rather not think about what is happening or why, but only wants to get rid of a bothersome symptom, behavior modification may appear to be the therapy of choice.

As a rule of thumb, the types of psychotherapy that have been around the longest make the most modest claims. That they have survived in a market where new gimmicks and miracle cures appear and disappear with frightening regularity is worthy of note. It is prudent to stay away from the latest and the greatest, whichever therapeutic approach that happens to be. Physicians, clergy, or friends can often supply you with information, and there are books in public libraries with detailed descriptions of the various schools of psychotherapeutic thought.

Also available are psychotherapeutic self-help books; almost every week there is one on the best-seller list. Early in the century Freud characterized this genre as being as helpful as a menu is to a starving man, and there is little reason to modify his opinion now.

Although there is now convincing evidence that many forms of psychotherapy are more effective than nontreatment for nonpsychotic patients, the number of variables involved has made it difficult to compare success rates among various psychotherapeutic approaches. The most important variable is the therapist.

Therapists

Because emotion influences the outcome of psychotherapy more often than does intellect (the best therapist uses both), one's choice of therapist is usually more important than one's choice of therapy.

Anyone, repeat *anyone*, can in most states put up a shingle reading "psychotherapist." The term is so broad that there is no regulation of it. Prior to 1900, counseling was performed mainly by religious and spiritual leaders. In the early part of this century, psychiatrists (who are physicians with additional training in emotional disorders) and psychologists (who have special skills in psychological testing) began to write about and do research in psychotherapy. More recently social workers, nurses, and paraprofessionals have in large numbers begun to do psychotherapy.

Knowing the therapist's professional background is helpful mainly in two areas. First, it often indicates there is a special skill. A physician can prescribe medication and has the most access to hospitalization, a member of the clergy has special training in spiritual matters, a psychologist can perform testing, and so on. Second, professional accrediting bodies and state licensing regulations in various states cover some disciplines—for example physicians, psychologists, and social workers. For these disciplines one can easily determine which individuals have met the academic and ethical criteria established by peers and legislatures. While licensing and length of study are not sure measures of skill, they do mean a therapist's work has been scrutinized, and they are a measure of who has the most to lose if unethical behavior occurs. In general, the more highly trained a therapist is, the higher the fees, the more likely at least part of the fee is covered by health insurance, and the more likely the therapist is covered by malpractice insurance.

We stress ethical behavior because a very strong emotional bond occurs routinely during psychotherapy. Feelings from the past and from other relationships are often brought into the psychotherapeutic process. Although the understanding of these feelings can have a lot to do with whether the therapy succeeds or not, they can also do harm if they are not handled well. If the therapist loses objectivity or only responds to the patient incorrectly in the same way that others have in the past, the patient can be harmed rather than helped. It is therefore best to seek out therapists or clinics with good reputations or track records in the community. Out of this group, one should pick a therapist whose goals, values, and personality are compatible with one's own.

Common elements in psychotherapy

Relatively few adolescents who seek psychotherapy are "crazy," and this is important to know because the motivation of the patient is an important variable for therapeutic success. Many adolescents—and their parents—fear mental illness and put off treatment because of their fear that acknowledgment of problems will make them worse, or will prove that they *are* crazy. This is not the case. Until problems are acknowledged, no steps can be taken to combat them. In fact, one reason why so many different types of psychotherapy prove successful is probably that each in its own way allows the patient to make sense of his or her otherwise inexplicable thoughts and behavior. Self-motivation to seek relief from acute distress is a powerful factor leading to therapeutic success. Adolescents who are forced into therapy, who believe it will make them worse, or who do not believe it will be helpful are unlikely to gain much from it.

Psychotherapy and medication

Medications are now available that are helpful for the more severe mental illnesses, such as psychoses and deep depressions. Studies show that the effect of these medications on the adolescent is improved when combined with psychotherapy and attention to the problems of the family as a whole. Be suspicious whenever medication is offered over a long period of time without including psychotherapy too.

Leaving:
Adolescence to Adulthood

Parents' view

In *The Winter's Tale* Shakespeare noted, "I would there were no age between ten and twenty-three or that youth would sleep out the rest, for there is nothing in the between but getting wenches with child, wronging the ancientry, stealing and fighting." During the late teens to early twenties, most adolescents succeed at becoming young adults, and parents are, for the most part, relieved. It of course means children leaving home and sometimes astronomical educational costs, but family interactions usually become more peaceful. Sibling animosities tend to cool off by this age, and parent-child disagreements, when they are present, tend to be more focused. If disagreements are large, the child can now choose to leave home and become independent.

For better or for worse, parents know that by this age their children will hereafter be pretty much on their own. Such a realization is likely to give rise to feelings of pride, frustration, loneliness, satisfaction, fear, and/or relief. Second guessing about what one should or should not have done as a parent during the previous two decades is a useless task. In any case, trying to determine the relative strength of parents' genetic and parenting influences on their children is like asking which blade of a scissors is more important. Mao Tse-tung commented that experience is a comb that Nature gives us when we are bald, but most parents profit from their past experience by becoming better grandparents.

As for loneliness when children leave home, there is usually some of this, but the specter of "empty nest" depression seldom comes true. Without exception, surveys show that couples whose children have grown up and have left the house feel more satisfaction with life than do couples with younger children.

As a parent's young adult children become more committed vocationally and sexually, there is often a final intrapsychic conflict over letting go. Although one knows that one should allow adult children to make their own decisions and that one no longer has the power to do otherwise, the temptation to say what is "right" may linger out of habit. While such wishes to intervene may occasionally be warranted, they should usually be stifled. They generally have more to do with the parent's need than the child's. At times parents react negatively to youths' dreams because these dreams awaken old dreams and frustrations in themselves. They may even fear that the youth will succeed, thus suggesting that the parent's own renunciations may have been in vain or unnecessary.

In most families, however, young adulthood is a time when children grow closer again to the philosophical and moral values of their parents. Adolescents tend in the beginning to believe that they will mark the world, only to discover increasingly that the world has marked them. As one grows older, one's parents' ways seem more sensible in retrospect than they did at the time. When it comes to raising one's own new family, the constantly shifting contemporary child-rearing fads are seldom as comfortable as reaching back for the "old ways." For unsure young parents, hindsight seems better than no sight at all.

Adolescents' view

The end of adolescence is more difficult to delineate than the onset, since the beginning is physiologically defined while the ending is psychosocially defined. The law states that adolescents are adults when they reach age 18. By cultural definition adolescents who are living away from their parents and supporting themselves are adults. The transition to adulthood is least clear for offspring who work but remain at home, or who live at college or graduate school but continue for another four, six, or eight years to be supported financially by their parents.

For the child, vocational and sexual decisions are often crucial in defining when psychological adulthood is obtained. An important task of late adolescence is giving up the belief that one can do everything. Although every commitment necessarily limits potential, priorities must be ordered if adult adjustment is to occur. This task requires renunciations, which some people find so difficult that they continue jumping from job to job or from sexual partner to sexual partner whenever even minor dissatisfactions occur. Such behavior is commonly labeled "adolescent," even if the person is 40 years old. Although it is important to retain some flexibility, by early adulthood a person should have the capacity to stick with reasonable choices, even when difficulties arise. The development of the ability to put periods of time in perspective, especially in relation to one's long-term future, is crucial for this accomplishment. It is hard to settle down, for example, when one cannot yet imagine ever being older than 25 or 30. Although it usually takes another two decades before one is struck palpably with the fact that life is necessarily a fatal endeavor, it is not uncommon by the early twenties to realize that one's time is not endless and that perhaps one way to have more is to desire less. With the development of firm love and work commitments, the late adolescent's ties to the parents change in quality and degree. When the contemporary commitments are exciting, the adolescent is usually relatively un-

301

aware of the process of separation or of the discomfort it may be causing the parents. This indifference may strike parents as unfeeling ingratitude after all they have done, and the parents may be right. Usually, however, the unfeelingness is due to the child's absorption in endeavors that are new and seem compelling, rather than dissatisfaction with parents or a conscious wish to hurt them. As noted before, Nature seems aware that if youth were not endowed with the enthusiasm typical for the age and a built-in ignorance for problems yet to come, few would be willing to begin at the bottom of vocational ladders or to start families of their own. In short, the single-mindedness of young adults may seem hurtful to parents, but it is indispensable for beginning the new generation.

For a sad minority of adolescents, this push to leave the family and take on the world never occurs. These children, once they are in their twenties and thirties, find it increasingly difficult to consider separating from their parents. The phenomenon is reminiscent of the school avoidance problems of some children in the early grades. Indeed, there is an anecdote about a mother who comes in the morning to awaken her daughter for school. In response to her mother's entreaties the daughter says, "The kids hate me, and the teachers are nasty. I won't go, you can't make me go, and there's no good reason why I should go!" "Well," answers the mother, "there are *two* good reasons. You're 42 years old and you're the principal."

When parents and adult child live together without concern about or wish for separation, the child's social development is usually stunted, but problems may not develop until the parents die. At this time the offspring's social constriction and lack of separation and individuation usually cause major problems. When either the parent or the adult child is unhappy with the situation of prolonged adolescence and is unable to modify it alone, counseling is indicated.

The Group for the Advancement of Psychiatry has suggested six criteria to be used to determine the resolution of adolescence. Although they are somewhat idealistic, they pinpoint the areas of maturation that have the greatest importance. (Many of us would be pleased to have reached these goals no matter what our age.)

1. Attainment of separation and independence from parents
2. Establishment of a sexual identity
3. A commitment to work
4. Development of a personal moral value system
5. Attainment of a capacity for lasting relationships
6. An emotional return to the parents based on relative equality

This section began with a quote, and it seems fitting to end with one. Dickens, in the opening lines of *A Tale of Two Cities*, describes an era in time, the French Revolution. His words can just as well describe an era of life, adolescence. "It was the best of times, it was the worst of times; it was the age of foolishness, it was the epoch of belief; it was the season of light, it was the season of darkness; it was the spring of hope, it was the winter of despair."

Index

Index

lung, 276; lymphatic system, 228;
  skin, 185, 235
Candida albicans, 188
carbohydrates, 25, 26
carbon dioxide, 214
cardiovascular system, 202, 215–21,
  227
cars, 80–2
cavity, tooth, 35, 36
cervicitis, 187–8
cervix, 125, 160; chancre, 190;
  infection of, 186–8; and Pap
  smear, 125, 196
chancres, 190
chest, 123; pain, 219, 220
chills, 238
Chlamydia trachomatis, 188, 189
cholera, 132
cholesterol, 25, 145, 217–18
chorea, 220
cigarette smoking, 87, 217, 275–9,
  280; and birth control pill, 196
clinical psychologists, 248–9
clitoris, 124
clothing, 73–8
clotrimazole, 181
clubs, 42
cocaine, 285, 290
codeine, 287
cohabitation, 55, 56
cold: common, 28; sensitivity to,
  156; sores, 190
colitis, 136
colon, 225–7
comedones, 176, 178
communes, 97
compulsive behavior, 246
computerized axial tomography
  (CAT) scan, 130
condoms, 195
conformity, 40, 41
congenital heart disease, 136,
  219–20
conjunctiva, 122
constipation, 226
contraception, 56, 160, 193; barrier
  agents, 194–6; intrauterine
  device, 195, 197; morning-after
  pill, 195, 198; oral, 163, 196–7, 224

contrast material, 129
conversion reactions, 245–6
Cooley's anemia, 131, 136
coordination, 229
cornea, 122
coronary artery disease, 217
corpus luteum, 20
cortisone, 235
cosmetic surgery, 171
cosmetics, 76
coughing, 207, 209, 210
counterphobic reactions, 245
crabs, 191
cramps, 222; menstrual, 162–3
cranial nerves, 124
crime, 291, 292
Crohn's disease, 136, 225, 226, 227
cultures, 128–9
cystic fibrosis, 207, 212
cystitis, 236

dating, 51–6, 98
Daytop, 289
death: alcohol-related automobile,
  79, 81, 82–3, 279, 281; anxiety
  about, 243; major causes, 227;
  preoccupation with, 66
decongestants, 207
dehydration, 204
delinquency, 45, 69, 107, 108,
  290–1; depression and, 250;
  prevention and treatment,
  292–3; types of, 291–2
delusions, 264–5
dementia praecox, 266
Demerol, 287
dental health, 35–8
deodorant, 175, 183
depression, 249–63; and headache,
  237; manic, 255; physiological
  factors, 253–4; psychological
  factors, 251–3; suicide, 57, 227,
  243, 256–60; treatment, 260–3
dermabrasion, 179
Dexedrine, 289
diabetes insipidus, 34
diabetes mellitus, 31, 34, 146, 217;
  juvenile, 203–5
diaphragm, 195–6

307

Index

A Note About the Authors

John E. Schowalter attended the University of Wisconsin, where he received his M.D. in 1960, and is trained in psychiatry, child psychiatry, and psychoanalysis. He has been associated with the Yale Child Study Center since 1963, and is now Director of Training there. Dr. Schowalter is also Professor of Pediatrics and Psychiatry in the Yale University School of Medicine, the author of more than fifty scientific articles, and a member of many professional groups, including the American Academy of Child Psychiatry, in which he is chairperson of the Committee on Adolescent Psychiatry. He lives in New Haven with his wife and two adolescent children.

Walter R. Anyan, Jr., was educated at Dartmouth and the Harvard Medical School. He received his M.D. at Harvard in 1961, and did postgraduate work at Yale. He is Associate Professor of Pediatrics in the Yale University School of Medicine, and Director of Medical Studies in the Department of Pediatrics. Dr. Anyan is the author of a medical text on adolescent medicine, and is in charge of the Medical Program for Adolescence at the Yale–New Haven Hospital. He lives in Guilford, Connecticut, with his wife and two sons, both of whom are approaching adolescence.

A Note on the Type

The text of this book was set, via computer-driven cathode ray tube, in Video Gael, an adaptation of Caledonia, a typeface originally designed by W. A. Dwiggins. It belongs to the family of printing types called "modern faces" by printers—a term used to mark the change in style of type letters that occurred in about 1800. Caledonia borders on the general design of Scotch Modern, but is more freely drawn than that letter.

Composed, printed, and bound
by The Haddon Craftsmen, Inc., Scranton, Pennsylvania

Typography and binding design by Judith Henry